Geoffrey Chaucer

Troilus and Criseyde

Geoffrey Chaucer

Troilus and Criseyde

Edited by

R. A. SHOAF

from the text of A. C. Baugh

COLLEAGUES PRESS

1989

ISBN 0–937191–10–8
ISBN 0–937191–11–6 (pbk.)
Library of Congress Catalog Card Number 88–72033
British Library Cataloguing in Publication Data available
Copyright © 1989 R. A. Shoaf

Albert C. Baugh, Editor, *Chaucer's Major Poetry*,
© 1963, pp. 74–211. Reprinted by permission of
Prentice-Hall, Inc., Englewood Cliffs, NJ

Published by Colleagues Press Inc.
Post Office Box 4007
East Lansing, MI 48826

Distribution outside North America
Boydell and Brewer Ltd.
Post Office Box 9
Woodbridge, Suffolk IP12 3DF
England

Printed in the United States of America

this book is for Judy

Contents

Acknowledgments

In John A. Alford, I had a publisher, also a friend, in every way ideal for this project. I cannot thank him enough. Stephen A. Barney read the manuscript for Colleagues Press and (as he has done so often for so many) offered numerous valuable comments and suggestions. My gratitude is great; his desert, I confess, far greater. Helen Cooper read part of Book Two in 1986, as I got underway with the project, and made pertinent comments; I am grateful for her help.

My students in the University of Florida in the fall term of 1987 used the edition in photocopy format. They made many valuable comments, and I have tried to learn from their experience of it what exactly it ought to do for those just getting underway with the poem.

Ms. Katrina Ruth, Research Assistant in the Department of English in the fall term of 1987, proofread the entire text. Her able work eliminated many errors. Those that remain are entirely my own responsibility.

This book is dedicated to Judy, my wife. Among our very first conversations, over 15 years ago now, were discussions of *Troilus and Criseyde* and Henryson's *Testament of Cresseid*. It is obvious to me that without her, my appreciation and understanding of these poems would never have come as far as they have or go as far as they someday might.

Gainesville, Florida
May 23, 1988

Preface and Guide to the Edition

And for ther is so gret diversite
In Englissh and in writyng of oure tonge,
So pray I God that non myswrite the,
Ne the mysmetre for defaute of tonge.
And red wherso thow be, or elles songe,
That thow be understonde, God I biseche!

Troilus 5.1793–98

OUR TIME has seen the publication of many important editions of *Troilus and Criseyde*: Skeat, Root, Robinson, Donaldson, Baugh, Fisher, and Windeatt have all greatly contributed to our understanding of Chaucer's masterpiece. And, of course, *The Riverside Chaucer* now continues this tradition with the edition of Stephen Barney. The edition of *Troilus and Criseyde* offered here is not intended to replace any of these editions; on the contrary, it is intended to complement them and, in doing so, to supply a need frequently felt by Chaucerians—namely, an edition of the poem prepared especially for those setting out for the first time on the extraordinary adventure of reading one of the greatest love poems in English.

Troilus and Criseyde is also, we know, one of the most difficult poems in English. Indeed, in all the years I have been teaching Chaucer, the most constant complaint from students I have heard is, "this poem is *hard*." Numerous colleagues around the country have reported much the same response: their students admire the poem but bemoan its difficulty. The principal end of the present undertaking is to improve this situation with an edition that approximates a translation in ease of reading and that offers apparatus designed to reduce the frustration and to maximize the pleasure in the first encounter with the poem.

Even veteran readers of *Troilus and Criseyde* will not have forgotten how difficult and laborious it is to look up words in a glossary or dictionary as one is reading the poem. Some would argue that the solution here is a translation. And indeed many translations or "modernizations" do exist—Krapp, Lumiansky, and Stanley-Wrench, for examples. But the obvious objection occurs immediately to everyone that in a translation, Chaucer's text is no longer there.

The solution adopted here to this dilemma is the continuous marginal gloss, as in the following example (*Troilus* 2.1–7):

°Owt of thise blake wawes for to saylle,	*out, black, waves*
O wynd, o wynd, the weder gynneth clere;	*weather, begins (to)*
°For in this see the boot hath swych travaylle,	
Of my °connyng, that unneth I it steere.	
This see clepe I the tempestous matere	*call*
Of disespeir that Troilus was inne;	*despair*
But now of hope the °kalendes bygynne.	

1–4 See *Purg.* 1.1–3.

3–4 for in this sea the boat of my understanding has such toil that I barely steer it

4 Parallel to Dante's "ingegno," "connyng" can be modernized as "genius" or "wit" if we understand by these terms something like the innate capacity to make poetry.

7 the inauguration begins ("kalendes"—the first day of the month and hence the "first" of any thing or action)

Here, I hope, are the virtues of a translation without its principal defect, the absence of the original. *Chaucer's* text is here, along with various helps in reading it.

As this example should also make clear, I have elected to err in the direction of over- rather than under-glossing: my primary goal is to facilitate the *first* encounter with the poem. Implicit in such a goal is the assumption of *subsequent* encounters with the poem, especially in the classroom where, it is hoped, the instructor will use the glosses as departures for his or her commentary, either in agreement or disagreement, but always with awareness that no two readers of the poem would always gloss every word in the same way.

To improve the glossing further, I have added explanatory notes on unusually difficult words or phrases. These and all other annotations at the foot of the page are marked in the text by the symbol ° before the relevant word or line. To continue with the present example, we have:

4　Parallel to Dante's "ingegno," this word can be modernized as "genius" or "wit" if we understand by these terms something like the innate capacity to make poetry.

7　the inauguration begins ("kalendes"—the first day of the month and hence the "first" of any thing or action)

These notes never attempt to "solve a crux"; they seek only to provide sufficient information for an adequate construal of the word or phrase.

Allusions are identified throughout the edition—as in the reference to Dante in the note on "connyng." Generally, the edition attempts to identify all allusions that are immediately relevant to understanding the poem; no attempt is made, however, to identify all allusions in the poem since this would not only make for an unwieldy page appearance and a much longer book, it would also needlessly duplicate the efforts of others. Where an allusion is still being debated by professional readers of the poem, that debate is duly recorded.

The present stanza also exemplifies one other frequent procedure. Often, a line or lines in a stanza are still difficult to understand even after glosses, explanations, and allusions have been offered and identified. In such cases, I have provided a "modernization" in the apparatus. At all times I have tried to keep the "modernization" to minimal interpretative interference. Even so, instructors will often take issue with the "modernizations," and this is only as it should be—this edition is not concerned with the last word, only with a helpful first word.

Finally, I should observe that a list is provided of words difficult or otherwise special and occurring frequently, in the hope that readers will familiarize themselves early with these words and become accustomed to consulting the list for them. The list is printed on the back end-paper of the book for easy access.

This edition of *Troilus and Criseyde* is based on A. C. Baugh's text, from *Chaucer's Major Poetry*, partly because, as reviewers observed when it first appeared, "his text is eminently sound" (John Burrow). But the primary motive has been the excellence of his glossary and annotations, which I have used as an important part of our common fund of knowledge about *Troilus and Criseyde*. Baugh's edition, then, especially in conjunction with the excellent *Chaucer Glossary* published by Norman Davis and his colleagues (Oxford, 1979), has enabled me to produce this edition with considerable confidence about my decisions on definitions and annotations.

Given the recent appearance of the monumental works of Windeatt and Barney, it seems appropriate to observe here that when I have elected to use any of their findings, I cite them explicitly and *in situ*. I prepared the first draft of my glosses and annotations without consulting their editions; since completing the first draft, however, I have regularly checked their editions to corroborate my information.

In conclusion, I would like to mention my ideal conception of the fate of this edition. It would eventually enjoy a happy obsolescence in the hands of all who used it. As they transcended it, en route to greater understanding of *Troilus and Criseyde*, they would cease to use it regularly in favor of one of the major scholarly editions. But they would not, even so, discard it. On occasion, they might have trouble remembering a passage exactly; then, as I imagine it, they would return to their personal, scribbled-in copy of the present edition where they would not only find the passage in question but also recall the sense of excitement and pleasure with which they first encountered that passage and, indeed, the whole poem.

Introduction to the Poem

THE PRIMARY goal of the Introduction is to help readers start the poem. The poem will thereafter be their principal and their best guide to Chaucer's insights.

1. Date

Chaucer wrote the *Troilus* probably in the 1380s. In this decade, he also translated Boethius's *Consolation of Philosophy* and worked on the *Knight's Tale*, itself in part a translation of Boccaccio's *Teseida*. If, as we believe, he was born about 1343, then he was in his 40's when he wrote the *Troilus* and had been writing poetry for more than half his life. He would continue to write for roughly another decade and a half (dying, as tradition has it, October 25, 1400). When he wrote the *Troilus*, then, he was a seasoned poet; he was also, at least, a cosmopolitan diplomat (he had by now traveled extensively in France and Italy), a tested military man, a successful courtier, an experienced civil servant—in short, a mature adult.

2. Sources

Chaucer's principal source is Boccaccio's *Il Filostrato* ("The Love-Stricken One"); this is the text Chaucer is translating, although, as numerous scholars remark, his "translation" is hardly slavish (Baugh observes that over 5500 lines of the *Troilus* are Chaucer's own). Chaucer's Narrator cites as his "auctour" or "authority" a man named Lollius (*Troilus* 1.394), possibly an invented character (though see *The House of Fame* 1468) but at any rate someone by whose hand no work is extant for us to consult; who Lollius was and what he signifies in the *Troilus*, therefore, remain uncertain.

In addition to Boccaccio, Chaucer also consulted and used at least Boethius's *Consolation of Philosophy*, *The Romance of the Rose*, Dante's *Comedy*, lyrics of Petrarch, Virgil's *Aeneid*, Statius's *Thebaid*, Ovid's *Metamorphoses*; he may also have known in addition to other sources a French prose translation of *Il Filostrato*, by one Beauvau, Seneschal of Anjou, *Le Roman de Troyle et de Criseida* (but see Windeatt, pp. 19–24, who disputes this source).

Crucially, Chaucer did not know Homer; in fact, Homer was only a name throughout the medieval period, becoming available to the West again only in the Renaissance. Knowledge of the Trojan War in the Middle Ages came primarily (though not exclusively) through the Latin versions of two prose works, the *De Excidio Trojae Historia* by Dares Phrygius and the *Ephemeris Belli Trojani* by Dictys Cretensis (see *The House of Fame* 1466–70). These two works (second century A.D. if not earlier) provided the material for a lengthy French poem, the *Roman de Troie* (containing 30,000 lines), which was written about 1155–60 by Benoît de Sainte-Maure; this work, in turn, was translated into Latin in 1287 by a Sicilian lawyer, Guido delle Colonne, as the *Historia Trojana* or *Historia Destructionis Troiae*. It is in Benoît's *Roman* that the story of Troilus and Criseyde first appears (Benoît calls her Briseida), and it is from Benoît's and Guido's accounts of the story that Boccaccio developed his own narrative of Troilo and Criseida (the form of her name chosen by Boccaccio). As Baugh notes, we assume that Chaucer first encountered Boccaccio's poem during his second mission to Italy, in 1378, and that he brought back a manuscript of it when he returned to England on that trip.

Immediately evident from this précis is one fact which readers should never forget: Chaucer's *Troilus* is the learned poem of a learned man. This fact entails important corollaries. First, the poem is allusive or, we can also say, citational; the poem, in other words, is always looking back, looking back to prior authorities which it regularly and often openly cites. Such practice, to be sure, is common in medieval poetry, which often privileges "auctoritas" ("authority") over originality, but it is probably fair to say that in no other medieval poems except the *Comedy* and *The Romance of the Rose* is this practice pursued so consistently and so noticeably as in the *Troilus*. Second, the poem is written by a reader, a reader moreover who frequently calls attention not just to his reading but also to the fact that he is reading. Third, the poem is a version of the story which its many sources tell, and like any version, it is only *a* version (that is, one version)—hence the Narrator's repeated editorializing about his sources, a feature of the poem to which readers must quickly become sensitive.

3. Language

The one word both most accurate and most useful for describing the language of the poem is *conversational*. This means not only that there is a great deal of dialogue in the *Troilus*, though that is certainly true, but also that even the large narrative portions of the poem are often like dialogue: the Narrator, in other words, is most often conversing with his audience (Chaucer, by the way, probably read the poem aloud to his original audiences). Readers, thus, will hear a voice that is frequently and often at the same time familiar, divulging, confessional, apologetic, self-exculpating, collusive, indignant, remorseful, and more. And the sooner readers become attuned to this voice, the sooner they will begin to understand the *Troilus*.

Brief remarks on the *structure* of Chaucer's language will aid the reader in this process of becoming attuned to the Narrator's voice. Chaucer wrote in the period of the language now called Middle English (c. 1100–1500). Since that time the language has undergone considerable change. Modern English has a different sound, its grammar has changed, and many words no longer have the same meanings they had in Chaucer's day. Although it would be impossible to give a full account here of the differences, the following discussion may help to identify some of the important ones that readers of *Troilus and Criseyde* will need to know.

Among the chief differences between Chaucer's English and ours are the effects of what is called the Great Vowel Shift (dated to the fifteenth century). As a result of this Shift, the pronunciation of English long vowels was raised, except for *i* and *u*, which became diphthongs. To pronounce Chaucer's English, then, we must go back behind the Great Vowel Shift, and this means that we pronounce his vowels in much the same way that the vowels of French, German, and Italian are pronounced today. The following table exemplifies the approximate pronunciation of Chaucer's vowels and diphthongs (This and other tables in the Introduction are cited from Baugh's edition, pp. xxiii–xxix).

Sound	Pronunciation	Spelling	Examples
ā	like *a* in *father*	a, aa	fader, caas
a	like *a* in *what*	a	what
ē	like *a* in *mate*	e, ee	swete, neede
ę̄	like *e* in *there*	e, ee	bere, heeth
e	like *e* in *met*	e	hem
ə	like *a* in *about*	e	yonge
ī	like *i* in *machine*	i, y	blithe, nyce
i	like *i* in *bit*	i, y	list, nyste
ō	like *o* in *so*	o, oo	dom, roote
ǭ	like *o* in *cloth*	o, oo	lore, goon
o	like *o* in *or*	o	for
ū	like *oo* in *root*	ou, ow	hous, how
u	like *oo* in *book*	u, o	ful, nonne
ü	like Fr. *u* in *tu*	u	vertu
au	like *ow* in *how*	au, aw	cause, drawe
ęi	like *ay* in *day*	ai, ay, ei, ey	fair, may, feith, eyr
ęu	ę + u	ew	fewe, shewe
iu	like *ew* in *few*	eu, ew	reule, newe
ǫi	like *oy* in *boy*	oi, oy	point, joye
ou	like *ow* in *grow*	ou, ow	thought, knowe

Chaucer pronounced his consonants much as we do today. However, he pronounced some consonants which are now silent: *k* and *g* (in *knowe* and *gnawe*, for examples); *gh*, which is pronounced like *ch* in German *ich* (in *knyght*); *l* before *f, v, k, m* (*calf, halve, folk, palmer*); w (*write*). Numerous other observations on consonants in Chaucer's English could be made, but a useful rule of thumb is: when in doubt, pronounce.

Chaucer's English is still inflected, if only slightly, a sign of its descent from Old English. In nouns, the genitive singular and the plural end usually in *-es*, sometimes in *-is*. We are familiar with this phenomenon in Modern English, too, where the genitive singular ends in *'s* and many nouns have their plurals in *s*. Frequently in Middle English (as sometimes in Modern English) plurals are formed with *-n* or *-en* (*oxen, asshen*).

Adjectives also in Chaucer's English are declined, in keeping with what are termed *strong* and *weak* declensions. The *weak* declension shows a final *-e* when the adjective is preceded by a demonstrative, a definite article, or a possessive pronoun. Hence Chaucer would say "yong man" but "the yonge man." Some adjectives always have a final *-e* (e.g., *swete*), and all adjectives, strong or weak, have a final *-e* in the plural.

Because of the frequency with which readers will meet the personal pronouns, a complete table of them is provided here (N. = nominative; G. = genitive; D. = dative; A. = accusative):

SINGULAR

	First Person	*Second Person*		*Third Person*	
N.	I, ich (ik)	thou	he(e)	she	hit, hyt
G.	my, myn	thy, thyn	his	hir(e), her	his
D.	me	the(e)	him	hir(e), her(e)	him
A.	me	the(e)	him	hir(e), her(e)	hit, hyt

PLURAL

N.	we	ye	they
G.	oure	youre	hir(e), her(e)
D.	us	yow, you	hem
A.	us	yow, you	hem

The only two forms here that may cause confusion are *the*, meaning "thee," but spelled like the article, and *hir(e)*, which means either "her" or "their" depending on the context.

Like other Germanic languages and like Modern English, Middle English shows a distinction between strong verbs (we call them "irregular") and weak verbs (we call them "regular"). Strong verbs, like *sing – sang – sung*, form the past tense and past participle by changing the stem vowel (*i – a – u*, in this example); weak verbs, like *walk – walked – walked*, form the past tense and past participle by adding *d* or *t*.

In Middle English, the infinitive ends in *-en* or *-n* (*speken* and *gon* are examples), though it is common for the *-n* to be dropped (*speke, go*).

For the reader's convenience, the present and past indicative inflections of a strong and a weak verb are illustrated below:

PRESENT INDICATIVE

		Strong	*Weak*
Sing.	1.	bere	love
	2.	berest	lovest
	3.	bereth	loveth
Pl.		bere(n)	love(n)

PAST INDICATIVE

		Strong	*Weak*
Sing.	1.	bar	loved(e)
	2.	bere, bare	lovedest
	3.	bar, beer	loved(e)
Pl.		bere(n), bare(n)	lovede(n), loved

4. Chaucer as Translator

Chaucerians never tire (nor should they) of citing the fourteenth-century French poet Eustace Deschamps's accolade for Chaucer: "grant translateur." Indeed, Chaucer is a "great translator"; but this means many different things, depending on one's perspective, and all of them relevant. Here, for the sole purpose of an introduction, the concern is with the consistent tendency within the poem to call attention to the act of translating (e.g., 1.393–99; 2.8–49; 3.1195–97 and 1324–37). Indeed, one of the most distinctive features of the *Troilus* is the Narrator's self-consciousness as translator—

And of his song naught only the sentence,	*meaning*
As writ myn auctour called Lollius,	
But pleinly, save oure tonges difference,	*tongue's*
I dar wel seyn, in al that Troilus	*dare*
Seyde in his song, loo! every word right thus	
As I shal seyn.	

Troilus 1.393–98

And as readers come to terms with this feature of the poem, they should remember that the principal motive of Deschamps's accolade is the fact that throughout his career Chaucer's poems usually began as translations—he almost always started his poems (at least, his major poems) from his translation of a given text. To understand Chaucer without understanding also the difficulties and ramifications of translation is probably impossible (see further the *Prologue* to *The Legend of Good Women*, esp. lines 321–34).

5. Characters

To help readers relate initially to each character, a *keyword* is provided here for that character with a brief explanation of its relevance. Obviously, one word can hardly be decisive or exhaustive for characters as complex as Chaucer's, but still one word can, in my experience, help readers get started in forming judgments about each character.

Criseyde Hardly anyone would dispute that the keyword here is *changeable*. Beautiful, experienced, shrewd, Criseyde is also, in Chaucer's famous phrase, "slydynge of corage" (*Troilus* 5.825)—that is, unstable, mutable, lacking in steadfastness. Here readers may want to pay special attention to the meteorological imagery that Chaucer continually applies to Criseyde—she changes even as the sky changes in variable weather (*Troilus* 1.175, e.g.). Her changeableness finally is Troilus's undoing since as much as her actual betrayal of him for Diomede it is her *being* "slydynge of corage" that diseases Troilus's imagination and breaks his will to live.

Troilus Here the keyword is probably *idealist*. Although Troilus initially is a scorner of Love, when finally he falls in love, his commitment is so fierce, his idealism so pure, that death really is his only alternative to having Criseyde. Even at those moments when he most nearly resembles Pandarus (e.g., *Troilus* 3.407–13), Troilus is still not as coarse as Pandarus—his idealism is so intense, it keeps him even then if not pure, at least, purer. Here readers will want perhaps to keep in mind the various imagery of transcendence which Chaucer consistently applies to Troilus so as to suggest the surging and striving of his idealism (e.g., 3.1599–1600).

Pandarus Pandarus is *expedient*; no other word sums him up quite so well. If his friend Troilus has a desire which he can fulfill, then one way or another he will find the means to fulfill it. No matter how elaborate the ruse and no matter how much time and energy it may take, Pandarus will not stint to devote himself to it entirely. So absolute is his expediency that we early realize that his serving Troilus is also self-serving; unsuccessful himself in love (e.g., *Troilus* 2.1107), he enjoys vicariously the love-affair he orchestrates between Troilus and his niece (e.g., *Troilus* 3.1566–68).

Narrator The keyword here initially is *diffident*. The Narrator is lacking in confidence on a number of fronts: he is hardly a lover (*Troilus* 2.19); he is insecure about following his author (*Troilus* 2.49); he repeatedly defers to his audience (e.g., *Troilus* 3.1324–37); and even at the end he is still deferential, paying respect to the ladies in his audience (*Troilus* 5. 1772–78) and paying homage, humbly, to the great epic poets who have preceded him (*Troilus* 5.1791–92). Here readers will benefit most perhaps from keeping in mind these basic questions: is the Narrator uniformly diffident in the poem or does he change and, if he changes, in what ways and how does Chaucer alert us to them?

6. Contexts

Among many minor ones, there are three major contexts for the *Troilus*: the Trojan War or matter of Troy, *fin'amors* (often called "courtly love"), and Boethian philosophy, derived from the *Consolation of Philosophy* (which Chaucer translated entire). The first of these has been discussed already.

Fin'amors is arguably the most influential and enduring legacy of the Middle Ages. Although no single definition can be adequate to so complicated a term, Chaucer's succinctest and (to my mind) most beautiful expression of it occurs in a song sung by Antigone, Criseyde's niece, in Book 2:

> Whom shulde I thanken but yow, god of Love,
> Of al this blisse, in which to bathe I gynne?   *begin*
> And thanked be ye, lord, for that I love!
> This is the righte lif that I am inne,
> To flemen alle manere vice and synne: *banish*
> This dooth me so to vertu for t'entende,
> That day by day I in my wille amende.
> *Troilus* 2.848–54

Here, especially in the last four lines, is the essential of *fin'amors*: "fine or refined love" renders virtuous those who love, ennobling them, by making them naturally abhor vice and pursue rectitude. From its inception, *fin'amors* was such a motive for moral excellence, and no matter how corrupt *fin'amors* became (and it did become corrupt), this motive never completely decayed.

Clearly, *fin'amors* was a code or, say, a discourse for governing or expressing relations among the sexes. Its premise throughout was the sovereignty of the lady in amorous relations (she was early called *midons*, a masculine-feminine hybrid signalling the dominance of the lady over her lover—something like "my lady-lord"). The lady's sovereignty implied a chastening and a channelling of male aggression—hence also the marked civilizing tendency of *fin'amors* wher-

xxii

ever it was followed. This tendency rapidly made itself felt in the public realm of politics and society, extending its influence from the private realm of amorous relations, and in this realm it became, in effect, a set of customs and manners.

However "antiquated" *fin'amors* may have become by the late fourteenth century, Chaucer would nonetheless have been intimately familiar with it as a set of customs and manners if as nothing else. Furthermore, if *fin'amors* to some extent was "quaint" in Chaucer's day, it was by no means passé. It had always been an elitist phenomenon and was probably even more so in the late fourteenth century, but it remained nonetheless a *lingua franca* throughout Europe which united otherwise disparate political, national, and linguistic groups. Men and women all across Europe were united by *fin'amors* even as they were united, for example, by their Catholicism or by the Latin language.

Chaucer should probably be thought of as more a historian of *fin'amors* than a devotee; that is to say, whatever his own social practice, he was learned in the code or discourse and wrote within it, as well as about it, fluently. His first extant long poem, *The Book of the Duchess*, amply illustrates this knowledge and this fluency. And throughout the rest of his career, he returned regularly to *fin'amors* for matter and for inspiration alike. And clearly one of the features of *fin'amors* that continually drew him to it was its distinct tendency to express itself as a "religion." Much has been written on this matter (and much that is suspect for exaggeration and special pleading). But it does seem generally agreed that *fin'amors* was so complete a code that it took on the forms and rituals of a religion. It is impossible to enter into the controversy surrounding this issue here, but it is all the same necessary to alert readers to the controversy and its origins. After all, different as they are, Dante's *Comedy* and *The Romance of the Rose*, for example, clearly demonstrate that *fin'amors* as an expression of human eroticism was "felt" as a religion, a kind of worship. And as readers will see before they have finished the first 50 lines of *Troilus*, Chaucer's Narrator openly assumes that love is a religion.

An efficient as well as informative means of introducing *fin'amors*, both as a code or discourse and also as a "religion" with its rituals, is to refer to the "rules of love" supplied in Andreas Capellanus's *De arte honesti amandi* (*The Art of Courtly Love*), a book written in the twelfth century in the milieu of the court of Champagne, then under the rule of Marie de Champagne, daughter of Eleanor of Aquitaine. Hence, for this introduction, the 31 rules are quoted in full (Andreas Capellanus, *The Art of Courtly Love*, trans. John Jay Parry [New York: Norton, 1969), pp. 184–86]); readers should study them briefly and then consult them regularly as they work their way through the *Troilus* (especially, through the early books of the poem, Rules 2, 10, 13, 14, 16, 20, 23, and 30).

The Rules of Love

1. Marriage is no real excuse for not loving.
2. He who is not jealous cannot love.
3. No one can be bound by a double love.
4. It is well known that love is always increasing or decreasing.
5. That which a lover takes against the will of his beloved has no relish.
6. Boys do not love until they arrive at the age of maturity.
7. When one lover dies, a widowhood of two years is required of the survivor.
8. No one should be deprived of love without the very best of reasons.
9. No one can love unless he is impelled by the persuasions of love.
10. Love is always a stranger in the home of avarice.
11. It is not proper to love any woman whom one would be ashamed to seek to marry.
12. A true lover does not desire to embrace in love anyone except his beloved.
13. When made public love rarely endures.
14. The easy attainment of love makes it of little value; difficulty of attainment makes it prized.
15. Every lover regularly turns pale in the presence of his beloved.
16. When a lover suddenly catches sight of his beloved his heart palpitates.
17. A new love puts to flight an old one.
18. Good character alone makes any man worthy of love.
19. If love diminishes, it quickly fails and rarely survives.
20. A man in love is always apprehensive.
21. Real jealousy always increases the feeling of love.
22. Jealousy, and therefore love, are increased when one suspects his beloved.
23. He whom the thought of love vexes eats and sleeps very little.
24. Every act of a lover ends in the thought of the beloved.

25. A true lover considers nothing good except what he thinks will please his beloved.
26. Love can deny nothing to love.
27. A lover can never have enough of the solaces of his beloved.
28. A slight presumption causes a lover to suspect his beloved.
29. A man who is vexed by too much passion usually does not love.
30. A true lover is constantly and without intermission possessed by the thought of his beloved.
31. Nothing forbids one woman being loved by two men or one man by two women.

The third major context for the *Troilus* to which readers should be introduced is Boethian philosophy. This matter is both easier and more difficult to address than *fin'amors*—easier because Chaucer's intimate acquaintance with and reliance on Boethius is obvious, more difficult because Boethius is everywhere in Chaucer's work so evident that it is hard to know where to begin.

One approach, certainly useful, is straightforward documentation. For example, much of Troilus's long and climactic internal debate in Book 4 on fate and free-will (lines 958–1082) is a virtual translation of Boethius (Book 5 of the *Consolation*), and the notes to these lines will show the extent to which Chaucer felt intimate with Boethius's complex arguments on this thorny problem.

It is equally useful to wonder, and to try to characterize, what inspired Chaucer's attraction to and lifelong engagement with Boethius. The keyword is *resignation* (a resignation of which Troilus is incapable). Boethius was imprisoned and condemned to death after a long and distinguished political career; eventually he was put to death but not before he wrote the *Consolation of Philosophy* in his prison cell (Troilus could not have done this). The sense of resignation that emerges from this book and that spoke deeply to Chaucer has nothing in it of sloth—Boethius was not a quitter. It is rather a sense of resignation as *vigilant patience*, a wakeful waiting that is convinced that understanding will come, comprehension will occur, order will appear. One man in and of himself, it is true, may not in his own lifetime be able to wait long enough—his vigilance and his patience may finally be exhausted by death's inevitability. But if resigned in Boethius's way, a man may until that final exhaustion experience within himself evocations of a comprehensibility within the universe that is somehow more than just the cheat of rationalization or the artificiality of imposed order. Or so I believe Chaucer believed Boethius believed.

7. Conclusion

Troilus and Criseyde is a long, learned poem—part epic, part tragedy, part comedy, part romance—in which Chaucer draws on all of his wide learning to examine human relationships, primarily erotic relationships, in a context dominated by the idea of worldly mutability, and against the historical backdrop of the Trojan War: *fin'amors* is the code or discourse that supplies the primary vocabulary of the poem; the matter of Troy is the source of the poem's major historical events; and Boethian philosophy is the intellectual structure within which Chaucer develops his main ideas and eventually arrives at his principal conclusions—and these number among them, but are by no means restricted to, a sober conviction of the short-term untrustworthiness of the world, a healthy scepticism toward idealism and pragmatism alike, and a profound belief, all the same, in the ennobling virtues of human love, its near kinship to divine love.

8. Select Bibliography

The problem with a select bibliography, of course, is that it is selective—not exhaustive—and thus some principle of selection, also therefore necessarily a slant if not a bias, is always at work in it. The following bibliography emphasizes works that will be of immediate use and help in interpreting and judging a crux or a figure or an image or a plot device or an allusion, etc. It does not list more specialized or technical studies of manuscripts, sources, language, contemporary events, etc: for these, readers may wish to consult the *New Cambridge Bibliography of English Literature*, vol. 1 [600–1660], ed. Watson (1974), John Leyerle and Anne Quick, *Chaucer: A Bibliographical Introduction* (Toronto: University of Toronto Press, 1986), and the annual bibliographies published in *Studies in the Age of Chaucer* (since 1979); also useful is the bibliography in Windeatt, pp. 567–84.

Two remarks on the format of the following bibliography are in order. To facilitate ease of reference, abbreviations are not used. Also multiple reprint information is not included; such information can be found in advanced bibliographies, such as those listed above (especially Leyerle and Quick).

EDITIONS

Stephen A. Barney. *The Riverside Chaucer*, gen. ed. Larry D. Benson, based on *The Works of Geoffrey Chaucer*, ed. F. N. Robinson. Boston: Houghton Mifflin, 1987.

A. C. Baugh. *Chaucer's Major Poetry*. Englewood Cliffs, NJ: Prentice Hall, 1963.

E. T. Donaldson. *Chaucer's Poetry: An Anthology for the Modern Reader*. 2nd edition. New York: Ronald Press, 1975.

John H. Fisher. *The Complete Poetry and Prose of Geoffrey Chaucer*. New York: Holt, Rinehart, and Winston, 1977.

F. N. Robinson. *The Works of Geoffrey Chaucer*. Boston: Houghton Mifflin, 1957.

Robert K. Root. *The Book of Troilus and Criseyde by Geoffrey Chaucer*. Princeton: Princeton University Press, 1926.

W. W. Skeat. *The Complete Works of Geoffrey Chaucer*, 7 vols. Oxford: Oxford University Press, 1894–97.

Barry A. Windeatt. *Troilus and Criseyde*. London: Longman, 1984.

MODERNIZATIONS

George P. Krapp. *Troilus and Criseyde, Englished Anew*. New York: Random House, 1932.

Robert M. Lumiansky. *Geoffrey Chaucer's Troilus and Criseyde, Rendered into Modern English Prose*. Columbia, SC: University of South Carolina Press, 1952.

Margaret Stanley-Wrench. *Troilus and Criseyde*. Fontwell, Sussex: Centaur Press, 1965.

STUDIES

David Aers. "Criseyde: Woman in Medieval Society." *Chaucer Review* 13 (1978–79): 177–200.

David Anderson. "Theban History in Chaucer's *Troilus*." *Studies in the Age of Chaucer* 4 (1982): 109–33.

———. "Cassandra's Analogy: *Troilus* V.1450–1521." *Hebrew University Studies in Literature and the Arts* 13 (1985): 1–17.

Stephen A. Barney. "Troilus Bound." *Speculum* 47 (1972): 445–58.

———. Ed. *Chaucer's "Troilus": Essays in Criticism*. Hamden, CT: Archon, 1980.

C. David Benson. *The History of Troy in Middle English Literature: Guido delle Colonne's "Historia destructionis Troiae" in Medieval England*. Totowa, NJ: Rowman and Littlefield, 1980.

Morton W. Bloomfield. "Distance and Predestination in *Troilus and Criseyde*." *Publications of the Modern Language Association* 72 (1957): 14–26.

Roger Boase. *The Origin and Meaning of Courtly Love*. Manchester: Manchester University Press, 1977.

Piero Boitani. *Chaucer and the Italian Trecento*. Cambridge: Cambridge University Press, 1983.

Evan Carton. "Complicity and Responsibility in Pandarus' Bed and Chaucer's Art." *Publications of the Modern Language Association* 94 (1979): 47–61.

F. G. Cassidy. "'Don Thyn Hood' in Chaucer's *Troilus*." *Journal of English and Germanic Philology* 57 (1958): 739–42.

S. L. Clark and Julian N. Wasserman. "The Heart in *Troilus and Criseyde*: The Eye of the Breast, the Mirror of the Mind, the Jewel and Its Setting." *Chaucer Review* 18 (1984): 316–27.

Paul M. Clogan. "Chaucer and the *Thebaid* Scholia." *Studies in Philology* 61 (1964): 599–615.

Alfred David. "The Hero of the *Troilus*." *Speculum* 37 (1962): 566–81.

Norman Davis. "The *Litera Troili* and English Letters." *Review of English Studies*, n.s. 16 (1965): 233–44.

Sheila Delany. "Techniques of Alienation in *Troilus and Criseyde*." In *The Uses of Criticism*, ed. A. P. Foulkes, 77–95. Bern: H. Lang, 1976.

E. T. Donaldson. "The Ending of Chaucer's *Troilus*." In *Early English and Norse Studies Presented to Hugh Smith in Honour of His Sixtieth Birthday*, ed. Arthur Brown and Peter Foote, 26–45. London: Methuen, 1963.

———. "Criseide and her Narrator." In *Speaking of Chaucer*, 65–83. New York: Norton, 1972.

Penelope B. R. Doob. "Chaucer's 'corones tweyne' and the Lapidaries." *Chaucer Review* 7 (1972): 85–96.

Peter Dronke. "The Conclusion of *Troilus and Criseyde*." *Medium Aevum* 23 (1964): 47–52.

Laurence Eldredge. "Boethian Epistemology and Chaucer's *Troilus* in Light of Fourteenth-Century Thought." *Mediaevalia* 2 (1976): 50–75.

John Fleming. "Deiphebus Betrayed: Virgilian Decorum, Chaucerian Feminism." *Chaucer Review* 21 (1986): 182–99.

William Frost. "A Chaucerian Crux." *Yale Review* 66 (1977): 551–61.

John Fyler. "The Fabrications of Pandarus." *Modern Language Quarterly* 41 (1980): 115–30.

John M. Ganim. *Style and Consciousness in Middle English Narrative*. Princeton: Princeton University Press, 1983.

Alan Gaylord. "Friendship in Chaucer's *Troilus*." *Chaucer Review* 3 (1968–69): 239–64.

―――. "Uncle Pandarus as Lady Philosophy." *Papers of the Michigan Academy of Science, Arts, and Letters* 46 (1961): 571–95.

Ida L. Gordon. *The Double Sorrow of Troilus: A Study of Ambiguities in "Troilus and Criseyde"*. Oxford: Clarendon Press, 1970.

R. K. Gordon. *The Story of Troilus as Told by Benoît de Sainte-Maure, Giovanni Boccaccio, Geoffrey Chaucer, and Robert Henryson*. 1934. Rpt. Medieval Academy Reprints for Teaching 2. Toronto: University of Toronto Press, 1978.

Richard F. Green. "Troilus and the Game of Love." *Chaucer Review* 13 (1978–79): 201–20.

Elizabeth R. Hatcher. "Chaucer and the Psychology of Fear: Troilus in Book V." *English Literary History* 40 (1973): 307–24.

Donald R. Howard. "Experience, Language, and Consciousness: *Troilus and Criseyde*, II, 596–931." In *Medieval Literature and Folklore Studies: Essays in Honor of Francis Lee Utley*, ed. Jerome Mandel and Bruce A. Rosenberg, 173–92. New Brunswick: Rutgers University Press, 1970.

Lynn Staley Johnson. "The Medieval Hector: A Double Tradition." *Mediaevalia* 5 (1979): 165–82.

Alice R. Kaminsky. *Chaucer's "Troilus and Criseyde" and the Critics*. Columbus, OH: Ohio University Press, 1980.

R. E. Kaske. "Pandarus's 'Vertu of Corones Tweyne.'" *Chaucer Review* 21 (1986): 226–33.

Alfred L. Kellogg. "On the Tradition of Troilus's Vision of the Little Earth." *Mediaeval Studies* 22 (1960): 204–13.

Henry A. Kelly. *Love and Marriage in the Age of Chaucer*. Ithaca: Cornell University Press, 1975.

Peggy A. Knapp. "The Nature of Nature: Criseyde's 'Slydynge Corage.'" *Chaucer Review* 13 (1978): 133–40.

Mark Lambert. "*Troilus*, Books I–III: A Criseydan Reading." In *Chaucer Studies III: Essays on "Troilus and Criseyde"*, ed. Mary Salu, 105–25. Cambridge: D. S. Brewer, 1979.

C. S. Lewis. "What Chaucer Really Did to *Il Filostrato.*" *Essays & Studies* 17 (1932): 56–75.

John Leyerle. "The Heart and the Chain." In *The Learned and the Lewed: Studies in Chaucer and Medieval Literature*, ed. Larry D. Benson, 113–45. Harvard English Studies 5. Cambridge: Harvard University Press, 1974.

R. M. Lumiansky. "Calchas in the Early Versions of the Troilus Story." *Tulane Studies in English* 4 (1954): 5–20.

Monica McAlpine. *The Genre of "Troilus and Criseyde.*" Ithaca: Cornell University Press, 1978.

John P. McCall. "Five-Book Structure in Chaucer's *Troilus.*" *Modern Language Quarterly* 23 (1962): 297–308.

Sanford B. Meech. *Design in Chaucer's "Troilus.*" Syracuse: Syracuse University Press, 1959.

Dieter Mehl. "The Audience of Chaucer's *Troilus and Criseyde.*" In *Chaucer and Middle English Studies: In Honor of Rossell Hope Robbins*, ed. Beryl Rowland, 173–89. London: Allen and Unwin, 1974.

Barbara Newman. " 'Feynede Loves,' Feigned Love, and Faith in Trouthe." In Barney, 257–75.

Glending Olson. *Literature as Recreation in the Later Middle Ages.* Ithaca: Cornell University Press, 1982.

Charles A. Owen. "The Problem of Free Will in Chaucer's Narratives." *Philological Quarterly* 46 (1967): 433–56.

Howard R. Patch. "Troilus on Determinism." *Speculum* 6 (1931): 225–43.

——. "Troilus on Predestination." *Journal of English and Germanic Philology* 17 (1918): 399–422.

Robert A. Pratt. "Chaucer and *Le Roman de Troyle et de Criseida.*" *Studies in Philology* 53 (1956): 509–39.

D. W. Robertson, Jr. "Chaucerian Tragedy." *English Literary History* 19 (1952): 1–37.

Donald W. Rowe. *O Love! O Charite! Contraries Harmonized in Chaucer's "Troilus.*" Carbondale: Southern Illinois University Press, 1976.

Paul G. Ruggiers. "The Italian Influence on Chaucer." In *Companion to Chaucer Studies*, ed. Beryl Rowland, 160–84. 2nd ed. Oxford: Oxford University Press, 1979.

Elizabeth Salter. "*Troilus and Criseyde*: Poet and Narrator." In *Acts of Interpretation: The Text in its Contexts, 700–1600: Essays on Medieval and Renaissance Literature in Honor of E. Talbot Donaldson*, ed. Mary J. Carruthers and Elizabeth D. Kirk, 281–91. Norman, OK: Pilgrim Books, 1982.

Richard J. Schoeck and Jerome Taylor, eds. *Chaucer Criticism, II: "Troilus and Criseyde" and the Minor Poems*. Notre Dame: University of Notre Dame Press, 1961.

R. A. Shoaf. *Dante, Chaucer, and the Currency of the Word: Money, Images, and Reference in Late Medieval Poetry*. Norman, OK: Pilgrim Books, 1983.

John M. Steadman. *Disembodied Laughter: "Troilus" and the Apotheosis Tradition: A Reexamination of Narrative and Thematic Contexts*. Berkeley: University of California Press, 1972.

Paul Strohm. "Storie, Spelle, Geste, Romaunce, Tragedie: Generic Distinctions in the Middle English Troy Narratives." *Speculum* 46 (1971): 348–59.

Yasunari Takada. "'Hevene' in Criseyde: Dante's 'Festa' and Chaucer's 'Feste.'" *Philologia Anglica: Festschrift for Prof. Y. Terasawa*, 299–305. Tokyo: Kenkyusha, 1988.

M. Teresa Tavormina. "The Moon in Leo: What Chaucer Really Did to *Il Filostrato*'s Calendar." *Ball State University Forum* 22 (1981): 14–19.

Karla Taylor. "Proverbs and the Authentication of Convention in *Troilus and Criseyde*." In Barney, 277–96.

Eugene Vance. "Mervelous Signals: Poetics, Sign Theory, and Politics in Chaucer's *Troilus*." *New Literary History* 10 (1979): 293–337.

Mary F. Wack. "Lovesickness in *Troilus*." *Pacific Coast Philology* 19 (1984): 55–61.

David Wallace. "Chaucer's 'Ambages.'" *American Notes & Queries* 23 (1984): 1–4.

Julian N. Wasserman. See under S. L. Clark.

Winthrop Wetherbee. *Chaucer and the Poets: An Essay on "Troilus and Criseyde"*. Ithaca: Cornell University Press, 1984.

James I. Wimsatt. "Medieval and Modern in Chaucer's *Troilus and Criseyde*." *PMLA* 92 (1977): 203–16.

Barry Windeatt. "'Love that oughte ben secree' in Chaucer's *Troilus*." *Chaucer Review* 14 (1979–80): 116–31.

Robert F. Yeager. "'O Moral Gower': Chaucer's Dedication of *Troilus and Criseyde*." *Chaucer Review* 19 (1984): 87–99.

Karl Young. *The Origin and Development of the Story of Troilus and Criseyde*. Chaucer Society 2nd ser. 40. 1908. Rpt. New York: Gordian, 1968.

Abbreviations

The following abbreviations (listed in alphabetical order) are used in the notes to the text throughout the book.

Ch	=	Chaucer
CP	=	*Consolation of Philosophy*
C	=	Criseyde
CT	=	*Canterbury Tales*
MA	=	Middle Ages
ME	=	Middle English
N	=	Narrator
P	=	Pandarus
RR	=	*Romance of the Rose*
T&C	=	*Troilus and Criseyde*
T	=	Troilus

Geoffrey Chaucer

Troilus and Criseyde

Troilus and Criseyde

BOOK ONE

The °double sorwe of Troilus to tellen,
That was the kyng Priamus sone of Troye, *Priam's*
In lovynge, how his aventures °fellen *proceeded*
Fro wo to wele, and after out of joie, *woe, felicity, afterwards*
5 My purpos is, er that I parte fro ye. *leave you*
°Thesiphone, thow help me for t'endite *compose*
Thise woful vers, that wepen as I write. *verses that weep*

To the clepe I, thow goddesse of torment, *call*
Thow cruwel Furie, sorwynge evere yn peyne, *pain*
10 Help me, that am the sorwful instrument,
That helpeth loveres, as I kan, to pleyne. *complain*
For wel sit it, the sothe for to seyne, *it is fitting, truth, say*
A woful wight to han a drery °feere, *person, sad companion*
And to a sorwful tale, a sory chere. *sad countenance*

---

1 The phrase "double sorwe" probably is meant to evoke the legend of Thebes and "la doppia tristizia di Iocasta" ("the double sorrow of Jocasta"), as Dante phrases it in the encounter between Statius, author of the *Thebaid*, and Virgil (*Purg.* 22. 56).

3 lit., "happened" or "fell out"

6 one of the three Furies of the classical world—Alecto, Tisiphone (Ch's Thesiphone), Megæra (See also 4. 22–4.)

13 The "companion," in this case, is probably Thesiphone; possibly, however, the "drery feere" of lovers who complain is the Narrator.

15 For I, that °God of Loves servantz serve,
   °Ne dar to Love, for myn unliklynesse,
   Preyen for speed, al sholde I therfore sterve,
   So fer am I from his help in derknesse.   *far, darkness*
   But natheles, if this may don gladnesse,   *nevertheless, cause*
20 To any lovere, and his cause availle,   *further*
   Have he my thonk, and myn be this travaille!   *good will, labor*

   But ye loveres, that bathen in gladnesse,   *bathe*
   If any drope of pyte in yow be,   *drop, pity*
   Remembreth yow on passed hevynesse   *depression that has passed*
25 That ye han felt, and on the adversite
   Of othere folk, and thynketh how that ye
   Han felt that Love dorste yow displese,   *dared*
   Or ye han wonne hym with to grete an ese.   *else, won, too easily*

   And °preieth for hem that ben in the cas   *plight*
30 Of Troilus, as ye may after here,   *hear*
   That Love hem brynge in hevene to solas.   *solace*
   And ek for me preieth to God so dere   *also, dear*
   That I have myght to shewe, in som manere,   *demonstrate*
   Swich peyne and wo as Loves folk endure,   *Love's*
35 In Troilus °unsely aventure.   *Troilus's unhappy adventure*

   And biddeth ek for hem that ben despeired   *pray also, in despair*
   In love, that nevere nyl recovered be,   *will never recover*

---

15 Cf. the designation of the Pope, "servant of the servants of God."

16–17 do not dare, since I am ill-suited (to it), to pray to Love for furtherance, although I should therefore die

29 pray for them who are

35 The pair "sely"/"unsely" are frequent words in Ch's poetry. Often they carry something like the valence of Virgil's crucial pair "felix"/"infelix" (see esp. *Legend of Good Women* 3, *Dido* 1157 –"sely Dido," evoking Virgil's "infelix Dido"); "sely" can mean "happy," "blessed," "fortunate," but, just so, it can connote an individual's dependence on fortune or happenstance, and thus, like "felix," can carry with it the connotation of its (imminent) opposite, "unsely," or, as in the present case, "poor," "simple," "hapless," "wretched," "unhappy."

4

And ek for hem that falsly ben apeired   *also, injured*
Thorugh wikked tonges, be it he or she;   *tongues (i. e., rumor)*
40 Thus biddeth God, for his benignite,   *pray*
So graunte hem soone owt of this world to pace,   *out, pass*
That ben °despeired out of Loves grace.   *in despair of*

And biddeth ek for hem that ben at ese,   *ease*
That God hem graunte ay good perseveraunce,
45 And sende hem myght hire ladies so to plese
That it to Love be worship and plesaunce.   *(may) be*
For so hope I my sowle best avaunce,   *soul, to promote in well-being*
To prey for hem that Loves servauntz be,   *by praying*
And write hire wo, and lyve in charite,   *(by) writing of, living*

50 And for to have of hem compassioun,   *by having on them*
As though I were hire owne brother dere.   *dear*
Now herkneth with a good entencioun,   *listen, will*
For now wil I gon streght to my matere,   *straight, subject matter*
In which ye may the double sorwes here   *hear*
55 Of Troilus, in lovynge of Criseyde,
And how that she forsook hym er she deyde.   *before, died*

Yt is wel wist how that the Grekes, stronge   *known*
In armes, with a thousand shippes, wente
To Troiewardes, and the cite longe
60 Assegeden, neigh ten yer er they stente,   *besieged, nearly, ceased*
And in diverse wise and oon entente,   *ways, one*
The ravysshyng to wreken of Eleyne,   *avenge*
°By Paris don, they wroughten al hir peyne.   *applied all their effort*

Now fel it so that in the town ther was   *it so happened*
65 Dwellynge a lord of gret auctorite,
A gret devyn, that clepid was Calkas,   *soothsayer, named*

---

42 Cf. 5. 713.
63 "By Paris don" complements "ravysshyng."

That in science so expert was that he
Knew wel that Troie sholde destroied be,
By answere of his god, that highte thus,   *was called*
70 °Daun Phebus or Appollo Delphicus.

So whan this Calkas knew by calkulynge,   *by calculation*
And ek by answer of this Appollo,   *also*
That Grekes sholden swich a peple brynge,
Thorugh which that Troie moste ben fordo,   *destroyed*
75 He caste anon out of the town to go;   *planned, immediately*
For wel wiste he by sort that Troye sholde   *knew, divination*
Destroyed ben, ye, °wolde whoso nolde.   *yes*

°For which for to departen softely
Took purpos ful this forknowynge wise,
80 And to the Grekes oost ful pryvely   *host, secretly*
He stal anon; and they, in curteys wise,   *stole, courteously*
Hym diden bothe worship and servyse,   *showed*
In trust that he hath konnynge hem to rede   *knowledge to counsel them*
In every peril which that is to drede.   *that is to be feared*

85 The noise up ros, whan it was first aspied   *rose, discovered*
Thorugh al the town, and generaly was spoken,   *(it) was said*
That Calkas °traitour fled was and allied
With hem of Grece, and °casten to be wroken
On hym that falsly hadde his feith so broken,   *faith*
90 And seyden he and al his kyn at-ones   *said, at once*
Ben worthi for to brennen, fel and bones.   *deserved to burn, skin*

---

70 Phebus Apollo, god of oracles, prophets and diviners
77 equivalent to "willy-nilly," in the past tense
78-9 Because of which this foreknowing wise man took full purpose to depart
quietly
87 as a traitor had fled and (was)
88 and they of Troy determined to be avenged

Now hadde Calkas left in this meschaunce, *unfortunate circumstance*
Al unwist of this false and wikked dede, *ignorant*
His doughter, which that was in gret penaunce, *agony*
95 For of hire lif she was ful sore in drede, *sorely in dread*
°As she that nyste what was best to rede;
For bothe a widewe was she and allone *widow*
Of any frend to whom she dorste hire mone. *dared reveal her sorrow*

Criseyde was this lady name al right. *lady's*
100 As to my doom, in al Troies cite *judgment*
Nas non so fair, for passynge every wight *there was none, creature*
So aungelik was hir natif beaute, *angelic, native*
That lik a thing inmortal semed she, *immortal*
As doth an hevenyssh perfit creature, *heavenly perfect*
105 That down were sent in scornynge of nature. *scorning*

This lady, which that alday herd at ere *continually, heard, ear*
Hire fadres shame, his falsnesse and tresoun, *father's*
Wel neigh out of hir wit for sorwe and fere, *nigh, fear*
°In widewes habit large of samyt broun,
110 On knees she fil biforn °Ector adown; *fell, Hector*
With pitous vois, and tendrely wepynge, *pitiful voice, weeping*
His mercy bad, hirselven excusynge. *asked for*

Now was this Ector pitous of nature, *compassionate*
And saugh that she was sorwfully bigon, *saw, overwhelmed*
115 And that she was so fair a creature;
Of his goodnesse he gladede hire anon, *cheered, right away*
And seyde, "Lat youre fadres treson gon *let, go*
Forth with meschaunce, and ye youreself in joie *bad luck (on it)*
Dwelleth with us, whil yow good list, in Troie. *as long as you like*

---

96 as one who didn't know what was the best advice to give herself or to follow
109 in a widow's garment of flowing brown silk
110 Hector, Priam's eldest son and principal defender of Troy

7

120 "And al th'onour that men may don yow have,   *may cause you to have*
    As ferforth as youre fader dwelled here,   *as much as when*
    Ye shul have, and youre body shal men save,
    As fer as I may °ought enquere or here."   *far*
    And she hym thonked with ful humble chere,   *thanked, demeanor*
125 And °ofter wolde, and it hadde ben his wille,   *if*
    And took hire leve, and hom, and held hir stille.   *and (went) home*

    And in hire hous she abood with swich meyne   *household company*
    As til hire honour nede was to holde;   *to, it was necessary to keep*
    And whil she was dwellynge in that cite,
130 Kepte hir estat, and both of yonge and olde   *(she) kept, position*
    °Ful wel biloved, and wel men of hir tolde.   *men spoke well*
    °But wheither that she children hadde or noon,
    I rede it naught, therfore I late it goon.   *read, ignore it*

    The thynges fellen, as they don of werre,   *happened, war*
135 Bitwixen hem of Troie and Grekes ofte;
    For som day boughten they of Troie it derre,   *more dearly (in battle)*
    And eft the Grekes founden nothing softe   *(then) again, in no way*
    The folk of Troie; and thus Fortune on lofte,   *on high*
    And under eft, gan °hem to whielen bothe   *again (in turn)*
140 Aftir hir cours, ay whil that thei were wrothe.

    But how this town com to destruccion
    Ne falleth naught to purpos me to telle;   *falls not to my purpose*
    For it were here a long digression
    Fro my matere, and yow to long to dwelle.   *would delay you too long*

---

123 in any way learn or hear
125 and would have more often
131 (was) very well beloved
132 Boccaccio, however, in Ch's source, says that she had neither son nor daughter.
139 turn them on her wheel along her path (up and down), all the while that they were enraged against each other (Note the auxiliary "gan" here, equivalent to "did"— i.e., "did turn them on her wheel.")

145 But the Troian gestes, as they felle,   *Trojan deeds, happened*
    °In Omer, or in Dares, or in Dite,
    Whoso that kan may rede hem as they write.   *whoever can may read*

    But though that Grekes hem of Troie shetten   *shut up*
    And hir cite bisegede al aboute,   *besieged*
150 Hire olde usage nolde they nat letten,   *customs, discontinue*
    As for to honoure hir goddes ful devoute;   *devoutly*
    But aldirmost in honour, out of doute,   *most of all*
    Thei hadde a relik, heet °Palladion,   *relic, called*
    That was hire trist aboven everichon.   *was what they trusted, all*

155 And so bifel, whan comen was the tyme   *it befell*
    Of Aperil, whan clothed is the mede   *meadow*
    With newe grene, of lusty Veer the pryme,   *at the beginning of spring*
    And swote smellen floures white and rede,   *sweet*
    In sondry wises shewed, as I rede,   *ways, showed, read*
160 The folk of Troie hire observaunces olde,
    Palladiones feste for to holde.   *festival, in order to hold*

    And to the temple, in al hir beste wise,   *their best manner*
    In general ther wente many a wight,   *person*
    To herknen of Palladion the servyse;   *attend and hear*
165 And namely, so many a lusty knyght,   *especially*
    So many a lady fressh and mayden bright,

---

146 During most of the Middle Ages in the Latin West, Homer was known by name, but his Greek text was largely unread; it began to be available again in the West only in Petrarch's time (see, further, the Introduction above, pp. xvi). Ch cites him along with Dares (*De Excidio Trojae Historia*) and Dite (Dictys, *Ephemeris de Historia Belli Trojani*) as the authorities known to him, not as his immediate sources—see, further, Introduction 2, "Sources."

153 On the preservation of the Palladium, or image of Pallas Athena, the safety of Troy depended. According to Greek legend it was stolen by Diomede and Odysseus, but the *Roman de Troie* makes Antenor and Aeneas the traitors (24301ff.); see, further, below, 4. 204 and 5. 977.

Ful wel arayed, bothe meste and leste,   *dressed, greatest and least*
Ye, bothe for the seson and the feste.   *season, festival*

Among thise othere folk was Criseyda,
170 In widewes habit blak; but natheles,   *widow's weeds, nevertheless*
Right as oure first lettre is now an A,
In beaute first so stood she, makeles.   *matchless*
Hire goodly lokyng gladed al the prees.   *gladdened all the crowd*
Nas nevere yet seyn thyng °to ben preysed derre,   *seen*
175 °Nor under cloude blak so bright a sterre   *star*

As was Criseyde, as folk seyde everichone   *people said everyone*
That hir behelden in hir blake wede.   *saw, garments*
And yet she stood ful lowe and stille allone,   *humble, alone*
Byhynden other folk, in litel brede,   *space*
180 And °neigh the dore, ay under shames drede,
Simple of atire and debonaire of chere,
With ful assured lokyng and manere.

This Troilus, as he was wont to gide   *accustomed to guide*
His yonge knyghtes, lad hem up and down   *led*
185 In thilke large temple on every side,   *this same*
Byholding ay the ladyes of the town,
Now here, now there; for no devocioun
Hadde he to non, to reven hym his reste,   *deprive him of*
But gan to °preise and lakken whom hym leste.

190 And in his walk ful faste he gan to wayten   *closely, did observe*
If knyght or squyer of his compaignie   *squire*

---

174 to be more dearly valued
175 Meteorological imagery—planets, weather, etc.—is used consistently of C throughout the poem; see, further, e.g., 2. 764–70 and 806.
180-2 and near the door, ever under the dread of shame, simply clothed and courteous of countenance, with fully confident composure and demeanor
189 did praise and fault whom he pleased

Gan for to syke, or lete his eighen baiten	*did sigh, eyes feast*
On any womman that ke koude espye,	*see*
He wolde smyle and holden it folye,	*folly*
195 And seye hym thus, "God woot, she slepeth softe	*say, knows*
For love of the, whan thow turnest ful ofte!	

"I have herd told, pardieux, of youre lyvynge,	*how you live*
Ye loveres, and youre lewede observaunces,	*foolish*
And which a labour folk han in wynnynge	*what, winning*
200 Of love, and in the kepyng which doutaunces;	*what anxieties*
And whan youre prey is lost, °woo and penaunces.	
O veray fooles, nyce and blynde be ye!	*true, foolish*
°Ther nys nat oon kan war by other be."	

And with that word he gan caste up the browe,	*eyebrow*
205 Ascaunces, "Loo! is this naught wisely spoken?"	*as if to say, not*
At which the God of Love gan loken rowe	*look angrily*
Right for despit, and °shop for to ben wroken.	*despite*
He kidde anon his bowe nas naught broken,	*showed soon*
For sodeynly he hitte hym atte fulle;	*hit him (with an arrow)*
210 °And yet as proud a pekok kan he pulle.	

O blynde world, O blynde entencioun!	*blind*
How often falleth al the effect contraire	*turns out contrary*
Of surquidrie and foul presumpcioun;	*pride*
For kaught is proud, and kaught is debonaire.	
215 This Troilus is clomben on the staire,	*has climbed*
And litel weneth that he moot descenden;	*supposes, must*
But alday faileth thing that fooles wenden.	*continually, imagine*

As proude °Bayard gynneth for to skippe	
Out of the weye, so pryketh hym his corn,	*pricks*

---

201 (what) woe and suffering
203 there isn't one who can be aware (of the trials of love) by (example of) another
207 determined to be avenged
210 and he can still pluck as proud a peacock (as T)
218 the name of a horse in several French *chansons de geste* (narrative poems)

11

220 Til he a lasshe have of the longe whippe;
Than thynketh he, "Though I praunce al byforn
°First in the trays, ful fat and newe shorn,
Yet am I but an hors, and horses lawe   *horse's law*
I moot endure, and with my feres drawe";   *must, fellow horses pull*

225 °So ferde it by this fierse and proude knyght: *it happened with*
Though he a worthy kynges sone were,
And wende nothing hadde had swich myght   *assumed*
Ayeyns his wille that shuld his herte stere,   *against, control*
Yet with a look his herte wax a-fere,   *was set afire*
230 That he that now was moost in pride above,   *who*
Wax sodeynly moost subgit unto love.   *became suddenly*

Forthy ensample taketh of this man,   *hence example take*
Ye wise, proude, and worthi folkes alle,
To scornen Love, which that so soone kan   *(should you decide) to scorn*
235 The fredom of youre hertes to hym thralle;   *enslave*
For evere it was, and evere it shal byfalle,
That Love is he that alle thing may bynde,
For may no man fordon the lawe of kynde.   *abolish the law of nature*

That this be soth, hath preved and doth yit.   *true, proved (so)*
240 For this trowe I ye knowen alle or some,   *believe*
Men reden nat that folk han gretter wit   *read*
Than they that han be most with love ynome;   *those who, taken*
And strengest folk ben therwith overcome,   *strongest*
The worthiest and grettest of degree: *greatest*
245 This was, and is, and yet men shal it see.

And trewelich it sit wel to be so.   *it is fitting*
For alderwisest han therwith ben plesed;   *the wisest of all, pleased*
And they that han ben aldermost in wo,   *most of all*

---

222 as the fore horse in a tandem—i.e., as leader of the team
225 The simile begun in the previous stanza ("As," 218) is concluded here ("So . . .").

With love han ben comforted moost and esed;   *eased*
250 And ofte it hath the cruel herte apesed,   *appeased*
And worthi folk maad worthier of name,   *made*
And causeth moost to dreden vice and shame.   *most (people), dread*

Now sith it may nat goodly ben withstonde,
And is a thing so vertuous in kynde,   *its nature*
255 Refuseth nat to Love for to ben bonde,   *to be bound*
Syn, as hymselven liste, he may yow bynde.   *since, as it pleases him*
The yerde is bet that bowen wole and wynde   *branch, will bow, bend*
Than that that brest; and therfore I yow rede   *which bursts, counsel*
To folowen hym that so wel kan yow lede.   *follow him who, lead*

260 But for to tellen forth in special   *especially*
As of this kynges sone of which I tolde,
And leten other thing collateral,   *leave aside, incidental*
Of hym thenke I my tale forth to holde,   *I determine*
Bothe of his joie and of his cares colde;
265 And al his werk, as touching this matere,
For I it gan, I wol therto refere.   *since, return*

Withinne the temple he wente hym forth °pleyinge,
This Troilus, of every wight aboute,   *person*
On this lady, and now on that, lokynge,
270 Wher so she were of town or of withoute;   *whether*
And upon cas bifel that thorugh a route   *by chance it befell, crowd*
His eye percede, and so depe it wente,   *pierced, deep*
Til on Criseyde it smot, and ther it stente.   *hit upon, stopped*

And sodeynly he wax therwith astoned,   *became, astonished*
275 And gan hir bet biholde in thrifty wise.   *better, prudent*
"O mercy, God," thoughte he, "wher hastow woned,   *have you dwelt*
That art so feyr and goodly to devise?"   *fair, portray (within)*
Therwith his herte gan to sprede and rise,

267-8 "pleyinge . . . of": joking at the expense of

And softe sighed, lest men myghte hym here, *quietly (he), hear*
280 And caught ayeyn his firste pleyinge chere. *previous playful manner*

She nas nat with the °leste of hire stature,
But alle hire lymes so wel answerynge *all parts of her body*
Weren to wommanhode, that creature
Was nevere lasse mannysh in semynge. *less mannish in appearance*
285 And ek the pure wise of hire mevynge *very manner, moving*
Shewed wel that men myght in hire gesse *guess*
Honour, estat, and wommanly noblesse. *breeding*

To Troilus right wonder wel with alle *withal*
Gan for to like hire °mevynge and hire chere, *to be pleasing*
290 Which somdel deignous was, for she let falle *somewhat haughty*
Hire look a lite aside in swich manere, *little*
Ascaunces, "What! may I nat stonden here?" *as if to say, stand*
And after that hir lokynge gan she lighte, *brighten*
That °nevere thoughte hym seen so good a syghte.

295 And of hire look in him ther gan to quyken *quicken*
So gret desir and such affeccioun,
That in his hertes botme gan to stiken *bottom, stick*
Of hir his fixe and depe impressioun. *fixed, deep*
And though he erst hadde poured up and down, *formerly, gazed*
300 He was tho glad his hornes in to shrinke; *pull in his horns*
°Unnethes wiste he how to loke or wynke. *hardly knew, shut his eyes*

Lo, he that leet hymselven so konnynge, *considered, smart*
And scorned hem that Loves peynes dryen, *pains, suffer*
Was ful unwar that Love hadde his dwellynge *unaware*
305 Withinne the subtile stremes of hire yën; *streams, eyes*

---

281 i.e., she was not short
289 her comportment and her demeanor
294 it seemed to him he had never seen
301 i.e., he scarcely knew what to do

14

That sodeynly hym thoughte he felte dyen,   *it seemed to him, die*
Right with hire look, the spirit in his herte.   *with her very look*
Blissed be Love, that kan thus folk converte!   *blessed*

    She, this in blak, likynge to Troilus   *this (woman), pleasing*
310 Over al thing, he stood for to biholde;
    Ne his desir, ne wherfore he stood thus,   *neither, nor why*
    °He neither chere made, ne worde tolde;
But from afer, °his manere for to holde,   *afar*
On other thing his look som tyme he caste,   *gaze*
315 And eft on hire, while that the servyse laste.   *again, lasted*

    And after this, nat fullich al awhaped,   *disconcerted*
Out of the temple al esilich he wente,   *quietly*
Repentynge hym that he hadde evere ijaped   *joked at the expense*
Of Loves folk, lest fully the descente   *descent*
320 Of scorn fille on hymself; but what he mente,   *fell, meant (within)*
Lest it were wist on any manere syde,   *known, anywhere*
His woo he gan dissimulen and hide.   *woe, dissimulate*

    Whan he was fro the temple thus departed,
He streght anon unto his paleys torneth,   *straightway, turns*
325 °Right with hire look thorugh-shoten and thorugh-darted,
Al feyneth he in lust that he sojorneth;
And al his chere and speche also he °borneth,
And ay of Loves servantz every while,   *ever, all the time*
Hymself to wrye, at hem he gan to smyle,   *to cover himself*

---

312 he made no sign (of it) by his countenance
313 in order to maintain his outward bearing
325 with her look indeed shot through and pierced, although he pretends he dwells in happiness
327 (lit., "burnishes") and all his demeanor and his speech he is careful of (i.e., in order to hide his real feelings)

15

330 And seyde, "Lord, so ye lyve al in lest,   *in bliss*
    Ye loveres! for the konnyngeste of yow,   *most intelligent*
    That serveth most ententiflich and best,   *diligently*
    Hym tit as often harm therof as prow.   *there happens to him, profit*
    Youre hire is quyt ayeyn, ye, God woot how!   *service, paid, knows*
335 Nought wel for wel, but scorn for good servyse.   *not well for well*
    In feith, youre °ordre is ruled in good wise!   *manner*

    "In nouncerteyn ben alle youre observaunces,   *uncertainty are*
    But it a sely fewe pointes be;   *unless, minor*
    Ne no thing asketh so gret attendaunces
340 As doth youre lay, and that knowe alle ye;   *law*
    But that is nat the worste, as mote I the!   *may I prosper*
    But, tolde I yow the worste point, I leve,   *(if) I told, believe*
    Al seyde I soth, ye wolden at me greve.   *though, truth, complain*

    °"But take this: that ye loveres ofte eschuwe,
345 Or elles doon, of good entencioun,
    Ful ofte thi lady wol it mysconstruwe,
    And deme it harm in hire opynyoun;   *judge, harmful*
    And yet if she, for other enchesoun,   *reason*
    Be wroth, than shaltow have a groyn anon.   *angry, grumbling*
350 °Lord, wel is hym that may ben of yow oon!"   *well is it for, one*

    But for al this, whan that he say his tyme,   *saw*
    He held his pees; non other boote hym gayned;   *remedy, profited*
    °For love bigan his fetheres so to lyme,
    That wel unnethe until his folk he fayned

---

336 in the sense of a religious order—as of monks, or nuns, or canons, etc.

344-5 but consider this: what you lovers often refrain from doing, or else do with good intention

350 The sense of the line is ironic, if not mildly sarcastic.

353-4 for love began to smear his feathers with bird lime (with which birds are hunted and caught) so that hardly could he even pretend to his household (Cf. further, 5. 1546.)

16

355 That other besy nedes hym destrayned;   *needs, preoccupied*
For wo was hym, that what to doon he nyste,   *he didn't know what to do*
But bad his folk to gon wher that hem liste.   *bade, it pleased them*

And whan that he in chambre was allone,
He doun upon his beddes feet hym sette,   *the foot of his bed*
360 And first he gan to sike, and eft to grone,   *sigh, then to groan*
And thought ay on hire so, withouten lette,   *cease*
That, as he sat and wook, his spirit mette   *sat awake, dreamed*
That he hire saugh a-temple, and al the wise   *in the temple, manner*
Right of hire look, °and gan it newe avise.

365 Thus gan he make a mirour of his mynde,   *mirror out of*
In which he saugh al holly hire figure;   *saw, wholly*
°And that he wel koude in his herte fynde,
It was to hym a right good aventure   *piece of luck*
To love swich oon, and if he dede his cure   *a one, devoted his care*
370 To serven hir, yet myghte he falle in grace,
Or ellis for oon of hire servantz pace;   *else, pass*

Imaginynge that travaille nor grame   *neither labor nor suffering*
Ne myghte for so goodly oon be lorn   *a one be wasted*
As she, ne hym for his desir no shame,   *on account of*
375 Al were it wist, °but in pris and up-born   *though it were known*
Of alle lovers wel more than biforn.
Thus argumented he in his gynnynge,   *beginning*
Ful unavysed of his woo comynge.   *unaware, to come*

Thus took he purpos loves craft to suwe,   *decided, pursue*
380 And thoughte he wolde werken pryvely,   *work secretly*
First to hiden his desir in °muwe

---

364 and he began to reflect upon it anew
367 and this (fact) he could certainly find in his heart, that
375-6 but (that he would be) in esteem and respected by all lovers
381 A mew was a cage, esp. for hawks when moulting (shedding and replacing feathers) — hence, a secret place.

From every wight yborn, al-outrely,   *person, absolutely*
°But he myghte ought recovered be therby;
Remembryng hym that love to wide yblowe   *too widely rumored about*
385 Yelt bittre fruyt, though swete seed be sowe.   *yields, sweet, sown*

And over al this, yet muchel more he thoughte
What for to speke, and what to holden inne;   *speak*
And what to arten hire to love he soughte,   *how, induce*
And on a song anon-right to bygynne,   *immediately (he decided)*
390 And gan loude on his sorwe for to wynne;   *complain*
For with good hope he gan fully assente
Criseyde for to love, and nought repente.   *regret*

And of his song naught only the sentence,   *meaning*
As writ myn auctour called °Lollius,   *writes*
395 But pleinly, save oure tonges difference,   *tongue's*
I dar wel seyn, in al that Troilus   *dare*
Seyde in his song, loo! every word right thus
As I shal seyn; and whoso list it here,   *whoever wishes to hear it*
Loo, next this vers he may it fynden here.   *in this next verse*

Troilus's Song

400 "If no love is, O God, what fele I so?   *feel*
And if love is, what thing and which is he?
If love be good, from whennes cometh my woo?
If it be wikke, a wonder thynketh me,   *wicked, it seems to me*
Whenne every torment and adversite
405 That cometh of hym, may to me savory thinke,   *seem savory to me*
For ay thurst I, the more that ich it drynke.   *thirst*

"And if that at myn owen lust I brenne,   *desire, burn*
From whennes cometh my waillynge and my pleynte?   *complaint*

---

383 unless he might in any way be benefitted thereby
394 the N's putative source, probably fictitious (See Introduction 2, "Sources")

18

If harme agree me, wherto pleyne I thenne?	*is agreeable to*
410 I noot, °ne whi unwery that I feynte.	*don't know*
O quike deth, O swete harm so queynte,	*living death, strange*
How may of the in me swich quantite,	*may (there be)*
But if that I consente that it be?	*unless*

"And if that I consente, I wrongfully	
415 Compleyne, iwis. Thus possed to and fro,	*tossed*
Al sterelees withinne a boot am I	*rudderless, boat*
Amydde the see, bitwixen wyndes two,	*amidst, sea, winds*
That in contrarie stonden evere mo.	*contrary (to each other), stand*
Allas! what is this wondre maladie?	*strange*
420 °For hete of cold, for cold of hete, I dye."	

And to the God of Love thus seyde he	
With pitous vois, "O lord, now youres is	*piteous*
My spirit, which that oughte youres be.	
Yow thanke I, lord, that han me brought to this.	*have*
425 But wheither goddesse or womman, iwis,	*whether, indeed*
She be, I not, which that ye do me serve;	*know not, cause me to*
But as hire man I wol ay lyve and sterve.	*ever, die*

"Ye stonden in hir eighen myghtily,	*stand, eyes*
As in a place unto youre vertu digne;	*worthy*
430 Wherfore, lord, if my service or I	
May liken yow, so beth to me benigne;	*please*
For myn estat roial I here resigne	*royal estate*
Into hire hond, and with ful humble chere	*demeanor*
Bicome hir man, as to my lady dere."	*dear*

---

410 nor do I know why, without being weary, I faint

420 Expand thus: I die of cold when I have a fever and of fever when I am cold. Oxymorons such as these are typical of love poetry of the age, especially of Petrarch's sonnets—see *Rime sparse* 105, line 90 and see also *T&C* 2. 1099 and 4. 280.

19

435 In hym ne deyned spare blood roial   *condescended to*
    The fyr of love—°the wherfro God me blesse—   *fire*
    Ne him forbar in no degree for al   *spared*
    His vertu or his excellent prowesse,
    But held hym as his thral lowe in destresse,   *slave*
440 And brende hym so in soundry wise ay newe,   *burned, sondry, ever*
    That sexti tyme a day he loste his hewe.   *sixty, color*

    So muche, day by day, his owene thought,
    For lust to hire, gan quiken and encresse,   *desire for, quicken*
    That every other charge he sette at nought.   *responsibility*
445 Forthi ful ofte, his hote fir to cesse,   *hence, hot fire, end*
    To sen hire goodly lok he gan to presse,   *see, press on*
    For therby to ben esed wel he wende;   *comforted, expected*
    And ay the ner he was, the more he brende.   *nearer, burned*

    For ay the ner the fir, the hotter is,—   *nearer, (it) is*
450 This, trowe I, knoweth al this °compaignye.   *believe*
    But were he fer or ner, I dar sey this: *far, dare*
    By nyght or day, for wisdom or folye,   *folly*
    His herte, which that is his brestes yë,   *breast's eye*
    Was ay on hire, that fairer was to sene   *see*
455 Than evere was °Eleyne or Polixene.

    Ek of the day ther passed nought an houre
    That to hymself a thousand tyme he seyde,   *he did (not) say*
    "Good goodly, °to whom serve I and laboure,   *pleasing one*
    As I best kan, now wolde God, Criseyde,
460 Ye wolden on me rewe, er that I deyde!   *have pity, died*

---

436 from which God defend me ("The fire" is the subject of this sentence.)
450 Ch asks us to imagine the Narrator reading his poem aloud to an audience.
455 Helen, for whom the Trojan war was fought; Polyxena, daughter of Priam, beloved by Achilles
458 to whom I am a servant and for whom I labor to serve

My dere herte, allas! myn hele and hewe   *well-being, color*
And lif is lost, but ye wol on me rewe."   *(all are) lost, unless*

Alle other dredes weren from him fledde,   *dreads*
Both of th'assege and his savacioun;   *siege (by the Greeks), safety*
465 °N'yn him desir noon other fownes bredde,
But argumentes to this conclusioun,   *except*
That she of him wolde han compassioun,
And he to ben hire man, while he may dure.   *last*
Lo, here his lif, and from the deth his cure!   *death, redemption*

470 °The sharpe shoures felle of armes preve,
That Ector or his othere bretheren diden,
Ne made hym only therfore ones meve;
And yet was he, where so men °wente or riden,   *wherever*
Founde oon the beste, and lengest tyme abiden
475 Ther peril was, and dide ek swich travaille   *performed also such work*
In armes, that to thynke it was merveille.   *was a wonder*

But for non hate he to the Grekes hadde,   *on account of no hate that*
Ne also for the rescous of the town,   *rescue*
Ne made hym thus in armes for to madde,   *rage*
480 But only, lo, for this conclusioun: *purpose*
To liken hire the bet for his renoun.   *please, better, fame*
Fro day to day in armes so he spedde,
That the Grekes as the deth him dredde.   *death, dreaded*

And fro this forth tho refte hym love his sleep,   *then took from*
485 And made his mete his foo; and ek his sorwe   *food, foe*
Gan multiplie, that, whoso tok keep,   *whoever paid any attention*

---

465 nor in him did desire breed any other fawns (i.e., lesser desires, as children)
470-2 the sharp, cruel combats, proof of arms, that Ector and his other brothers engaged in, did not make him move once on that account
473-5 walked or rode, found to be the very best and (one of those who remained) the longest time where there was danger

21

It shewed in his hewe both eve and morwe.   *countenance*
Therfor a title he gan him for to borwe   *name (as cover), borrow*
Of other siknesse, lest men of hym wende   *suspected*
490 That the hote fir of love hym brende,   *fire, burned*

And seyde he hadde a fevere and ferde amys.   *(he) said, wasn't well*
But how it was, certeyn, kan I nat seye,   *say*
If that his lady understood nat this,
°Or feynede hire she nyste, oon of the tweye;
495 But wel I rede that, by no manere weye,   *read, in no way at all*
Ne semed it as that she of hym roughte,   *cared about him*
Or of his peyne, or whatsoevere he thoughte.

But thanne felte this Troilus swich wo,
That he was wel neigh wood; for ay his drede   *mad, anxiety*
500 Was this, that she som wight hadde loved so,   *man*
That nevere of hym she wolde han taken hede,—   *him (Troilus), heed*
°For which hym thoughte he felte his herte blede;
Ne of his wo ne dorste he nat bygynne   *dared*
To tellen hir, for al this world to wynne.   *win*

505 But whan he hadde °a space from his care,
Thus to hymself ful ofte he gan to pleyne;   *complain*
He seyde, "O fool, now artow in the snare,   *are you*
That whilom japedest at loves peyne.   *made fun of, pain*
Now artow hent, now gnaw thin owen cheyne!   *caught, chain*
510 Thow were ay wont eche lovere reprehende   *accustomed, each*
Of thing fro which thou kanst the nat defende.   *not defend yourself*

"What wol now every lovere seyn of the,   *will, say of you*
If this be wist? but evere in thin absence   *known*
Laughen in scorn, and seyn, "Loo, ther goth he   *goes*

---

494 or pretended that she didn't know, one of the two
502 because of which it seemed to him that he felt his heart bleed
505 a period of freedom from his concerns

22

515 That is the man of so gret sapience,	*wisdom*
That held us loveres leest in reverence.	*least*
°Now, thanked be God, he may gon in the daunce	*dance*
Of hem that Love list febly for to avaunce.	*it pleases, weakly*

"But, O thow woful Troilus, God wolde,	*would God*
520 Sith thow most loven °thorugh thi destine,	*since, must*
That thow beset were on swich oon that sholde	*fixed, such a one*
Know al thi wo, al lakked hir pitee!	*though pity were lacking in her*
But also cold in love towardes the	*as*
Thi lady is, as frost in wynter moone,	*moon*
525 And thow fordon, as snow in fire is soone.	*done for*

"God wold I were aryved in the port	*would God*
Of deth, to which my sorwe wol me lede!	*lead*
A, Lord, to me it were a gret comfort;	
Than were I quyt of languisshyng in drede.	*finished with, anxiety*
530 For, °by myn hidde sorwe iblowe on brede,	
I shal byjaped ben a thousand tyme	*be mocked*
More than that fool of whos folie men ryme.	*folly, make rhymes*

"But now help, God, and ye, swete, °for whom	*sweetheart*
I pleyne, ikaught, ye, nevere wight so faste!	
535 O mercy, dere herte, and help me from	
The deth, for I, while that my lyf may laste,	*death*
More than myself wol love yow to my laste.	
And with som frendly look gladeth me, swete,	*gladden, sweetheart*
Though nevere more thing ye me byhete."	*should promise*

540 Thise wordes, and ful many an other to,	*too*
He spak, and called evere in his compleynte	*spoke*

---

517 The sense is that T is now among those whom Love does not favor.
520 on account of your destiny
530 through my hidden sorrow once it is blown abroad (by rumor)
533-4 for whom I, caught—indeed, never a man so fast—complain

23

Hire name, for to tellen hire his wo,
Til neigh that he in salte teres dreynte.   *nearly, tears drowned*
Al was for nought: she herde nat his pleynte;   *complaint*
545 And whan that he bythought on that folie,   *considered*
A thousand fold his wo gan multiplie.

Bywayling in his chambre thus allone,   *bewailing*
A frend of his, that called was Pandare,
Com oones in unwar, and herde hym groone,   *once, unawares, groan*
550 And say his frend in swich destresse and care.   *saw*
"Allas," quod he, "who causeth al this fare?   *carrying on*
O mercy, God! what unhap may this meene?   *misfortune, mean*
Han now thus soone Grekes maad yow leene?   *made, lean*

"Or hastow som remors of conscience,   *have you, remorse*
555 And art now falle in som devocioun,
And wailest for thi synne and thin offence,   *wail*
And hast for ferde caught °attricioun?   *fear*
God save hem that biseged han oure town,
That so kan leye oure jolite on presse,   *put away our cheerfulness*
560 And bringe oure lusty folk to holynesse!"

Thise wordes seyde he for the nones alle,   *nonce*
That with swich thing he myght hym angry maken,
And with an angre don his wo to falle,   *fit of anger, cause*
As for the tyme, and his corage awaken.   *for the moment, courage*
565 But wel he wist, as fer as tonges spaken,   *knew, spoke*
Ther nas a man of gretter hardinesse   *wasn't*
Thanne he, ne more desired worthinesse.

"What cas," quod Troilus, "or what aventure   *accident, chance*
Hath gided the to sen me langwisshinge,   *guided*
570 That am refus of every creature?   *rejected by*
But for the love of God, at my preyinge,   *prayer*

---

557 a mild form of contrition

Go hennes awey, for certes my deyinge   *dying*
Wol the disese, and I mot nedes deye;   *distress, must needs*
Therfore go wey, ther is na more to seye.

575 "But if thow wene I be thus sik for drede,   *suppose, sick, dread*
It is naught so, and therfore scorne nought.
Ther is another thing I take of hede   *am preoccupied with*
Wel more than aught the Grekes han yet wrought,   *done*
Which cause is of my deth, for sorowe and thought. *through sorrow*
580 °But though that I now telle it the ne leste,
Be thow naught wroth; I hide it for the beste."   *angry*

This Pandare, that neigh malt for wo and routhe,   *melted, pity*
Ful ofte seyde, "Allas! what may this be?
Now frend," quod he, "if evere love or trouthe
585 Hath ben, or is, bitwixen the and me,
Ne do thow nevere swich a crueltee
To hiden fro thi frend so gret a care!   *(as) to hide from*
Wostow naught wel that it am I, Pandare?   *don't you know*

"I wol parten with the al thi peyne,   *share*
590 If it be so I do the no comfort,   *I (can) do*
As it is frendes right, soth for to seyne,   *truth to tell*
To entreparten wo as glad desport.   *share, as (well as), joy*
I have, and shal, for trewe or fals report,
In wrong and right iloved the al my lyve: *loved, life*
595 Hid nat thi wo fro me, but telle it blyve."   *hide, quickly*

Than gan this sorwful Troylus to syke,   *then, sigh*
And seide hym thus: "God leve it be my beste   *grant*
To telle it the; for sith it may the like,   *to you, since, please*
Yet wol I telle it, though myn herte breste.   *burst*
600 And wel woot I thow mayst do me no reste;   *know*

---

580 but though I don't like to tell it to you now

25

But lest thow deme I truste nat to the,   *suppose, in you*
Now herke, frend, for thus it stant with me.   *listen, stands*

"Love, ayeins the which whoso defendeth   *against*
Hymselven most, hym alderlest avaylleth, *it avails him least of all*
605 With disespeyr so sorwfulli me offendeth,   *despair*
That streight unto the deth myn herte sailleth. *straight, sails*
Therto desir so brennyngly me assailleth,   *burningly*
That to ben slayn it were a gretter joie
To me than kyng of Grece ben and Troye.   *than to be*

610 "Suffiseth this, my fulle frend Pandare,
That I have seyd, for now wostow my wo;   *said, you know*
And for the love of God, my colde care
So hide it wel—I tolde it nevere to mo.   *to others*
For harmes myghten folwen mo than two,
615 If it were wist; but be thow in gladnesse,   *known*
And lat me sterve, °unknowe, of my destresse."   *die*

"How hastow thus unkyndely and longe   *unnaturally*
Hid this fro me, thow fol?" quod Pandarus.   *fool*
°"Paraunter thow myghte after swich oon longe,
620 That myn avys anoon may helpen us."   *counsel*
"This were a wonder thing," quod Troilus. *would be a strange*
"Thow koudest nevere in love thiselven wisse: *you could, manage*
How devel maistow brynge me to blisse?" *the devil may you*

"Ye, Troilus, now herke," quod Pandare;   *listen*
625 "Though I be nyce, it happeth often so, *ignorant, happens*
°That oon that excesse doth ful yvele fare
By good counseil kan kepe his frend therfro.
I have myself ek seyn a blynd man goo   *seen*

———————————————

616 unknown (i.e., in secret)
619 you may perhaps long for such a one
626 that one whom excess causes to fare badly

°Ther as he fel that couthe loken wide;
630 A fool may ek a wis man ofte gide. *also, wise, guide*

"A wheston is no kervyng instrument, *whetstone, carving*
But yet it maketh sharpe kervyng tolis. *carving tools*
°And there thow woost that I have aught myswent,
Eschuwe thow that, for swich thing to the scole is;
635 Thus often wise men ben war by foolys. *are aware by (example of)*
If thow do so, thi wit is wel bewared; *employed*
°By his contrarie is every thyng declared.

"For how myghte evere swetnesse han ben knowe *sweetness, known*
To him that nevere tasted bitternesse?
640 Ne no man may ben inly glad, I trowe, *inwardly*
That nevere was in sorwe or som destresse.
Eke whit by blak, by shame ek worthinesse,
°Ech set by other, more for other semeth,
As men may se, and so the wyse it demeth. *wise judge it*

645 "Sith thus of two contraries is o lore, *comes one single lesson*
I, that have in love so ofte assayed *experienced*
Grevances, oughte konne, and wel the more, *should be able*
Counseillen the of that thow art amayed. *to advise, dismayed*
°Ek the ne aughte nat ben yvel appayed,
650 Though I desyre with the for to bere *with you to bear*
Thyn hevy charge; it shal thee lasse dere. *burden, harm you less*

───────────

629 where he fell who could see clearly
633-4 and where you know me to have erred in any way, avoid that, for such a
matter is a lesson to you
637 by its opposite is everything known for what it is (Cf. *RR* 21543-52.)
643 each thing set beside its opposite seems more distinct because of the other
649 and you ought not be dissatisfied

°"I woot wel that it fareth thus be me   *know, with*
As to thi brother, Paris, an herdesse,   *shepherdess*
Which that icleped was °Oënone,   *called*
655 Wrot in a compleynte of hir hevynesse.
Yee say the lettre that she wrot, I gesse."   *saw*
"Nay nevere yet, ywys," quod Troilus.   *no, certainly*
"Now," quod Pandare, "herkne, it was thus: *listen*

°"'Phebus, that first fond art of medicyne,'   *invented the art*
660 Quod she, 'and couthe in every wightes care   *knew, person's*
Remedye and reed, by herbes he knew fyne,   *advice, thoroughly*
Yet to hymself his konnyng was ful bare;   *useless*
For love hadde hym so bounden in a snare,   *bound*
Al for the doughter of the kyng Amete,
665 That al his craft ne koude his sorwes bete.'   *cure*

"Right so fare I, unhappily for me,
I love oon best, and that me smerteth sore;   *one, pains*
And yet, peraunter, kan I reden the,   *advise you*
And nat myself; repreve me na more.   *chide*
670 I have no cause, I woot wel, for to sore   *know, soar*
As doth an hauk that listeth for to pleye;   *hawk, is pleased*
But to thin help yet somwhat kan I seye.

"And of o thyng right siker maistow be,   *one, sure*
That certein, for to dyen in the peyne,   *even to dying under torture*
675 That I shal nevere mo discoveren the;   *betray you at all*

---

652 Construe the syntax thus: "I know it fares with me (in the same way) as a shepherdess, called Oënone, wrote, in a complaint about her sorrow, to your brother Paris (that it fared with her). . ." (i.e., my situation is like that which Oënone wrote about).

654 The nymph Oënone, deserted by Paris when he went to fetch Helen, pleaded with him by letter to be faithful to her. The letter constitutes Ovid's *Heroides* 5.

659 The story of Phebus Apollo's love for the daughter of Admetus is probably from a gloss to lines 151–2 of the epistle mentioned in the note to 654. Admetus was a king in Thessaly, whose flocks for a time were tended by Apollo.

Ne, by my trouthe, I kepe nat restreyne   *care not to restrain*
The fro thi love, theigh that it were Eleyne   *although*
That is thi brother wif, if ich it wiste: *brother's wife, knew*
°Be what she be, and love hire as the liste!   *pleases you*

680 Therfore, as frend, fullich in me assure,   *trust in me fully*
And telle me plat now what is th'enchesoun   *flatly, reason*
And final cause of wo that ye endure;
For douteth nothyng, myn entencioun   *fear not*
Nis nat to yow of reprehencioun,   *rebuke*
685 To speke as now, for no wight may byreve   *person, bar*
A man to love, °tyl that hym list to leve.   *from loving*

"And witteth wel that bothe two ben vices,   *understand*
°Mistrusten alle, or elles alle leve.
But wel I woot, the mene of it no vice is,   *know, mean*
690 For for to trusten som wight is a preve   *since to, one, proof*
Of trouth, and forthi wolde I fayn remeve   *hence, gladly remove*
Thi wronge conseyte, and °do the som wyght triste   *notion*
Thi wo to telle; and tel me, if the liste.   *it pleases you*

"The °wise seith, 'Wo hym that is allone,   *woe to him*
695 For, and he falle, he hath non helpe to ryse';   *if*
And sith thow hast a felawe, tel thi mone;   *friend, moan*
For this nys naught, certein, the nexte wyse   *the nearest way*
To wynnen love, as techen us the wyse,   *teach*

---

679 whoever she may be
686 until it suits him to leave off loving
688 either to mistrust everyone or else believe everyone
692-3 and cause you to trust some person (enough) to tell your woe (to him)
694 the wise man—i.e., Solomon; cf. Eccles. 4:10 (Although St. Isidore, e. g., in his *Book of Etymologies* [5.29.11 and 13], records that Priam ["third age"] reigned in Troy *before* Solomon ["fourth age"] was born, Ch probably did not bother much about such anachronisms, which are common in ME poetry.)

To walwe and wepe as °Nyobe the queene,   *wallow and weep, like*
700 Whos teres yet in marble ben yseene.   *tears*

"Lat be thy wepyng and thi drerynesse,   *weeping, dreariness*
And lat us lissen wo with oother speche;   *alleviate*
So may thy woful tyme seme lesse.   *seem*
Delyte nat in wo thi wo to seche,   *delight, seek (obsessively)*
705 As don thise foles that hire sorwes eche   *fools, increase*
With sorwe, whan thei han mysaventure,   *misfortune*
And listen naught to seche hem other cure.   *are not pleased to seek*

"Men seyn, 'to wrecche is consolacioun   *say, a miserable man it is*
To have another felawe in hys peyne.'   *fellow (companion), pain*
710 That owghte wel ben oure opynyoun,   *ought, opinion*
For, bothe thow and I, of love we pleyne.   *complain*
So ful of sorwe am I, soth for to seyne,   *truth to tell*
That certeinly namore harde grace   *misfortune*
May sitte on me, for-why ther is no space.   *because*

715 "If God wol, thow art nat agast of me,   *wills, afraid*
Lest I wolde of thi lady the bygyle!   *trick you (to take her away)*
Thow woost thyself whom that I love, parde,   *you know, certainly*
As I best kan, gon sithen longe while.   *it's been a long time now*
And sith thow woost I do it for no wyle,   *on account of no wiles*
720 And seyst I am he that thow trustest moost,   *say*
Telle me somwhat, syn al my wo thow woost."   *all my woe you know*

Yet Troilus for al this no word seyde,
But longe he ley as stylle as he ded were;   *still as if, dead*
And after this with sikynge he abreyde,   *sighing, started up*
725 And to Pandarus vois he lente his ere,   *Pandarus's voice*
And up his eighen caste he, that in feere   *eyes, (such) that*

---

699 Niobe was queen of Thebes; her pride was punished by the death of all of her children. As she wept, she was turned to stone, even to her tears. See Ovid, *Metam.* 6. 311–12.

30

Was Pandarus, lest that in frenesie   *frenzy*
He sholde falle, or elles soone dye;   *else, die*

And cryde "Awake!" ful wonderlich and sharpe;   *wondrously (loud)*
730 "What! slombrestow as in a litargie?   *do you slumber, lethargy*
Or artow °lik an asse to the harpe,   *are you, donkey*
That hereth sown whan men the strynges plye,   *sound, handle*
But in his mynde of that no melodie   *no melody from that*
May sinken hym to gladen, for that he   *because*
735 So dul ys of his bestialite?"   *dull, animal nature*

And with that, Pandare of his wordes stente;   *ceased*
And Troilus yet hym nothyng answerde,
°For-why to tellen nas nat his entente
To nevere no man, for whom that he so ferde.
740 For it is seyd, "man maketh ofte a yerde   *rod*
With which the maker is hymself ybeten   *beaten*
In sondry manere," °as thise wyse treten;   *sundry ways*

°And namelich in his counseil tellynge
That toucheth love that oughte ben secree;
745 For of himself it wol °ynough out sprynge,
But if that it the bet governed be.   *unless, better*
Ek som tyme it is a craft to seme fle   *expedient, to seem to flee*
Fro thyng whych in effect men hunte faste:
Al this gan Troilus in his herte caste.   *consider*

750 But natheles, whan he hadde herd hym crye
"Awake!" he gan to syken wonder soore,   *sigh*

---

731 See Boethius, *CP* 1, prose 4.
738-9 because it was not his intent ever to tell any man on account of whom he fared this way
742 as these wise (men) tell
743 and especially in his counsel telling that which concerns love that ought to be secret
745 spring out enough (i.e., come to light)

31

And seyde, "Frend, though that I stylle lye,   *still*
I am nat deef. Now pees, and crye namore,   *deaf, peace*
For I have herd thi wordes and thi lore;   *teaching*
755 But suffre me my meschief to bywaille,   *misfortune, bewail*
For thi proverbes may me naught availle.   *help*

"Nor other cure kanstow non for me.   *can you (perform)*
Ek I nyl nat ben cured; I wol deye.   *won't, die*
What knowe I of the queene Nyobe?
760 Lat be thyne olde ensaumples, I the preye." *examples, pray you*
"No," quod tho Pandarus, "therfore I seye,
Swych is delit of foles to bywepe   *delight, fools, weep for*
Hire wo, but seken bote they ne kepe. *they don't care to seek a cure*

"Now knowe I that ther reson in the failleth. *reason in you fails*
765 But telle me if I wiste what she were   *knew who*
For whom that the al this mysaunter ailleth. *misadventure, ails*
Dorste thow that I tolde hir in hire ere *would you dare, ear*
Thi wo, sith thow darst naught thiself for feere, *since, fear*
And hire bysoughte on the to han som routhe?" *to have some pity*
770 "Why, nay," quod he, "by God and by my trouthe!"

"What? nat as bisyly," quod Pandarus,   *solicitously*
"As though myn owene lyf lay on this nede?" *depended on (fulfilling)*
"No, certes, brother," quod this Troilus.   *indeed, said*
"And whi?"–"For that thow scholdest nevere spede." *should, succeed*
775 "Wostow that wel?" – "Ye, that is out of drede," *do you know, doubt*
Quod Troilus; "for al that evere ye konne, *might be able to do*
She nyl to noon swich wrecche as I ben wonne." *wretch, be won*

Quod Pandarus, "Allas! what may this be,
That thow dispeired art thus causeles?   *despaired, causeless*
780 What! lyveth nat thi lady, *bendiste*?   *lives, bless us*
How wostow so that thow art graceles? *do you know, without favor*
Swich yvel is nat alwey booteles.   *remediless*
Why, put nat impossible thus thi cure,   *assume*
Syn thyng to come is oft in aventure.   *often uncertain*

32

785 "I graunte wel that thow endurest wo
    As sharp as doth he °Ticius in helle,
    Whos stomak foughles tiren evere moo   *fowls tear*
    That hightyn volturis, as bokes telle.   *are called vultures*
    But I may nat endure that thow dwelle
790 In so unskilful an oppynyoun   *unreasonable*
    That of thi wo is no curacioun.   *(there) is no cure*

    °"But oones nyltow, for thy coward herte,
    And for thyn ire and folissh wilfulnesse,
    For wantrust, tellen of thy sorwes smerte,
795 Ne to thyn owen help don bysynesse
    As much as speke a resoun moore or lesse,
    But lyest as he that lest of nothyng recche.
    What womman koude loven swich a wrecche?   *wretch (as you)*

    "What may she demen oother of thy deeth,   *think otherwise*
800 If thow thus deye, and she not why it is,   *die, not know*
    But that for feere is yolden up thy breth,   *except, fear, yielded*
    For Grekes han biseged us, iwys?   *because*
    Lord, which a thonk than shaltow han of this!   *what gratitude*
    Thus wol she seyn, and al the town attones,   *at once*
805 'The wrecche is ded, the devel have his bones!'   *wretch, dead*

    "Thow mayst allone here wepe and crye and knele,   *alone, kneel*
    But love a womman that she woot it nought,   *who knows it not*
    And she wol quyte it that thow shalt nat fele.   *requite, feel (it)*
    Unknowe, unkist, and lost, that is unsought!   *unknown, unkissed*

---

786 Tityus is a giant who attempted violence on Diana and was cast into Hades where he lay stretched out while two vultures devoured his liver.

792-7 not even once, because of your coward's heart, and because of your rage and foolish wilfullness, because of (your) mistrust, will you tell of your painful sorrows (and not even once will you) be active in your own help (at least) as much as speak a reason more or less, but rather you lie (about) like him who's pleased to care about nothing.

33

810 What! many a man hath love ful deere ybought   *dearly paid for*
    Twenty wynter that his lady wiste,   *whom his lady knew*
    That nevere yet his lady mouth he kiste.   *kissed*

    "What? sholde he °therfore fallen in dispayr,   *despair*
    Or be recreant for his owne tene,   *vanquished, vexation*
815 Or slen hymself, al be his lady fair?   *slay, though*
    Nay, nay, but evere in oon be fressh and grene   *constantly*
    To serve and love his deere hertes queene,   *heart's*
    And thynk it is a guerdon, hire to serve,   *reward*
    A thousand fold moore than he kan deserve."

820 And of that word took hede Troilus,   *heed*
    And thoughte anon what folie he was inne,   *folly*
    And how that soth hym seyde Pandarus,   *the truth*
    °That for to slen hymself myght he nat wynne,
    But bothe don unmanhod and a synne,   *an unmanly deed, sin*
825 And of his deth his lady naught to wite;   *(would) not be at fault*
    For of his wo, God woot, she knew ful lite.   *little*

    And with that thought he gan ful sore syke,   *sigh*
    And seyde, "Allas! what is me best to do?"
    To whom Pandare answerde, "If the like,   *it pleases you*
830 The beste is that thow telle me al thi wo;
    And have my trouthe, but thow it fynde so   *unless*
    I be thi boote, °or that it be ful longe,   *(that) I am your healer*
    To pieces do me drawe, and sithen honge!"

    "Ye, so thow seyst," quod Troilus tho, "allas!   *then*
835 But, God woot, it is naught the rather so.   *knows, sooner*
    Ful hard were it to helpen in this cas,

---

813 i.e., because, for twenty years, he has not kissed her
823 that he would not gain anything by slaying himself
832-3 before too much time has passed, cause me to be drawn to pieces and then hanged

34

For wel fynde I that Fortune is my fo;
Ne al the men that riden konne or go   *can ride or walk*
May of hire cruel whiel the harm withstonde;   *wheel*
840 °For, as hire list, she pleyeth with free and bonde."

Quod Pandarus, "Than blamestow Fortune   *do you blame*
For thow art wroth, ye, now at erst I see.   *angry, at last*
Woost thow nat wel that Fortune is comune   *don't you know, common*
To everi manere wight in som degree?   *person*
845 And yet thow hast this comfort, lo, parde,   *indeed*
That, as hire joies moten overgon,   *must pass away*
So mote hire sorwes passen everechon.   *must, everyone*

"For if hire whiel stynte any-thyng to torne,   *ceased at all to turn*
Than cessed she Fortune anon to be.   *immediately*
850 Now, sith hire whiel by no way may sojourne,   *stop*
What woostow if hire mutabilite   *what do you know but that*
Right as thyselven list, wol don by the,   *suits you, will do by you*
Or that she be naught fer fro thyn helpynge?   *not far from, aid*
Paraunter thow hast cause for to synge.   *perhaps, sing*

855 "And therfore wostow what I the biseche?   *do you know, beseech you*
Lat be thy wo and tornyng to the grounde;   *turning*
For whoso list have helyng of his leche,   *is pleased, physician*
To hym byhoveth first unwrye his wownde.   *it is necessary, uncover*
°To Cerberus yn helle ay be I bounde,
860 Were it for my suster, al thy sorwe,   *sister*
By my wil she sholde al be thyn to-morwe.

"Look up, I seye, and telle me what she is
Anon, that I may gon aboute thy nede.   *go about (for) your needs*

---

840 for as she likes she plays with free and bound (No one, in other words, is exempt from her "play.")
859-61 P is swearing an oath. Cerberus is the three-headed dog guarding the entrance to Hades.

Knowe ich hire aught? For my love, telle me this. *at all*
865 Thanne wolde I hopen rather for to spede." *hope sooner to succeed*
Tho gan the veyne of Troilus to blede, *then, vein, bleed*
For he was hit, and wax al reed for shame. *grew, red*
"A ha!" quod Pandare, "here bygynneth game." *now the hunt begins*

And with that word he gan hym for to shake,
870 And seyde, "Thef, thow shalt hyre name telle." *thief*
But tho gan sely Troilus for to quake *poor, shake and quiver*
As though men sholde han led hym into helle,
And seyde, "Allas! of al my wo the welle, *well-spring*
Thanne is my swete fo called Criseyde!"
875 And wel neigh with the word for feere he deide. *nigh, fear, died*

And whan that Pandare herde hire name nevene, *named*
Lord, he was glad, and seyde, "Frend so deere,
Now fare aright, for Joves name in hevene.
Love hath byset the wel; be of good cheere! *done well by you*
880 For of good name and wisdom and manere
She hath ynough, and ek of gentilesse.
If she be fayr, thow woost thyself, I gesse. *fair, know, guess*

"Ne I nevere saugh a more bountevous *kind*
Of hire estat, n'a gladder, ne of speche *nor a*
885 A frendlyer, n'a more gracious
For to do wel, ne lasse hadde nede to seche *need to seek*
What for to don; and al this bet to eche, *to make even better*
In honour, to as fer as she may strecche, *reach*
A kynges herte semeth by hyrs a wrecche. *hers a wretch's (heart)*

890 "And forthy loke of good comfort thou be; *hence look*
For certainly, the firste poynt is this:
Of noble corage and wel ordayné, *regulated (within himself)*
A man to have pees with himself, ywis. *(ought) to have peace*
So oughtest thou, for nought but good it is
895 To loven wel, and in a worthy place;
The oughte nat to clepe it hap, but grace. *call it luck*

36

"And also thynk, and therwith glade the,   *gladden yourself*
That sith thy lady vertuous is al,   *since, completely*
So foloweth it that there is som pitee   *pity*
900 Amonges alle thise other in general;   *these other (virtues)*
And forthi se that thow, in special,   *see*
Requere naught that is ayeyns hyre name; *seek nothing, against*
For vertu streccheth naught hymself to shame. *stretches*

"But wel is me that evere that I was born,
905 That thow biset art in so good a place;   *place (i. e., with Criseyde)*
For by my trouthe, in love I dorste have sworn *would have dared swear*
The sholde nevere han tid thus fayr a grace. *to you, have happened*
And wostow why? For thow were wont to chace *do you know, harass*
At Love in scorn, and for despit him calle   *despite*
910 'Seynt Idyot, lord of thise foles alle.'   *fools*

"How often hastow maad thi nyce japes,   *made, foolish jokes*
And seyd that Loves servantz everichone   *said, everyone*
°Of nycete ben verray Goddes apes;
And some wolde mucche hire mete allone,   *munch, meat*
915 Liggyng abedde, and make hem for to grone; *lying, groan*
And som, thow seydest, hadde a °blaunche fevere, *one, love-sickness*
And preydest God he sholde nevere kevere. *recover*

"And som of hem °tooke on hem, for the cold,
More than ynough, so seydestow ful ofte.   *you said, often*
920 And som han feyned ofte tyme, and told   *pretended*
How that they waken, whan thei slepen softe;
°And thus they wolde han brought hemself alofte,

---

913 through foolishness are true, natural born fools
916 (lit., a "white fever") a fever that made him pale, as in love-sickness
918 pulled over them, on account of the cold
922-3 and thus they would have brought themselves to the height (i.e., would have succeeded) and yet were underneath in the end (i.e., had failed)

And natheles were under at the laste.
Thus seydestow, and japedest ful faste.   *you said, joked*

925 "Yet seydestow, that for the moore part,
Thise loveres wolden speke in general,   *generally*
°And thoughten that it was a siker art,
For faylyng, for t'assayen overal.
Now may I jape of the, if that I shal;   *make fun of you*
930 But natheless, though that I sholde deye,   *nevertheless, die*
That thow art non of tho, I dorste saye.   *those, would dare*

°"Now bet thi brest, and sey to God of Love,   *beat*
'Thy grace, lord, for now I me repente,
If I mysspak, for now myself I love.'
935 Thus sey with al thyn herte in good entente."
Quod Troilus, "A, lord! I me consente,   *said*
And preye to the my japes thow foryive,   *pray, mockeries*
And I shal nevere more whyle I live."

"Thow seist wel," quod Pandarus, "and now I hope
940 That thow the goddes wrathe hast al apesed;   *appeased*
And sithen thow hast wopen many a drope,   *since, wept, drop*
And seyd swych thyng wherwith thi god is plesed,
Now wolde nevere god but thow were esed!   *except that, comforted*
And thynk wel, she of whom rist al thi wo   *arises*
945 Hereafter may thy comfort be also.

"For thilke grownd that bereth the wedes wikke   *the same, evil weeds*
Bereth ek thise holsom herbes, as ful ofte   *wholesome*
Next the foule netle, rough and thikke,   *next to, nettle*

927-8 and (you said they) thought that it was a sure method against failing to try
everywhere

932-8 P here acts as if he were a priest leading T in a confession of his sins; the
"confession" and "repentance" of the lover form a trope Ch most likely encountered
first in *RR*—see 4121–8, 4179–90, 6871–97.

The rose waxeth swoote and smothe and softe;   *grows sweet*
950 And next the valeye is the hil o-lofte;
And next the derke nyght the glade morwe;   *dark*
And also joie is next the fyn of sorwe.   *follows after the end*

"Now loke that atempre be thi bridel,   *restrained, bridle*
And for the beste ay °suffre to the tyde,
955 Or elles al oure labour is on ydel: *in vain*
He hasteth wel that wisely kan abyde.   *hastens, prudently, wait*
Be diligent and trewe, and °ay wel hide;   *be secret*
Be lusty, fre; persevere in thy servyse,   *pleasure-loving, generous*
And al is wel, if thow werke in this wyse.   *work*

960 "But he that parted is in everi place   *divided*
Is nowher hol, as writen clerkes wyse.   *whole*
What wonder is, though swich oon have no grace?   *such a one*
°Ek wostow how it fareth of som servise,
As plaunte a tree or herbe, in sondry wyse,   *ways*
965 And on the morwe pulle it up as blyve!   *immediately*
No wonder is, though it may nevere thryve.

"And sith that God of Love hath the bistowed   *since*
In place digne unto thi worthinesse,   *fitting*
Stond faste, for to good port hastow rowed;   *have you*
970 And of thiself, for any hevynesse,   *despite any sorrow*
Hope alwey wel; for, but if drerinesse   *unless gloominess*
Or over-haste oure bothe labour shende,   *both our efforts destroy*
I hope of this to maken a good ende.

"And wostow why I am the lasse afered   *do you know, less afraid*
975 Of this matere with my nece trete?   *to treat of this matter*
For this have I herd seyd of wyse lered,   *learned wise (men)*

---

954 submit to the time—i.e., be patient
957 See 1. 991-3.
963 also you know how it goes with

Was nevere man or womman yet bigete   *begotten*
That was unapt to suffren loves hete,   *love's heat*
Celestial, or elles love of kynde;   *heavenly or earthly love*
980 Forthy som grace I hope in hire to fynde.   *hence*

"And for to speke of hire in specyal,   *in particular*
Hire beaute to bithynken and hire youthe,   *consider*
It sit hire naught to ben celestial   *isn't appropriate for her*
As yet, though that hire list bothe and kowthe;   *she would and could*
985 But trewely, it °sate hire wel right nowthe
A worthi knyght to loven and cherice,   *cherish*
And but she do, I holde it for a vice.   *unless*

"Wherfore I am, and wol ben, ay redy   *will be, ever ready*
To peyne me to do yow this servyse;   *pain*
990 For bothe yow to plese thus hope I   *both of you*
Herafterward; for ye ben bothe wyse,
And konne it counseil kepe in swych a wyse   *can keep it a secret*
That no man schal the wiser of it be;
And so we may ben gladed alle thre.   *gladdened*

995 "And, by my trouthe, I have right now of the
A good conceyte in my wit, as I gesse,   *conceit, guess*
And what it is, I wol now that thow se.   *want you now to see*
I thenke, sith that Love, of his goodnesse,   *think, since*
Hath the converted out of wikkednesse,
1000 That thow shalt ben the beste post, I leve,   *supporter, believe*
Of al his lay, and °moost his foos to greve.   *law*

°"Ensample why, se now thise wise clerkes,   *see*
That erren aldermost ayeyn a lawe,   *most of all against*
And ben converted from hire wikked werkes   *wicked deeds*

---

985 it would certainly be appropriate to her right now
1001 and (the one) to grieve his foes the most
1002 Here's an example illustrating why I say this:

1005 Thorugh grace of God that °list hem to hym drawe,
    Thanne arn they folk that han moost God in awe,   *are, have*
    And strengest feythed ben, I undirstonde,   *are of the strongest faith*
    And °konne an errowr alderbest withstonde."

    Whan Troilus hadde herd Pandare assented   *(that) Pandarus (had)*
1010 To ben his help in lovyng of Cryseyde,
    °Weex of his wo, as who seith, untormented,
    But hotter weex his love, and thus he seyde,   *grew*
    With sobre chere, although his herte pleyde: *demeanor, played*
    "Now blisful Venus helpe, er that I sterve,   *die*
1015 °Of the, Pandare, I mowe som thank deserve.

    "But, deere frend, how shal my wo be lesse
    Til this be doon? And good, ek telle me this: *good (friend)*
    How wiltow seyn of me and my destresse,   *will you speak*
    Lest she be wroth—this drede I moost, ywys—   *angry, dread*
1020 Or nyl nat here or trowen how it is?   *won't hear, believe*
    Al this drede I, °and eke for the manere
    Of the, hire em, she nyl no swich thyng here."

    Quod Pandarus, "Thow hast a ful gret care
    Lest °that the cherl may fall out of the moone!
1025 Whi, Lord! I hate of the thi nyce fare!   *your foolish behavior*
    Whi, entremete of that thow hast to doone!   *mind your own affairs*

1005 that is pleased to draw them to him
1008 and can a false belief or heresy best of all withstand
1011 he became, regarding his woe, as one might say, untormented
1015 The syntax is elliptical. Construe as: "that I may do something (in return), P, to deserve thanks (from you)." The sense is: "that I may do something for you, P, that will give you cause to thank me as now I have cause to thank you (for what you have done for me)."
1021-2 and also considering your relation with her, that you are her uncle, she will no such thing hear
1024 that the man in the moon may fall out

For Goddes love, I bidde the a boone: *ask you a favor*
So lat m'alone, and it shal be thi beste."   *best for you*
Whi, frend," quod he, "now do right as the leste.   *it pleases you*

1030 "But herke, Pandare, o word, for I nolde   *listen, one, would not*
That thow in me wendest so gret folie,   *suspected, folly*
That to my lady I desiren sholde
That toucheth harm or any vilenye;   *that (which)*
For dredeles me were levere dye   *doubtless, I would rather die*
1035 Than she of me aught elles understode
But that that myghte sownen into goode."   *what might be conducive to*

Tho lough this Pandare, and anon answerde,   *then laughed*
°"And I thi borugh? fy! no wight doth but so.
I roughte naught though that she stood and herde   *wouldn't care*
1040 How that thow seist! but farewel, I wol go.
Adieu! be glad! God spede us bothe two!   *speed*
Yef me this labour and this bisynesse,   *give*
And of my spede be thyn al that swetnesse."   *success*

Tho Troilus gan doun on knees to falle,
1045 And Pandare in his armes hente faste,   *seized*
And seyde, "Now, fy on the Grekes alle!
Yet, parde, God shal helpe us atte laste.   *indeed*
And dredelees, if that my lyf may laste,   *doubtless*
And God toforn, lo, som of hem shal smerte;   *at my side, suffer*
1050 °And yet m'athinketh that this avant m'asterte!

"Now, Pandare, I kan na more seye,
But, °thow wis, thow woost, thow maist, thow art al!
My lif, my deth, hol in thyn honde I leye.   *whole, lay*
Help now!" Quod he, "Yis, by my trowthe, I shal."

1038 And am I your surety? ha, every lover says the same thing
1050 and yet I am sorry that this boast escaped from me
1052 you, being wise, you know, you may—you are all

1055 God yelde the, frend, and this in special,"	*reward, (for) this*
Quod Troilus, "that thow me recomaunde	
To hire that to the deth me may comande."	*death*

This Pandarus, tho desirous to serve	*then*
His fulle frend, than seyde in this manere:	
1060 "Farwell, and °thenk I wol thi thank deserve!	
Have here my trowthe, and °that thow shalt wel here,"—	*pledge*
And went his wey, thenkyng on this matere,	*thinking*
And how he best myghte hire biseche of grace,	*ask for*
And fynde a tyme therto, and a place.	

1065 For everi wight that hath an hous to founde	*one, a house to build*
Ne renneth naught the werk for to bygynne	*runs, work*
With °rakel hond, but he wol bide a stounde,	*rash, wait a while*
And sende his °hertes line out fro withinne	*imaginary line*
Aldirfirst his purpos for to wynne.	*first of all, achieve*
1070 Al this Pandare in his herte thoughte,	
°And caste his werk ful wisely or he wroughte.	

But Troilus lay tho no lenger down,	*then, longer*
But up anon upon his stede bay,	*bay steed*
And in the feld he pleyde the leoun;	*field, acted like the lion*
1075 Wo was that Grek that with hym mette a-day!	*met with him by day*
And in the town his manere tho forth ay	*thenceforth ever*
Soo goodly was, and gat hym so in grace,	*got*
That ecch hym loved that loked on his face.	*each, looked*

1060 and consider that I will be deserving of your thanks

1061 you shall indeed hear about that (i.e., about how I will deserve your thanks)

1067 On "rakel," cf. the important example in the ME alliterative poem, *Patience*, by the *Gawain*-poet, line 526; see also 3. 1630.

1068 The sense is that by considering the matter the builder will arrive at the best way to proceed; sending out the "hertes line," in other words, is an anticipatory imagining of the building to be erected. This passage is based on the *Poetria Nova* (43–5) of Geoffrey of Vinsauf (*fl ca* 1200), a manual of rhetoric and poetics known to Ch.

1071 and planned his work very prudently before he performed it

43

For he bicom the frendlieste wight,   *became, man*
1080 The gentilest, and ek the mooste fre,   *liberal*
       °The thriftiest and oon the beste knyght,
       That in his tyme was or myghte be.
       Dede were his japes and his cruelte,   *dead, jokes*
       °His heighe port and his manere estraunge,
1085 And ecch of tho gan for a vertu chaunge.   *each, those (vices)*

       Now lat us stynte of Troilus a stounde,   *cease, a while*
       That fareth lik a man that hurt is soore,   *fares like, sorely*
       °And is somdeel of akyngge of his wownde
       Ylissed wel, but heeled no deel moore,
1090 And, as an esy pacyent, the loore   *easy patient, advice*
       Abit of hym that gooth aboute his cure;   *complies with, goes*
       And thus he dryeth forth his aventure.   *continues to endure*

1081 "Thriftiest" here occurs in the sense of "the most thrifty managing" of his various endowments; hence the idea is that he is "the most successful and the very best knight in his time." Note, however, the interesting collocation "the mooste fre" / "the thriftiest."

1084 his haughty behavior and his distant manner

1088-9 and is somewhat well relieved of the aching of his wound, but is no nearer being cured

BOOK TWO

°Owt of thise blake wawes for to saylle,   *out, black, waves*
O wynd, o wynd, the weder gynneth clere;   *weather, begins (to)*
°For in this see the boot hath swych travaylle,
Of my °connyng, that unneth I it steere.
5 This see clepe I the tempestous matere   *call*
Of disespeir that Troilus was inne;   *despair*
But now of hope the °kalendes bygynne.

O lady myn, that called art °Cleo,
Thow be my speed fro this forth, and my Muse,   *help, henceforth*
10 To ryme wel this book til I have do;   *done*
Me nedeth here noon other art to use.
Forwhi to every lovere I me excuse,   *wherefore*
That of no sentement I this endite,   *from, compose*
But out of Latyn in my tonge it write.

15 Wherfore I nyl have neither thank ne blame   *will not*
Of al this werk, but prey yow mekely,   *work*
°Disblameth me, if any word be lame,
For as myn auctour seyde, so sey I.   *said*
Ek though I speeke of love unfelyngly,   *and, speak*

1-4 See *Purg.* 1. 1-3.
3-4 for in this sea the boat of my understanding has such toil that I barely steer it
4 Parallel to Dante's "ingegno," "connyng" can be modernized as "genius" or "wit" if we understand by these terms something like the innate capacity to make poetry.
7 the inauguration begins ("kalendes"—the first day of the month and hence the "first" of any thing or action)
8 Clio: the Muse of history
17 a frequent Chaucerian strategy (Cf. *CT* I A 3185.)

45

20 No wondre is, for it nothyng of newe is;
   A blynd man kan nat juggen wel in hewis.   *blind, judge, of hues*

   Ye knowe ek that in forme of speche is chaunge
   Withinne a thousand yeer, and °wordes tho
   That hadden pris, now wonder nyce and straunge
25 Us thinketh hem, and yet thei spake hem so,   *they seem to us*
   And spedde as wel in love as men now do;   *prospered*
   Ek for to wynnen love in sondry ages,   *win, various*
   In sondry londes, sondry ben usages.

   And forthi if it happe in any wyse,   *therefore, happen*
30 That here be any lovere in this place
   °That herkneth, as the storie wol devise,
   How Troilus com to his lady grace,
   And thenketh, "so nold I nat love purchace,"   *would I not*
   Or wondreth on his speche or his doynge,   *behavior*
35 I noot; but it is me no wonderynge.   *do not know, to me*

   For every wight which that to Rome went   *person, goes*
   Halt nat o path, or alwey o manere;   *holds, one*
   Ek in som lond were al the game shent,   *some, would be, spoiled*
   If that they ferde in love as men don here,   *behaved*
40 °As thus, in opyn doyng or in chere,
   In visityng, in forme, or seyde hire sawes;
   Forthi men seyn, ecch contree hath his lawes.   *hence, each, its*

   Ek scarsly ben ther in this place thre   *moreover, are*
   That have in love seid lik, and don, in al;   *alike*
45 °For to thi purpos this may liken the,

23-5 and words that had value then seem to us now wondrously foolish and strange
31-2 that listens, as the story will relate it, to how T came to stand in his lady's grace
40-1 as thus, in visible dealings, in manners, in visiting, in demeanor; or (if) they
expressed their sayings (as men do here)
45-6 for to the end you purpose, this (behavior) may please you (or: please some

And the right nought, yet al is seid or schal;
Ek som men grave in tree, some in ston wal,   *engrave*
As it bitit; but syn I have bigonne,   *happens, since*
Myn auctour shal I folwen, if I konne.   *follow, can*

50 In May, that moder is of monthes glade,   *mother*
That fresshe floures, blew and white and rede,   *when*
Ben quike agayn, that wynter dede made,   *are, alive, dead*
And °ful of bawme is fletyng every mede;
Whan Phebus doth his bryghte bemes sprede,
55 Right in the white °Bole, it so bitidde,   *it so happened*
As I shal synge, on °Mayes day the thrydde,

That Pandarus, for al his wise speche,   *speech*
Felt ek his part of loves shotes keene,   *also*
°That, koude he nevere so wel of lovyng preche,
60 It made his hewe a-day ful ofte greene.   *hue, in the daytime*
°So shop it that hym fil that day a teene
In love, for which in wo to bedde he wente,   *woe*
And made, er it was day, ful many a wente.   *tossing and turning*

°The swalowe Proigne, with a sorowful lay,   *song*
65 Whan morwen come, gan make hire waymentynge,   *morning, lamentation*

---

unspecified "you" in the audience) and (another) you not at all, yet everything is said or will be said (eventually)

53 suffused with balm is every meadow

55 the sign of Taurus (end of April through mid-May)

56 a particularly significant date for Ch (See *CT* I A 1462 and VII B 4380.)

59 that, though he could preach ever so well about loving, still . . .

61 it so turned out that that day a grief beset him

64 Ovid tells the story of Procne, the swallow, Philomela, the nightingale, and Tereus, the hoopoe at *Metam*. 6. 424–674; having married Procne, Tereus rapes her sister Philomela, who then conspires with Procne to punish Tereus by feeding him his son by Procne, whereupon the gods metamorphose (*forshapen*) all three of them into birds.

47

Whi she °forshapen was; and ever lay   *why*
Pandare abedde, half in a slomberynge,
Til she so neigh hym made hire cheterynge   *near, chattering*
How Tereus gan forth hire suster take,   *sister*
70 That with the noyse of hire he gan awake,

And gan to calle, and dresse hym up to ryse,   *prepare himself*
°Remembryng hym his erand was to doone
From Troilus, and ek his grete emprise;   *also, task*
And °caste and knew in good plit was the moone   *position*
75 To doon viage, and took his weye ful soone   *to make a trip*
Unto his neces palays ther biside.   *nearby*
Now °Janus, god of entree, thow hym gyde!   *entry, guide*

Whan he was come unto his neces place,
"Wher is my lady?" to hire folk quod he;   *said*
80 And they hym tolde, and he forth in gan pace,   *pass*
And fond two othere ladys sete, and she,   *sitting*
Withinne a paved parlour, and they thre
Herden a mayden reden hem the °geste   *heard, read, story*
Of the siege of °Thebes, while hem leste.   *while it pleased them*

85 Quod Pandarus, "Madame, God yow see,   *keep watch over*
With al youre book, and al the compaignie!"
"Ey, uncle myn, welcome iwys," quod she;   *ah, indeed*

---

66 A quasi-technical term, "forshapen" ("metamorphose") calls special attention to the Ovidian allusion.

72-3 recalling that he had an errand from T to perform and recalling also his great task

74 forecast astrologically

77 Janus is the deity whose province is gates and entryways; he is represented with two faces looking in opposite directions.

83 "Geste" is a technical generic term for "story."

84 Statius's *Thebaid* which also existed in a medieval French version, the *Roman de Thèbes*

And up she roos, and by the hond in hye	*rose, hand quickly*
She took hym faste, and seyde, "This nyght thrie,	*thrice*
90 To goode mot it turne, of yow I mette."	*may it turn, dreamed*
And with that word she doun on bench hym sette.	

"Ye, nece, yee shal faren wel the bet,	*prosper, the better*
If God wol, al this yeer," quod Pandarus;	*will*
"But I am sory that I have yow let	*hindered*
95 To herken of youre book °ye preysen thus.	*listen to*
For Goddes love, what seith it? telle it us!	
Is it of love? O, som good ye me leere!"	*teach*
"Uncle," quod she, "youre maistresse is nat here."	*mistress*

With that thei gonnen laughe, and tho she seyde,	*began to*
100 "This °romaunce is of Thebes that we rede;	*read*
And we han herd how that kyng Layus deyde	*died*
Thorugh Edippus his sone, and al that dede;	*deed*
And here we stynten at thise °lettres rede,	*stopped*
How the bisshop, as the book kan telle,	
105 °Amphiorax, fil thorugh the ground to helle."	*fell*

Quod Pandarus, "Al this knowe I myselve,
And al th'assege of Thebes and the care;
For herof ben ther maked bookes twelve.

---

95 which you set so much store by

100 "Romaunce" is a different generic term from "geste" (83), though such distinctions are much less fast in the MA than in modern discourse; significant here is that Ch's ME closely and etymologically translates the French title and not the Latin title of Statius's *Thebaid*.

103 "Letters red" probably refers to a rubric, of the kind that in medieval manuscripts would mark a break in the text or summarize, like a chapter title, a section of the story.

105 Amphiaurus (*Thebaid* VII) was swallowed up by the earth during the siege of Thebes; he was a soothsayer who foretold the sorrows which would result from the siege and who also foretold his own death; perhaps significant to *T&C* is that he was betrayed by his wife (*Thebaid* IV. 190–4 and VII. 787–8).

But lat be this, and telle me how ye fare.
110 Do wey youre °barbe, and shewe youre face bare;   *put aside*
Do wey youre book, rys up, and lat us daunce,   *rise*
And lat us don to May som observaunce."   *do*

"I? God forbede!" quod she, "be ye mad?
Is that a widewes lif, so God yow save?   *widow's*
115 By God, ye maken me ryght soore adrad!   *afraid*
Ye ben so wylde, it semeth as ye rave.
It sate me wel bet ay in a cave   *better, would befit, ever*
To bidde and rede on holy seyntes lyves;   *pray, read*
Lat maydens gon to daunce, and yonge wyves."

120 "As evere thryve I," quod this Pandarus,   *prosper*
"Yet koude I telle a thyng to doon yow pleye." *make you be merry*
"Now, uncle deere," quod she, "telle it us
For Goddes love; is than th'assege aweye?" *besieging force, away*
I am of Grekes so fered that I deye."   *afraid, die*
125 "Nay, nay," quod he, "as evere mote I thryve,   *might*
It is a thing wel bet than swyche fyve." *better, any five such*

"Ye, holy God," quod she, "what thyng is that?
What! bet than swyche fyve? I! nay, ywys!   *indeed*
For al this world ne kan I reden what   *guess*
130 It sholde ben; som jape, I trowe, is this; *should, joke, suspect*
And but youreselven telle us what it is,
My wit is for t'arede it al to leene.   *guess, lean*
As help me God, I not nat what ye meene." *know not, mean*

°"And I youre borugh, ne nevere shal, for me,
135 This thyng be told to yow, as mote I thryve!"

---

110 headdress worn by widows and nuns (a wimple), passing over or under the chin and extending down to the waist, sometimes only to the breast

134-5 and as I am your surety (i.e., you can take my word for it), never, if I have anything to do with it, shall this matter be told to you, so may I prosper

"And whi so, uncle myn? whi so?" quod she.
"By God," quod he, "that wol I telle as blyve!   *immediately*
For prouder womman is ther noon on lyve,   *alive*
And ye it wist, in al the town of Troye.   *if you knew it*
140 I jape nought, as evere have I joye!"   *jest, (may) I have*

Tho gan she wondren moore than biforn   *then did she wonder*
A thousand fold, and down hire eyghen caste;   *eyes*
For nevere, sith the tyme that she was born,
To knowe thyng desired she so faste;   *hard*
145 And with a syk she seyde hym atte laste,   *sigh*
"Now, uncle myn, I nyl yow nought displese,   *will you not*
Nor axen more that may do yow disese."   *ask, make you uncomfortable*

So after this, with many wordes glade,
And frendly tales, and with merie chiere,   *pleasant, happy spirits*
150 Of this and that they pleide, and °gonnen wade   *played*
In many an unkouth glad and dep matere,   *strange, deep subject*
As frendes doon whan thei ben mette yfere,   *get together*
Tyl she gan axen hym how Ector ferde,   *fared*
That was the townes wal and Grekes yerde.   *scourge*

155 "Ful wel, I thonk it God," quod Pandarus,
"Save in his arm he hath a litel wownde;
And ek his fresshe brother Troilus,
The wise, worthi Ector the secounde,   *Hector the second*
In whom that alle vertu list habounde,   *is pleased to abound*
160 As alle trouth and alle gentilesse,
Wisdom, honour, °fredom, and worthinesse."

"In good feith, em," quod she, "that liketh me;   *uncle, pleases*
Thei faren wel, God save hem bothe two!   *fare*

---

150 began to immerse (themselves)
161 combining the senses "freedom from" (poverty, meanness, niggardliness, etc.) and
"freedom to" (give or bestow—hence "liberal," "generous," "generosity")

For trewelich I holde it gret deynte,   *a rare treat*
165 A kynges sone in armes wel to do,
  °And ben of goode condiciouns therto;
For gret power and moral vertu here
Is selde yseyn in o persone yfere."   *seldom seen, one, together*

"In good faith, that is soth," quod Pandarus,   *true*
170 "But, by my trouthe, the kyng hath sones tweye,—   *two*
That is to mene, Ector and Troilus,—
That certeynly, though that I sholde deye,   *die*
Thei ben as voide of vices, dar I seye,   *devoid, dare*
As any men that lyven under the sonne.
175 Hire myght is wyde yknowe, °and what they konne.   *widely known*

"Of Ector nedeth it namore for to telle: *needs*
In al this world ther nys a bettre knyght   *is not*
Than he, that is of worthynesse welle;   *well*
And he wel moore vertu hath than myght.
180 That knoweth many a wis and worthi wight.   *wise, person*
The same pris of Troilus I seye;   *praise*
God help me so, I knowe nat swiche tweye."   *two*

"By God," quod she, "of Ector that is sooth.
Of Troilus the same thyng trowe I;   *believe*
185 For, dredeles, men tellen that he doth   *doubtless*
In armes day by day so worthily,
And bereth hym here at hom so gentily   *courteously*
To every wight, °that alle pris hath he
Of hem that me were levest preysed be."

---

166 and to be of proper moral bearing as well
175 and also what they can do
188-9 that he has all the esteem of those people by whom I would like most to be
esteemed

190 "Ye sey right sooth, ywys," quod Pandarus;	*say*
"For yesterday, whoso hadde with hym ben,	*whoever might have been*
He myghte han wondred upon Troilus;	
For nevere yet so thikke a swarm of been	*bees*
Ne fleigh, as Grekes from hym gonne fleen,	*flew, flee*
195 And thorugh the feld, in everi wightes eere,	*field, person's ears*
Ther nas no cry but 'Troilus is there!'	*was not any*

"Now here, now ther, he hunted hem so faste,	
Ther nas but Grekes blood,—and Troilus.	*was not (anything)*
Now hym he hurte, and hym al down he caste;	*this one, that one*
200 Ay wher he wente, it was arayed thus:	*everywhere, destined*
He was hir deth, and sheld and lif for us;	*their, shield*
That, as that day, ther dorste non withstonde,	*as for, dared*
Whil that he held his blody swerd in honde.	*sword*

"Therto he is the friendlieste man	*furthermore*
205 Of gret estat, that evere I saugh my lyve,	*estate, saw in my life*
°And wher hym lest, best felawshipe kan	
To swich as hym thynketh able for to thryve."	
And with that word tho Pandarus, as blyve,	*then, immediately*
He took his leve, and seyde, "I wol gon henne."	*go, hence*
210 "Nay, blame have I, myn uncle," quod she thenne.	*said*

"What aileth yow to be thus wery soone,	*ails, weary*
And namelich of wommen? wol ye so?	*especially, will you behave so*
Nay, sitteth down; by God, °I have to doone	
With yow, to speke of wisdom er ye go."	*matters needing wise counsel*
215 And everi wight that was aboute hem tho,	*person, them then*

206-7 and wherever it pleases him, he best can (show) fellowship to such as seem to him able to thrive

213-14 I have business with you before you go, to discuss serious affairs with you (Here *wisdom* has a strong connotation of *prudence*.)

That herde that, gan fer awey to stonde,   *began to*
Whil they two hadde °al that hem liste in honde.

Whan that hire tale al brought was to an ende   *their conversation*
Of hire estat and of hire governaunce,
220 Quod Pandarus, "Now is it tyme I wende.   *left*
But yet, I say, ariseth, lat us daunce,
And cast youre widewes habit to mischaunce!   *to a fate of bad luck*
What list yow thus youreself to °disfigure,   *why does it please you*
Sith yow is tid thus fair an aventure?"   *since to you has happened*

225 "A! wel bithought! for love of God," quod she,   *conceived*
"Shal I nat witen what ye meene of °this?"   *know, mean*
"No, °this thing axeth leyser," tho quod he,   *then said*
"And eke me wolde muche greve, iwys,   *also, it would upset me a lot*
If I it tolde, and ye it toke amys.   *took it wrongly*
230 Yet were it bet my tonge for to stille   *better, keep still*
Than seye a soth that were ayeyns youre wille.   *truth, against*

"For, nece, by the goddesse °Mynerve,
And Jupiter, that maketh the thondre rynge,   *thunder*
And by the blisful Venus that I serve,
235 Ye ben the womman in this world lyvynge,
Withouten paramours, to my wyttynge,   *except for lovers, knowledge*
That I best love, and lothest am to greve,   *loathest, grieve*
And that ye weten wel yourself, I leve."   *know, believe*

---

217 all the business they wished to transact

223 Obviously "disfigure" does not carry its literal modern sense; the idea seems to be that she is concealing herself under a figure or image (namely, widow's garments) which is not true to herself—hence we can gloss "to counterfeit yourself."

226 "This" refers to "thus fair an aventure" (line 224).

227 it cannot be hurried

232 Minerva (Athena) goddess of wisdom, a deity of special importance to Troy (See 1. 152–4 and 153n.)

"Iwis, myn uncle," quod she, "grant mercy.   *indeed, thank you*
240 Youre frendshipe have I founden evere yit;   *experienced*
I am to no man holden, trewely,   *obligated*
So muche as yow, and have so litel quyt;   *to you, repaid*
And with the grace of God, emforth my wit,   *as far as I am able*
As in my gylt I shal yow nevere offende;   *through my fault*
245 And if I have er this, I wol amende.   *before, will make amends*

"But, for the love of God, I yow biseche,
As ye ben he that I love moost and triste,   *are, trust*
Lat be to me youre fremde manere speche,   *strange manner of speech*
And sey to me, youre nece, what yow liste."   *say, pleases you*
250 And with that word hire uncle anoon hire kiste,   *kissed*
And seyde, "Gladly, °leve nece dere!   *dear*
Tak it for good, that I shal sey yow here."   *take*

With that she gan hire eighen down to caste,   *began, eyes*
And Pandarus to coghe gan a lite,   *coughed a little*
255 And seyde, "Nece, alwey, lo! to the laste,
How so it be that som men hem delite   *take pleasure*
With subtyl art hire tales for to endite,   *subtle, their, compose*
Yet for al that, in hire entencioun,   *their, intent*
Hire tale is al for som conclusioun.

260 "And sithen th'ende is every tales strengthe,   *since*
And this matere is so bihovely,   *matter, profitable*
What sholde I peynte or drawen it on lengthe   *embellish, draw it out*
To yow, that ben my frend so feythfully?"
And with that word he gan right inwardly   *began to*
265 Byholden hire and loken on hire face,   *look*
And seyde, "On swiche a mirour goode grace!"   *mirror*

---

251 The connotation of "leve" (lit., "dear") is something like "beloved."

55

Than thought he thus: "If I my tale endite   *compose*
Aught harde, or °make a proces any whyle,   *in any way difficult*
She shal no savour have therin but lite,   *taste, for it, little*
270 And trowe I wolde hire °in my wil bigyle;   *(will) believe*
For tendre wittes wenen al be wyle
Theras thei kan nought pleynly understonde;   *where, openly and fully*
Forthi hire wit to serven wol I fonde"–   *hence, accommodate, try*

And loked on hire in a bysi wyse,   *looked, attentively*
275 And she was war that he byheld hire so,   *aware*
And seyde, "Lord! so faste ye m'avise!   *steadily you gaze at me*
Sey ye me nevere er now—What sey ye, no?"   *saw, say*
"Yis, yis," quod he, "and bet wole er I go!   *better, will*
But, by my trouthe, I thoughte now if ye   *was wondering, whether*
280 Be fortunat, for now men shal it se,

"For to every wight som goodly aventure   *person, good fortune*
Som tyme is shape, if he it kan receyven;   *destined, receive*
And if that he wol take of it no cure,   *heed*
Whan that it commeth, but wilfully it weyven,   *waive*
285 Lo, neyther cas ne fortune hym deceyven,   *luck, deceive*
But °ryght his verray slouthe and wrecchednesse;
And swich a wight is for to blame, I gesse.   *person, guess*

"Good aventure, o beele nece, have ye   *fair*
Ful lightly founden, and ye konne it take;   *if, can*
290 And, for the love of God, and ek of me,
Cache it anon, lest aventure slake!   *seize, good fortune wane*
What sholde I lenger proces of it make?   *why, longer, argument*
Yif me youre hond, for °in this world is noon,   *give, hand*
If that yow list, a wight so wel bygon.

---

268 make a complex argument for any length of time
270-1 in my intention beguile her; for inexperienced minds assume all is cunning
286 just his very own laziness
293-4 in this world, there is no person, if you please, so fortunate (as you)

295 "And sith I speke of good entencioun,   *since, out of*
 As I to yow have told wel here-byforn,
 And love as wel youre honour and renoun
 As creature in al this world yborn,
 By alle the othes that I have yow sworn,   *oaths*
300 And ye be wrooth therfore, or wene I lye, *if, angry, suspect*
 Ne shal I nevere sen yow eft with yë. *again with eye (face to face)*

 "Beth naught agast, ne quaketh naught! Wherto? *Why*
 Ne chaungeth naught for fere so youre hewe! *fear, countenance*
 For hardely the werst of this is do, *assuredly, worst*
305 And though my tale as now be to yow newe,
 Yet trist alwey ye shal me fynde trewe;   *trust*
 And were it thyng that me thoughte unsittynge, *seemed to me improper*
 To yow wolde I no swiche tales brynge."   *such*

 "Now, my good em, for Goddes love, I preye," *uncle*
310 Quod she, "come of, and telle me what it is! *get on with it*
 For both I am agast what ye wol seye,
 And ek me longeth it to wite, ywys;   *know, indeed*
 For whethir it be wel or be amys,
 Say on, lat me nat in this feere dwelle."   *fear*
315 "So wol I doon; now herkeneth! I shal telle:

 "Now, nece myn, the kynges deere sone, *niece, dear*
 The goode, wise, worthi, fresshe, and free,
 °Which alwey for to don wel is his wone,
 The noble Troilus, so loveth the,
320 That, but ye helpe, it wol his bane be.   *unless*
 Lo, here is al! What sholde I moore seye?
 Do what yow lest, to make hym lyve or deye. *pleases you*

 "But if ye late hym deye, I wol sterve — *let, die*
 Have here my trouthe, nece, I nyl nat lyen —

---

318 whose custom or practice is always to behave well

325 Al sholde I with this knyf my throte kerve." *even if I had to, cut*
    With that the teris breste out of his yën, *tears, burst, eyes*
    And seide, "If that ye don us bothe dyen, *cause*
    Thus gilteles, °than have ye fisshed fayre! *guiltless*
    °What mende ye, though that we booth appaire?

330 "Allas! he which that is my lord so deere,
    That trewe man, that noble gentil knyght, *courteous*
    That naught desireth but youre frendly cheere, *countenance*
    °I se hym deyen, ther he goth upryght,
    And hasteth hym with al his fulle myght
335 For to ben slayn, if his fortune assente.
    Allas, that God yow swich a beaute sente!

    "If it be so that ye so cruel be,
    °That of his deth yow liste nought to recche,
    That is so trewe and worthi, as ye se, *who*
340 Namoore than of a japer or a wrecche,— *jester, wretch*
    If ye be swich, °youre beaute may nat strecche
    To make amendes of so cruel a dede.
    Avysement is good byfore the nede. *deliberation*

    "Wo worth the faire °gemme vertulees! *woe unto, powerless*
345 Wo worth that herbe also that dooth no boote! *provides no remedy*
    Wo worth that beaute that is routheles! *pitiless*

---

328 then have you done a fair day's work (sense ironic)

329 how do you gain by it if we both perish

333-5 I see him die, even where he appears to be walking upright, and (I see him) push himself hastily with all his might to get himself killed, if his luck will (only) assent (to it)

338 that it pleases you not to care about his death

341-2 your beauty would never compensate for so cruel a deed

344 an allusion to the belief that precious stones had magical and other useful properties

Wo worth that wight that °tret ech undir foote!   *person*
And ye, that ben of beaute °crop and roote,   *who are*
If therwithal in yow ther be no routhe,   *pity*
350 °Than is it harm ye lyven, by my trouthe!

"And also think wel that this is no gaude;   *trick*
For me were levere thow and I and he   *I would prefer*
Were hanged, than I sholde ben his baude,   *pimp*
As heigh as men myghte on us alle ysee!   *high*
355 I am thyn em; °the shame were to me,   *uncle*
As wel as the, if that I sholde assente,
Thorugh myn abet, that he thyn honour shente.   *abetting, ruined*

"Now understonde, for I yow nought requere   *require*
To bynde yow to hym thorugh no byheste,   *promise, any*
360 But only that ye make hym bettre chiere   *welcoming appearance*
Than ye han doon er this, and moore °feste,
So that his lif be saved atte leeste: *least*
This al and som, and pleynly oure entente.   *this is all, fully*
God help me so, I nevere other mente!

365 "Lo, this requeste is naught but skylle, ywys,   *only reasonable*
Ne doute of reson, pardee, is ther noon.   *reasonable fear, indeed*
°I sette the worste, that ye dreden this: *dread*
°Men wolde wondren sen hym come or goon.
Ther-ayeins answere I thus anoon,   *against that argument, promptly*

---

347 who treads each under foot
348 a common phrase signifying the whole of anything
350 then is it harm that you live (The world, in other words, is a worse place for your being alive in it.)
355–6 the shame would be as much mine as yours
361 "encouraging joy" (lit., "feast") where the sense is of festive, generous welcome and entertainment (Cf. *T&C* 3. 1312.)
367 I hypothesize the worst
368 people would speculate on seeing him

370 That every wight, but he be °fool of kynde,   *person, unless*
Wol deme it °love of frendshipe in his mynde.   *consider*

"What? who wol demen, though he se a man   *assume*
To temple go, that he th'ymages eteth?   *eats*
Thenk ek how wel and wisely that he kan
375 Governe hymself, that he no thyng foryeteth,   *forgets*
That where he cometh, he pris and thank hym geteth;   *praise*
And ek therto, he shal come here so selde,   *seldom*
°What fors were it though al the town byhelde?

"Swych love of frendes regneth al this town;   *friends, governs*
380 And °wry yow in that mantel evere moo;
And, God so wys be my savacioun,   *wise, salvation*
As I have seyd, youre beste is to do soo.   *best, behave this way*
But alwey, goode nece, to stynte his woo,   *put a stop to*
So lat youre °daunger sucred ben a lite,   *sugared be a little*
385 That of his deth ye be naught for to wite."   *blame*

Criseyde, which that herde hym in this wise,
Thoughte, "I shal felen what he meneth, ywis."   *feel out, means*
"Now em," quod she, "what wolde ye devise?   *uncle, suggest*
What is youre reed I sholde don of this?"   *advice*
390 "That is wel seyd," quod he. "Certein, best is,
That ye hym love ayeyn for his lovynge,   *in return*
As love for love is skilful guerdonynge.   *reasonable reward*

---

370 a "natural" fool
371 friendly affection (i.e., not a sexual affair)
378 what difference would it make if
380 and wrap yourself in this cover (the Trojan habit of friendship and hospitality) always
384 "Daunger" is a technical term of "fin'amors" ("refined love," often called "courtly love") representing one of the elements of the Lady's psyche personified in *RR*; it designates a complex combination of the "come-on" and "standoffishness."

"Thenk ek how elde wasteth every houre   *old age, wastes*
In eche of yow a partie of beautee;   *portion*
395 And therfore, er that age the devoure,   *devour you*
Go love; for olde, ther wol no wight of the.   *no one will want you*
Lat this proverbe a loore unto yow be: *lesson*
'To late ywar, quod beaute, whan it paste';   *on guard, has passed*
And elde daunteth daunger at the laste.   *quells haughtiness*

400 "The kynges fool is wont to crien loude,   *accustomed*
Whan that hym thinketh a womman °bereth hire hye,   *it seems to him*
'So longe mote ye lyve, and alle proude,   *may, all such proud ones*
Til crowes feet be growen under youre yë,   *eyes*
And sende yow than a myrour in to prye,   *(let someone) send, gaze*
405 In which that ye may se youre face a-morwe!'
Nece, °I bidde wisshe yow namore sorwe."

With this he stynte, and caste adown the heed,   *head, stopped*
And she began to breste a-wepe anoon,   *burst into tears right away*
And seyde, "Allas, for wo! Why nere I deed?   *were not*
410 For of this world the feyth is al agoon.   *faith*
Allas! what sholden straunge to me doon,   *strangers, do*
When he, that for my beste frend I wende,   *supposed*
Ret me to love, and sholde it me defende?   *advises, warn against*

"Allas! I wolde han trusted, douteles,
415 That if that I, thorugh my disaventure,   *misfortune*
Hadde loved outher hym or Achilles,   *either*
Ector, or any mannes creature,   *human creature*
Ye nolde han had no mercy ne mesure   *would not have, restraint*
On me, but alwey had me in repreve.   *reproof*
420 This false world, allas! who may it leve?   *trust*

---

401 acts uppity
406 I would not wish you more (i.e., worse) sorrow

"What! is this al the joye and al the feste?   *pleasure*
Is this youre reed? Is this my blisful cas?   *advice, lot*
°Is this the verray mede of youre byheeste?
Is al this °paynted proces seyd, allas!   *highly-colored account*
425 Right for this fyn? O lady myn, Pallas!   *purpose, Minerva*
Thow in this dredful cas for me purveye,   *provide*
For so °astoned am I that I deye."   *astonished, die*

Wyth that she gan ful sorwfully to syke.   *sigh*
"A! may it be no bet?" quod Pandarus;   *better*
430 "By God, I shal namore come here this wyke,   *week*
And God toforn, that am mystrusted thus!   *as God is my witness*
I se ful wel that ye sette lite of us,   *care little for us*
Or of oure deth! allas, I, woful wrecche!   *wretch*
°Might he yet lyve, of me is nought to recche.

435 "O cruel God, O dispitouse Marte,   *spiteful Mars*
O °Furies thre of helle, on yow I crye!
So lat me nevere out of this hous departe,   *may I*
If that I mente harm or vilenye!   *meant, anything improper*
But sith I se my lord mot nedes dye,   *since, must needs*
440 And I with hym, here I me shryve, and seye   *confess*
That wikkedly ye don us bothe deye.   *cause, to die*

---

423 A modern equivalent would be: "Is this the real return on the investment I would make in accordance with your promises to me?"
424 Note here the legal trope; "proces" is a ME word for a plea or argumentative brief at law (see 2. 1615); note further in "paynted" a probable reference to the *colores rhetorici* or "colors of rhetoric"; finally, we should observe the suggestion of hypocrisy since paint covers and conceals so that what is under it may be different from what the paint makes it appear to be.
427 Cf. the *Franklin's Tale* (*CT* V F 1339).
434 if he might yet live, what happens to me would not matter
436 See 1. 6n.

"But sith it liketh yow that I be ded,   *pleases, dead*
By Neptunus, that god is of the see,
Fro this forth shal I nevere eten bred   *henceforth, eat*
445 Til I myn owen herte blood may see;
For certeyn I wol deye as soone as he."
And up he sterte, and on his wey he raughte,   *jumped, started*
Til she agayn hym by the lappe kaughte.   *fold of a garment caught*

Criseyde, which that wel neigh starf for feere,   *nearly died, fear*
450 So as she was the ferfulleste wight   *most fearful person*
That myghte be, and herde ek with hire ere   *ear*
And saugh the sorwful ernest of the knyght,
And in his preier ek saugh noon unryght,   *prayer, offence*
°And for the harm that myghte ek fallen moore,
455 She gan to rewe, and dredde hire wonder soore,   *have regrets, dread*

And thoughte thus: "Unhappes fallen thikke   *misfortunes, thick*
Alday for love, and °in swych manere cas   *continually*
As men ben cruel in hemself and wikke;   *where, perverse*
And if this man sle here hymself, allas!   *slay*
460 In my presence, it wol be no solas.   *laughing matter*
What men wolde of hit deme I kan nat seye: *think*
°It nedeth me ful sleighly for to pleie."

And with a sorowful sik she sayde thrie,   *sigh, three times*
"A! Lord! °what me is tid a sory chaunce!
465 For myn °estat lith now in jupartie,   *lies, jeopardy*
And ek myn emes lif is in balaunce;   *uncle's*
But natheles, with Goddes governaunce,   *nevertheless*

---

454 and considering the further harm that might happen
457-8 and especially do they fall thick in such cases as this . . .
462 it is necessary for me to play cunningly, with all my wits about me
464 what a sad misfortune has befallen me
465 "condition," but the word can also mean "social rank" and "dignity" as well as "wealth" and "property"

°I shal so doon, myn honour shal I kepe,   *act, preserve*
And ek his lif,"– and stynte for to wepe.   *stopped weeping*

470 "Of harmes two, the lesse is for to chese;   *choose*
°Yet have I levere maken hym good chere
In honour, than myn emes lyf to lese.   *uncle's, lose*
Ye seyn, ye nothyng elles me requere?"   *say, require of*
"No, wis," quod he, "myn owen nece dere."   *indeed*
475 "Now wel," quod she, "and I wol doon my peyne;   *take the trouble*
I shal myn herte ayeins my lust constreyne.   *against my desire*

"But that I nyl nat holden hym in honde;   *except, deceive him*
Ne love a man ne kan I naught, ne may,
Ayeins my wyl; but elles wol I fonde,   *otherwise, try to*
480 Myn honour sauf, plese hym fro day to day.   *(with) my reputation safe*
Therto nolde I nat ones han seyd nay,   *would not, once have said*
But that I dredde, as in my fantasye;   *was afraid*
But cesse cause, ay cesseth maladie.   *(let) cease, ever*

"And here I make a protestacioun,
485 That in this °proces if ye depper go,   *matter, deeper*
That certeynly, for no salvacioun
Of yow, though that ye sterven bothe two,   *even though, die*
Though al the world on o day be my fo,   *one, foe*
Ne shal I nevere of hym han other routhe."   *have any other pity*
490 "I graunte wel," quod Pandare, "by my trowthe."

"But may I truste wel therto," quod he,
"That of this thyng that ye han hight me here,   *promised*
Ye wole it holden trewely unto me?"
"Ye, doutelees," quod she, "myn uncle deere."
495 "Ne that I shal han cause in this matere,"

---

468 I shall act in such a way that I shall, etc.
471 yet I would prefer to offer him a welcoming appearance
485 Cf. T&C 2. 424 and 1615.

64

Quod he, "to pleyne, or ofter yow to preche?"   *complain, more often*
"Why, no, parde; what nedeth moore speche?"   *indeed*

Tho fillen they in other tales glade,   *then they turned to, glad*
Tyl at the laste, "O good em," quod she tho,   *uncle, then*
500 "For his love, which that us bothe made,
Tel me how first ye wisten of his wo.   *learned, woe*
Woot noon of it but ye?"– He seyde, "No."–   *does anyone know*
"Kan he wel speke of love?" quod she; "I preye
Tel me, °for I the bet me shal purveye."

505 Tho Pandarus a litel gan to smyle,   *did smile a little*
And seyde, "By my trouthe, I shal yow telle.
This other day, naught gon ful longe while,   *recently*
In-with the paleis gardyn, by a welle,   *within, palace*
Gan he and I wel half a day to dwelle,
510 Right for to speken of an ordinaunce,   *plan*
How we the Grekes myghten disavaunce.   *repel*

"Soon after that bigonne we to lepe,   *exercise*
And casten with oure dartes to and fro,   *javelins*
Tyl at the laste he seyde he wolde slepe,   *sleep*
515 And on the gres adoun he leyde hym tho;   *grass, laid*
And I afer gan romen to and fro,   *afar, roam*
Til that I herde, as that I welk alone,   *walked*
How he bigan wofully to grone.   *groan*

"Tho gan I stalke hym softely byhynde,   *then*
520 And sikirly, the soothe for to seyne,   *certainly, truth to say*
As I kan clepe ayein now to my mynde,   *call*
Right thus to Love he gan hym for to pleyne: *complain*
He seyde, °'Lord, have routhe upon my peyne,   *pity, pain*

---

504 that I may be the better prepared
523ff Cf. this report of T's repentance with the scene of repentance at the end of book 1 (925–45).

Al have I ben rebell in myn entente;   *although*
525 Now, °*mea culpa*, lord, I me repente!

"'O god, that at thi disposicioun
Ledest the fyn, by juste purveiaunce,   *guides the end, providence*
Of every wight, my lowe confessioun   *person, humble*
Accepte in gree, and sende me swich penaunce   *graciously*
530 As liketh the, but from disesperaunce,   *pleases, despair*
That may my goost departe awey fro the,   *which, soul, exile from*
Thow be my sheld, for thi benignite.   *shield*

"'For certes, lord, so soore hath she me wounded,   *certainly*
That stood in blak, with lokyng of hire eyen,   *eyes*
535 That to myn hertes botme it is ysounded,   *plummeted*
Thorugh which I woot that I moot nedes deyen.   *know, must, die*
This is the werste, I dar me nat bywreyen;   *reveal my thoughts*
And wel the hotter ben the gledes rede,   *are, coals, red*
°That men hem wrien with asshen pale and dede.'

540 'Wyth that he smot his hed adown anon,   *hung*
And gan to motre, I noot what, trewely.   *mutter, I do not know*
And I with that gan stille awey to goon,
And leet therof as nothing wist had I,   *pretended, learned*
And com ayein anon, and stood hym by,   *came*
545 And seyde, 'awake, ye slepen al to longe!   *too*
°It semeth nat that love doth yow longe,

"'That slepen so that no man may yow wake.
Who sey evere or this so dul a man?'   *saw, before*

---

525 The Latin phrase— "my fault (I confess)" —is part of the formula of repentance in the Catholic church.

539 because men cover them with ashes pale and dead

546-7 it seems not that love causes you to pine with longing (or you wouldn't sleep so well)

'Ye, frend,' quod he, °'do ye youre hedes ake
550 For love, and lat me lyven as I kan.'
But though that he for wo was pale and wan,   *woe, drawn*
Yet made he tho as fressh a countenaunce   *then*
As though he sholde have led the newe daunce.

"This passed forth til now, this other day,
555 It fel that I com romyng al allone   *happened, came roaming*
Into his chaumbre, and fond how that he lay   *found*
Upon his bed; but man so soore grone   *grievously, groan*
Ne herde I nevere, and what that was his mone   *moan*
Ne wist I nought; for, as I was comynge,   *I could not find out*
560 Al sodeynly he lefte his complaynynge.   *ceased*

"Of whiche I took somwat suspecioun,   *became somewhat suspicious*
And ner I com, and fond he wepte soore;   *near*
And God so wys be my savacioun,   *wise, salvation*
°As nevere of thyng hadde I no routhe moore.
565 For neither with °engyn, ne with no loore,   *conventional wisdom*
Unnethes myghte I fro the deth hym kepe,   *hardly*
That yet fele I myn herte for hym wepe.   *(so) that, feel*

"And God woot, nevere, sith that I was born,   *knows, since*
Was I so besy no man for to preche,   *to preach to any man*
570 Ne nevere was to wight °so depe isworn,   *person*
Or he me told who myghte ben his leche.   *before, be, physician*
But now to yow rehercen al his speche,   *rehearse*
Or alle his woful wordes for to sowne,   *utter*
Ne bid me naught, but ye wol se me swowne.   *unless, swoon*

549-50 you lovers go ahead and make your heads ache for love
564 I never felt more pity regarding a matter
565 The word derives from Latin "ingenium" (cf. It. "ingegno" and 2. 4 above and
3. 274 below) and is perhaps best modernized by "imagination," but the range of senses
includes "ingenuity," "contrivance," "device," and "scheme."
570 so deeply sworn (to secrecy)

575 "But for to save his lif, and elles nought,   *nothing else*
     And to noon harm of yow, thus am I dryven;
     And for the love of God, that us hath wrought,   *made*
     °Swich cheer hym dooth, that he and I may lyven!
     Now have I plat to yow myn herte shryven;   *bluntly, confessed*
580 And sith ye woot that myn entent is cleene,   *since, know*
     Take heede therof, for I non yvel meene.   *evil mean*

     "And right good thrift, I prey to God, have ye,   *prosperity*
     That han swich oon ykaught withouten net!   *such a one*
     And, be ye wis as ye be fair to see,   *if you are as prudent*
585 Wel in the ryng than is the ruby set.
     Ther were nevere two so wel ymet,
     Whan ye ben his al hool, as he is youre: *wholly*
     Ther myghty God yet graunte us see that houre!"   *may*

     "Nay, therof spak I nought, ha, ha!" quod she;   *spoke*
590 "As helpe me God, ye shenden every deel!"   *spoil everything*
     "O, mercy, dere nece," anon quod he,   *immediately said*
     "What so I spak, I mente naught but wel,   *whatever, meant*
     By Mars, the god that helmed is of steel!   *helmeted*
     Now beth naught wroth, my blood, my nece dere."   *angry*
595 "Now, wel," quod she, "foryeven be it here!"

     With this he took his leve, and home he wente;
     And, Lord, so he was glad and wel bygon!   *begun*
     Criseyde aros, no lenger she ne stente,   *hesitated*
     But streght into hire closet wente anon,   *own room*
600 And set hire doun as stylle as any ston,
     And every word gan up and down to wynde   *turn over*
     That he had seyd, as it com hire to mynde;

     And was somdel astoned in hire thought,   *somewhat, astonished*
     Right for the newe cas; but whan that she   *situation*

---

578 show him such encouragement

68

605 Was ful avysed, tho fond she right nought	*had carefully considered*
Of peril, why she ought afered be.	
For man may love, of possibilite,	*hypothetically speaking*
A womman so, his herte may tobreste,	*burst*
And she naught love ayein, but if hire leste.	*unless it pleases her*

610 But as she sat allone and thoughte thus,	
Ascry aros at scarmuch al withoute,	*alarm arose, skirmish*
And men cride in the strete, "Se, Troilus	
Hath right now put to flighte the Grekes route!"	*crowd*
With that gan al hire meyne for to shoute,	*household*
615 "A, go we se! cast up the yates wyde!	*gates*
For thorwgh this strete he moot to paleys ride;	*through, palace*

"For other wey is fro the yate noon	
Of °Dardanus, there opyn is the cheyne."	*open, chain*
With that com he and al his folk anoon	
620 An esy pas rydyng, in routes tweyne,	*(at) an easy pace, companies*
°Right as his happy day was, sooth to seyne,	
For which, men seyn, may nought destourbed be	*regarding*
That shal bityden of necessitee.	*that (which) shall happen*

This Troilus sat on his baye steede,	
625 Al armed, save his hed, ful richely;	
And wownded was his hors, and gan to blede,	*wounded, began*
On which he rood a pas ful softely.	*at a walking pace*
°But swich a knyghtly sighte, trewely,	
As was on hym, was nought, withouten faille,	
630 To loke on Mars, that god is of bataille.	

---

618 The gate of Dardanus was one of the six gates of Troy.

621-3 in keeping with this being his lucky day, truth to tell, regarding which, as men say, what shall happen of necessity may not be disturbed (i.e., frustrated)

628-30 to look on Mars . . . was in no way such a knightly sight as to look on him

So lik a man of armes and a knyght
He was to seen, fulfilled of heigh prowesse;
For bothe he hadde a body and a myght
To don that thing, as wel as hardynesse;
635 And ek to seen hym in his gere hym dresse,   *gear, hold himself erect*
So fressh, so yong, so weldy semed he,   *vigorous*
It was an heven upon hym for to see.   *to look upon him*

His helm tohewen was in twenty places,   *hacked*
That by a tyssew heng his bak byhynde;   *tissue, hung*
640 His sheeld todasshed was with swerdes and maces,   *shattered*
In which men myght many an arwe fynde
That thirled hadde °horn and nerf and rynde;   *pierced*
And ay the peple cryde, "Here cometh oure joye,
And, next his brother, holder up of Troye!"   *next (to)*

645 For which he wex a litel reed for shame,   *turned, red*
Whan he the peple upon hym herde cryen,
That to byholde it was a noble game,   *beautiful sight*
How sobrelich he caste down his yën.   *soberly, eyes*
Criseÿda gan al his chere aspien,   *demeanor, contemplate*
650 And leet it so softe in hire herte synke,   *let*
That to hireself she seyde, "Who yaf me °drynke?"

For of hire owen thought she wex al reed,   *became, red*
Remembryng hire right thus, "Lo, this is he
Which that myn uncle swerith he moot be deed,   *swears, must, dead*
655 But I on hym have mercy and pitee."   *unless*
And with that thought, for pure ashamed, she   *out of very shame*
Gan in hire hed to pulle, and that as faste,   *very fast*
Whil he and alle the peple forby paste;   *passed by*

---

642 the materials with which shields were covered or bound—horn, sinew, and hide
651 The word suggests something which goes to her head or makes her head swim—
an "intoxicating beverage"; possibly there is a distant evocation of the Tristan legend,
in which a love-potion plays a crucial role.

And gan to caste and rollen up and down   *mull it over*
660 Withinne hire thought his excellent prowesse,
And his estat, and also his renown,
His wit, his shap, and ek his gentilesse;   *physique*
But moost hire favour was, °for his distresse   *to her liking*
Was al for hire, and thoughte it was a routhe   *(she) thought, pity*
665 To sleen swich oon, °if that he mente trouthe.   *slay*

Now myghte som envious jangle thus: *(person) snicker*
"This was a sodeyn love; how myght it be   *sudden*
That she so lightly loved Troilus,   *frivously*
Right for the firste syghte, ye, parde?"   *at*
670 Now whoso seith so, mote he nevere ythe!   *may, thrive*
For every thyng, a gynnyng hath it nede   *beginning, must it have*
Er al be wrought, withowten any drede.   *before, accomplished, doubt*

For I sey nought that she so sodeynly   *say*
Yaf hym hire love, but that she gan enclyne   *gave, began (to)*
675 To like hym first, and I have told yow whi;
And after that, his manhod and his pyne   *suffering*
Made love withinne hire herte for to myne,   *tunnel*
For which, by proces and by good servyse,   *at length*
He gat hire love, and in no sodeyn wyse.   *manner*

680 And also blisful Venus, wel arrayed,
Sat in hire °seventhe hous of hevene tho,   *then*

---

663 because his distress
665 if his intentions were honorable
681 The usual meaning of "hous" is a sign of the zodiac in which a given planet exerts its greatest influence, but here it seems to refer to one of the twelve equal sections of the heavens, six above and six below the horizon, marked by imaginary circles passing through the north and south points of the horizon. The houses are counted from the east, the first six being below the earth. The seventh house is the first above the horizon in the west, a propitious position for Venus, the planet concerned with matters of love. As Ch says at 684–5 Venus was also not unfavorably situated at T's birth.

Disposed wel, and °with aspectes payed,   *in propitious position*
To helpe sely Troilus of his woo.   *poor, woe*
And, soth to seyne, she nas not al a foo   *truth, was not, foe*
685 To Troilus in his nativitee;   *at his birth*
God woot that wel the sonner spedde he.   *knows, sooner, prospered*

Now lat us stynte of Troilus a throwe,   *cease, for a while*
That rideth forth, and lat us torne faste
Unto Criseyde, that heng hire hed ful lowe,   *hung*
690 Ther as she sat allone, and gan to caste   *began to consider*
Where on she wolde apoynte hire atte laste,   *on what, decide*
If it so were hire em ne wolde cesse   *uncle, would not*
For Troilus upon hire for to presse.   *in Troilus's behalf*

And, Lord! so she gan in hire thought argue   *began to*
695 In this matere of which I have yow told,
And what to doone best were, and what eschue,
That plited she ful ofte °in many fold.   *tossed and turned, often*
Now was hire herte warm, now was it cold;
And what she thoughte, somwhat shal I write,
700 As to myn auctour listeth for t'endite.   *it is pleasing, compose*

She thoughte wel that Troilus persone
She knew by syghte, and ek his gentilesse,
And thus she seyde, °"Al were it nat to doone
To graunte hym love, yet for his worthynesse
705 °It were honour, with pley and with gladnesse,
In honestee with swich a lord to deele,   *propriety, deal*
For myn estat, and also for his heele.   *position, welfare*

---

682 with aspects made favorable
697 in many a twist
703 although it wouldn't be the proper thing to do
705-7 Construe "for myn estat" with "It were honour."

"Ek wel woot I my kynges sone is he;   *know*
And sith he hath to se me swich delit,   *see*
710 If I wolde outreliche his sighte flee,   *utterly*
Peraunter he myghte °have me in dispit,   *perhaps*
Thorugh whicch I myghte stonde in worse plit.   *plight*
Now were I wis, me hate to purchase,   *prudent, for myself, to buy*
Withouten nede, ther I may stonde in grace?   *need, where*

715 "In every thyng, I woot, there lith mesure.   *know, lies*
For though a man forbede dronkenesse,   *forbid*
He naught forbet that every creature   *requires*
Be drynkeles for alwey, as I gesse.   *guess*
Ek sith I woot for me is his destresse,
720 I ne aughte nat for that thing hym despise,   *ought not*
Sith it is so, he meneth in good wyse.   *so (that), means favorably*

"And eke I knowe, of longe tyme agon,   *past*
His thewes goode, and that he is nat nyce.   *qualities, foolish*
°N'avantour, seith men, certein, he is noon;   *boaster*
725 To wis is he to doon so gret a vice;   *too, prudent*
Ne als I nyl hym nevere so cherice   *I will also, cherish*
That he may make avaunt, by juste cause,   *boast*
He shal me nevere bynde in swich a °clause.

°"Now sette a caas: the hardest is, ywys,   *worst*
730 Men myghten demen that he loveth me.   *surmise*
What dishonour were it unto me, this?
May ich hym lette of that? Why, nay, parde!   *prevent*
I knowe also, and alday heere and se,

---

711 bear a grudge against me
724 Cf. 3. 288ff.
728 stipulation (a legal metaphor)
729 now hypothesize a case

Men loven wommen al biside hire leve;   *without their permission*
735 And whan hem leste namore, °lat hem byleve!   *it pleases*

"I thenke ek how he able is for to have
Of al this noble town the thriftieste,   *the most worthy*
To ben his love, so she hire honour save.
For out and out he is the worthieste,
740 Save only Ector, which that is the beste;
And yet his lif al lith now in my cure.   *power and control*
But swich is love, and ek myn aventure.   *lot*

"Ne me to love, a wonder is it nought;   *nor to love me*
For wel woot I myself, so God me spede,   *know, prosper*
745 Al wolde I that noon wiste of this thought,   *although, might know*
I am oon the faireste, out of drede,   *the very fairest, doubt*
And goodlieste, whoso taketh hede,   *heed*
And so men seyn, in al the town of Troie.   *say*
What wonder is though he of me have joye?

750 "I am myn owene womman, wel at ese,   *own, ease*
I thank it God, as after myn estat,   *as regards, condition*
Right yong, and °stonde unteyd in lusty leese,
Withouten jalousie or swich debat.
Shal noon housbonde seyn to me "chek mat!"
755 For either they ben ful of jalousie,
Or maisterfull, or loven novelrie.   *domineering, novelty*

"What shal I doon? To what fyn lyve I thus?   *end*
Shal I nat love, in cas if that me leste?   *in case it pleases me*
What, par dieux! I am naught religious.   *of a religious order*
760 And though that I myn herte sette at reste
Upon this knyght, that is the worthieste,

---

735 let them remain (behind)
752 stand untied in pleasant pasture

And kepe alwey myn honour and my name,
By alle right, it may do me no shame."

But right as when the sonne shyneth brighte
765 In March, that chaungeth ofte tyme his face,
And that a cloude is put with wynd to flighte,
Which oversprat the sonne as for a space,   *overspreads*
°A cloudy thought gan thorugh hire soule pace,   *pass*
That overspradde hire brighte thoughtes alle,
770 So that for feere almost she gan to falle.

That thought was this: "Allas! syn I am free,   *since*
Sholde I now love, and put in jupartie   *jeopardy*
My sikernesse, and thrallen libertee?   *security, enslave*
Allas! how dorst I thenken that folie?   *dared, madness*
775 May I naught wel in other folk aspie   *observe*
Hire dredfull joye, hire constreinte, and hire peyne?
Ther loveth noon, that °she nath why to pleyne.

"For love is yet the mooste stormy lyf,
Right of hymself, that evere was bigonne;
780 For evere som mystrust or nice strif   *foolish contention*
°Ther is in love, som cloude is over that sonne.
Therto we wrecched wommen nothing konne,   *can (do)*
Whan us is wo, but wepe and sitte and thinke;
Oure wrecche is this, our owen wo to drynke.   *misfortune, own*

785 "Also thise wikked tonges ben so prest   *ready*
To speke us harm, ek men ben so untrewe,
That, right anon as cessed is hire lest,   *finished, desire*
So cesseth love, and forth to love a newe.   *off (they go)*
But harm ydoon is doon, whoso it rewe;   *no matter who regrets it*

768-9 Cf. 1. 175; 2. 781; 806.
777 she does not have reason to complain
781 Cf. 1. 175; 2. 768-9; 806.

75

790 For though thise men for love hem first torende,   *tear to pieces*
Ful sharp bygynnyng breketh ofte at ende.   *breaks*

"How ofte tyme hath it yknowen be,   *been known*
The tresoun that to wommen hath ben do!
To what fyn is swich love I kan nat see,   *end*
795 Or wher bycometh it, whan it is ago.   *what becomes of it, gone*
Ther is no wight that woot, I trowe so,   *person who knows, I think*
Where it bycometh; lo, no wight on it sporneth: *trips over it*
°That erst was nothing, into nought it torneth.

"How bisy, if I love, ek most I be   *must*
800 To plesen hem that jangle of love, and dremen,   *gossip, dream*
And coye hem, that they seye noon harm of me!   *flatter*
For though ther be no cause, yet °hem semen
Al be for harm that folk hire frendes quemen;
And who may stoppen every wikked tonge,
805 Or sown of belles whil that thei ben ronge?"   *sound*

°And after that, hire thought gan for to clere,
And seide, "He which that nothing undertaketh,   *(she) said*
Nothyng n'acheveth, °be hym looth or deere."
And with an other thought hire herte quaketh;   *quakes*
810 Than slepeth hope, and after drede awaketh;
Now hoot, now cold; but thus, bitwixen tweye,   *two*
She rist hire up, and went here for to pleye.   *rises, goes, relax*

Adown the steyre anon-right tho she wente   *stairs, right away*
Into the garden, with hire neces thre,   *nieces*
815 And up and down ther made many a wente,   *turn*

---

798 that which at first was nothing
802-3 to them, all things that people do to please their friends seem to be for harm
806 Cf. 1. 175; 2. 768-9; 2. 781.
808 be it to him repugnant or dear

76

°Flexippe, she, Tharbe, and Antigone,
To pleyen, that it joye was to see;
And other of hire wommen, a gret route,   *crowd*
Hire folowede in the garden al abowte.

820 This yerd was large, and °rayled alle th'aleyes,   *yard*
And shadewed wel with blosmy bowes grene,   *flowery boughs*
°And benched newe, and sonded alle the weyes,   *sanded, paths*
In which she walketh arm in arm bitwene,
Til at the laste Antigone the shene   *fair*
825 Gan on a Troian song to singen cleere,
That it an heven was hire vois to here.

She seyd: "O Love, to whom I have and shal
Ben humble subgit, trewe in myn entente,   *subject*
As I best kan, to yow, lord, yeve ich al,   *give*
830 For everemo, myn hertes lust to rente.   *desire in payment due*
For nevere yet thi grace no wight sente   *person*
°So blisful cause as me, my lif to lede
In alle joie and seurte, out of drede.   *security*

"Ye, blisful god, han me so wel byset
835 In love, iwys, that al that bereth lif   *are alive*
Ymagynen ne koude how to be bet;   *could not, better*
For, lord, withouten jalousie or strif,
I love oon which that is moost °ententif   *desirous*
To serven wel, unweri or unfeyned,   *unexhausted*
840 That evere was, and leest with harm desteyned.   *blemished*

---

816 Where Ch found the names of C's nieces is not known. Like the nieces themselves, the names (except for Antigone) seem to be Ch's invention.

820 all the walks enclosed

822 provided with benches

832 such blissful reason as to me to lead my life in . . .

838 "Desirous" conveys the sense, but the meaning also includes the notion of "intention," of "tending toward" with the mind; cf. 2. 853–4 and 923 below.

"As he that is the welle of worthynesse,
Of trouthe grownd, mirour of goodlihed,
Of wit Apollo, stoon of sikernesse,   *security*
Of vertu roote, of lust fynder and hed,   *pleasure, head*
845 Thorugh which is alle sorwe fro me ded,
Iwis, I love hym best, so doth he me;
Now good thrift have he, wherso that he be!   *prosperity*

"Whom shulde I thanken but yow, god of Love,
Of al this blisse, in which to bathe I gynne?   *begin*
850 And thanked be ye, lord, for that I love!
This is the righte lif that I am inne,
To flemen alle manere vice and synne: *banish*
This dooth me so to vertu for t'entende,
That day by day I in my wille amende.

855 "And whoso seith that for to love is vice,
Or thraldom, though he feele in it destresse,
He outher is envyous, or right nyce,   *either, foolish*
Or is unmyghty, for his shrewednesse,   *unable, wickedness*
To loven; for swich manere folk, I gesse,
860 Defamen Love, as nothing of him knowe:
°Thei speken, but thei benten nevere his bowe!

"What is the sonne wers, °of kynde right,   *in what respect, worse*
Though that a man, for feeblesse of his yën,   *weakness, eyes*
May nought endure on it to see for bright?
865 Or love the wers, though wrecches on it crien?   *worse, cry (out) on*
°No wele is worth that may no sorwe dryen.

---

861 A marginal gloss in two of the MSS refers to Robin Hood, presumably to the proverb recorded by Hazlitt: "Many talk of Robin Hood that never shot in (with) his bow."
862 in its proper nature
866 no prosperity is worthy that can endure no sorrow

78

And forthi, °who that hath an hed of verre,   *therefore, head, glass*
Fro caste of stones war hym in the werre!   *beware, war*

"But I with al myn herte and al my myght,
870 As I have seyd, wol love unto my laste,
My deere herte, and al myn owen knyght,
In which myn herte growen is so faste,
And his in me, that it shal evere laste.
Al dredde I first to love hym to bigynne,   *although I feared at first*
875 Now woot I wel, ther is no peril inne."   *in (love)*

And of hir song right with that word she stente,   *ceased*
And therwithal, "Now nece," quod Criseyde,
Who made this song now with so good entente?"
Antygone answerde anoon and seyde,   *immediately*
880 "Madame, iwys, the goodlieste mayde   *indeed*
Of gret estat in al the town of Troye,
And let hire lif in moste honour and joye."   *leads*

"Forsothe, so it semeth by hire song,"
Quod tho Criseyde, and gan therwith to sike,   *said, sigh*
885 And seyde, "Lord, is ther swych blisse among
Thise loveres, as they konne faire endite?"   *compose*
"Ye, wis," quod fresshe Antigone the white,   *certainly*
"For alle the folk that han or ben on lyve   *have been, are, alive*
Ne konne wel the blisse of love discryve.   *cannot, describe*

890 "But wene ye that every wrecche woot   *suppose, knows*
The parfite blisse of love? Why, nay, iwys!   *perfect, indeed*
They wenen all be love, if oon be hoot.   *suppose, one, hot*
Do wey, do wey, they woot no thyng of this!   *forget it!*
Men mosten axe at seyntes if it is   *must, ask*

867-8 let him who has a glass head beware of casting stones in the war (Cf. the modern proverb, "People who live in glass houses shouldn't throw stones.")

79

895 Aught fair in hevene (why? for they kan telle),
And axen fendes is it foul in helle."   *fiends*

Criseyde unto that purpos naught answerde,   *subject*
But seyde, "Ywys, it wol be nyght as faste."   *my, very quickly*
But every word which that she of hire herde,
900 °She gan to prenten in hire herte faste,   *print, began*
And ay gan love hire lasse for t'agaste   *ever did, less, frighten*
Than it dide erst, and synken in hire herte,   *before, (it) did sink*
That she wex somwhat able to converte.   *so that she grew, convert*

The dayes honour, and the hevenes yë,   *day's, eye*
905 The nyghtes foo—al this clepe I the sonne—   *foe, call, sun*
Gan westren faste, and downward for to wrye,   *sink in the west, turn*
As he that hadde his dayes cours yronne;
And white thynges wexen dymme and donne   *grow, dim, dark*
For lakke of lyght, and sterres for t'apere,   *appear*
910 That she and alle hire folk in went yfeere.   *together*

So whan it liked hire to go to reste,   *pleased*
And voided weren thei that voiden oughte,   *departed*
She seyde that to slepen wel hire leste.   *suited*
Hire wommen soone til hire bed hire broughte.   *to*
915 Whan al was hust, than lay she stille and thoughte   *hushed*
Of al this thing; °the manere and the wise
Reherce it nedeth nought, for ye ben wise.

A °nyghtyngale, upon a cedir grene,
Under the chambre wal ther as she ley,   *where, lay*
920 Ful loude song ayein the moone shene,   *in the moon light*
Peraunter, in his briddes wise, a lay   *perhaps, bird's way, song*

---

900 Cf. 2. 1241 and 3. 1356-7.
916-17 the manner and the mode it isn't necessary to rehearse, for you (the audience)
are informed
918 Cf. 2. 64 and n.

80

Of love, that made hire herte fressh and gay.
That herkned she so longe in good entente,   *(to) that she listened*
Til at the laste the dede slepe hire hente.   *dead, seized*

925 And as she slep, anon-right tho hire mette   *immediately she dreamed*
How that an °egle, fethered whit as bon,   *bone*
Under hire brest his longe clawes sette,
And out hire herte he rente, and that anon,   *tore*
And dide his herte into hire brest to gon,
930 Of which she nought agroos, °ne nothyng smerte;   *was not frightened*
And forth he fleigh, with herte left for herte.   *flew*

Now lat hire slepe, and we oure tales holde
Of Troilus, that is to paleis riden
Fro the scarmuch of the which I tolde,   *skirmish*
935 And in his chaumbre sit, and hath abiden,
Til two or thre of his messages yeden   *messengers went*
For Pandarus, and soughten hym ful faste,
Til they hym founde and broughte hym at the laste.

This Pandarus com lepyng in atones,   *leaping in at once*
940 And seyde thus, "Who hath ben wel ibete   *beaten*
To-day with swerdes and with slynge-stones,
But Troilus, that hath caught hym an hete?"   *fever*
And gan to jape, and seyde, "Lord, so ye swete!   *joke, sweat*
But ris, and lat us soupe and go to reste."   *sup*
945 And he answerde hym, "Do we as the leste."   *it pleases you*

With al the haste goodly that they myghte,   *were capable of*
They spedde hem fro the soper unto bedde;
And every wight out at the dore hym dyghte,   *betook himself*
And where hym liste upon his wey him spedde.   *it pleased him*

---

926 Cf. Dante's dream of the eagle in *Purg.* 9. 13–42; cf. also *Vita Nuova* 3, Dante's
vision of Love feeding his heart to the beloved.
930 in no way suffered

950 But Troilus, that thoughte his herte bledde
   For wo, til that he herde som tydynge,
   He seyde, "Frend, shal I now wepe or synge?"

   Quod Pandarus, "Ly stylle, and lat me slepe,
   And °don thyn hood; thy nedes spedde be!   *be at ease, are cared for*
955 And chese if thow wolt synge or daunce or lepe!   *choose, leap*
   At shorte wordes, thow shal trowen me: *trust*
   Sire, my nece wol do wel by the,   *niece*
   And love the best, by God and by my trouthe,
   °But lakke of pursuyt make it in thi slouthe.

960 "For thus ferforth I have thi werk bigonne,   *thus far*
   Fro day to day, til this day by the morwe   *until this morning*
   Hire love of frendshipe have I to the wonne,   *friendly affection*
   And also hath she leyd hire feyth to borwe.   *laid, faith in pledge*
   °Algate a foot is hameled of thi sorwe!"   *at any rate, cut off*
965 What sholde I lenger sermon of it holde?   *why, longer*
   As ye han herd byfore, al he hym tolde.

   °But right as floures, thorugh the cold of nyght
   Iclosed, stoupen on hire stalkes lowe,   *droop*
   Redressen hem ayein the sonne bright,   *stand up again toward*
970 And spreden °on hire kynde cours by rowe,   *spread*
   Right so gan tho his eighen up to throwe   *eyes*

---

954 Said to a person who has doffed his hat out of courtesy, the phrase may also
be construed through an interpretation derived from the sport of falconry, consistent
with the many other images in the poem derived from this sport: in this interpreta-
tion, the phrase means something like "be quiet and patient, bide your time" (the hawk
was hooded, its eyes covered, to keep it quiet and calm).
959 unless lack of suit (entreaty) make it a matter of negligence on your part
964 The image of laming suggests that T's sorrow has begun to diminish, to be less
powerful, unable therefore to dog him so fast.
967-70 Cf. *Inf.* 2. 127–31 for the identical figure of flowers rejuvenated.
970 in the natural course of events row by row

This Troilus, and seyde, "O Venus deere,
Thi myght, thi grace, yheried be it here!"   *praised*

And to Pandare he held up bothe his hondes,
975 And seyde, "Lord, al thyn be that I have!
For I am hool, al brosten ben my bondes.   *whole, broken*
A thousand Troyes whoso that me yave,   *gave*
Ech after other, God so wys me save,
Ne myghte me so gladen; lo, myn herte,
980 It spredeth so for joie, it wol tosterte!   *burst*

"But, Lord, how shal I doon? How shal I lyven?
Whan shal I next my deere herte see?
How shal this longe tyme awey be dryven,
Til that thow be ayein at hire fro me?
985 Thow maist answer, 'abid, abid,' but he   *wait*
That hangeth by the nekke, soth to seyne
In grete disese abideth for the peyne."   *pain*

"Al esily, now, for the love of Marte,"   *easily, Mars*
Quod Pandarus, "for °every thing hath tyme.
990 So longe abid, til that the nyght departe;
For al so siker as thow list here by me,   *certainly as you lie*
And God toforn, I wyl be ther at °pryme;   *as my witness*
And forthi, werk somwhat as I shal seye,   *therefore*
Or on som other wight this charge leye.   *person, duty, lay*

995 "For, pardee, God woot I have evere yit   *certainly, knows*
Ben redy the to serve, and to this nyght   *up to*
Have I naught fayned, but °emforth my wit   *nothing feigned*
Don al thi lust, and shal with al my myght.   *desire*
Do now as I shal seyn, and fare aright;

---

989 Cf. Ecclesiastes 3.1 and 17; see also *T&C* 2.694 and n.
992 prime (nine o'clock)
997 to the extent of

1000 And if thow nylt, °wite al thiself thi care!   *will not*
    On me is nought along thyn yvel fare.

    "I woot wel that thow wiser art than I
    A thousand fold, but if I were as thow,
    God help me so, as I wolde outrely,   *absolutely*
1005 Of myn owen hand, write hire right now
    A lettre, in which I wolde hire tellen how
    I ferde amys, and hire biseche of routhe.   *fared, beseech for pity*
    Now help thiself, and leve it nought for slouthe!   *leave, sloth*

    "And I myself wol therwith to hire gon;
1010 And whan thow woost that I am with hire there,
    Worth thow upon a courser right anon,   *mount*
    Ye, hardily, right in thi beste gere,   *gear*
    And ryd forth by the place, °as nought ne were,
    And thow shalt fynde us, if I may, sittynge
1015 At som wyndow, into the strete lokynge.   *street, gazing*

    "And if the list, than maistow us salue;   *you like, greet*
    And upon me make thow thi countenaunce;   *toward, cast, glance*
    But, by thi lif, be war and faste eschue   *alert, avoid*
    To tarien ought,—God shilde us fro meschaunce!   *linger, shield*
1020 Rid forth thi wey, and hold thi governaunce;   *behave properly*
    And we shal speek of the somwhat, I trowe,
    Whan thow art gon, °to don thyn eris glowe!   *ears glow*

    "Towchyng thi lettre, thou art wys ynough.   *concerning*
    I woot thow nylt it dygneliche endite,   *know, haughtily compose*
1025 As make it with thise argumentes tough;   *as (to), difficult*

1000-1 blame on yourself all the anxiety you'll have! On me is not to be blamed your evil condition

1013 as though nothing had been arranged

1022 Cf. the phrases "to make your ears burn," "your ears are burning" (said of persons aware of others talking about them).

Ne °scryvenyssh or craftily thow it write;   *stiltedly*
Biblotte it with thi teris ek a lite;   *blot, tears, little*
And if thow write a goodly word al softe,   *tender*
Though it be good, reherce it nought to ofte.   *repeat, too*

1030 "For though the beste harpour upon lyve   *harpist, alive*
Wolde on the beste sowned joly harpe   *of finest sound*
That evere was, with alle his fyngres fyve,
°Touche ay o streng, or ay o werbul harpe,
Were his nayles poynted nevere so sharpe,
1035 It sholde maken every wight to dulle,   *to become bored*
To here his glee, and of his strokes fulle.   *music, surfeited*

"Ne jompre ek no discordant thyng yfeere,   *jumble, together*
As thus, to usen termes of phisik   *medicine*
In loves termes; hold of thi matere   *obey*
1040 The forme alwey, and do that it be lik;   *perform (so), consistent*
For if a peyntour wolde peynte a pyk   *painter, pike (a fish)*
With asses feet, and hedde it as an ape,   *paint it with the head of*
It cordeth naught, °so nere it but a jape."   *accords*

This counseil liked wel to Troilus,   *was pleasing*
1045 But, as a dredful lovere, he seyde this: *anxious*
"Allas, my deere brother Pandarus,
I am ashamed for to write, ywys,
Lest of myn innocence I seyde amys,   *said*
Or that she nolde it for despit receyve;   *would not, on account of*
1050 Than were I ded, ther myght it nothyng weyve."   *make otherwise*

To that Pandare answerid, "If the lest,   *pleases you*
Do that I seye, and lat me therwith gon;
For by that Lord that formede est and west,

1026 in the manner of a scribe, in a formal or technical style
1033 touch always (only) one string or always harp (only) one tune
1043 unless it were only a joke

85

I hope of it to brynge answere anon
1055 Right of hire hond; and if that thow nylt noon,   *will have none*
Lat be, and sory mote he ben his lyve,   *sorry, may, all his life*
Ayeins thi lust that helpeth the to thryve."   *contrary to your wishes*

Quod Troilus, "Depardieux, ich assente!   *by God*
Sith that the list, I wil arise and write;   *since, it pleases you*
1060 °And blisful God prey ich with good entente,
The viage, and the lettre I shal endite,   *undertaking, compose*
So spede it; and thow, °Minerva, the white,   *cause it to prosper*
Yif thow me wit my lettre to devyse."   *give, compose*
And sette hym down, and wrot right in this wyse.   *(be) sat*

1065 First he gan hire his righte lady calle,   *own*
His hertes lif, his lust, his sorwes leche,   *pleasure, physician*
His blisse, and ek thise other termes alle
That in swich cas thise loveres alle seche;   *seek out*
And in ful humble wise, as in his speche,
1070 He gan hym recomaunde unto hire grace;   *did commend himself*
To telle al how, °it axeth muchel space.   *asks*

And after this, ful lowely he hire preyde   *humbly*
To be nought wroth, thogh he, of his folie,   *angry, folly*
So hardy was to hire to write, and seyde   *bold*
1075 That love it made, or elles most he die;   *caused, must*
And pitousli gan mercy for to crye;   *piteously*
And after that he seyde, and leigh ful loude,   *lied openly*
°Hymself was litel worth, and lasse he koude;   *knew*

1060-2 Construe "blisful God" and "so spede it" together—he prays God to further the "viage" and the "lettre."
1062 Minerva, goddess of wisdom (Note the epithet "white" and cf. 2. 887 and 3. 1567.)
1071 it would require too much space
1078 he was worth little and knew even less

And that she sholde han his konnyng excused,   *hold his understanding*
1080 °That litel was, and ek he dredde hire soo;   *held her in awe*
And his unworthynesse he ay acused;   *repeatedly blamed*
And after that than gan he telle his woo;   *then*
But that was endeles, withouten hoo;   *without ceasing*
And seyde he wolde in trouth alwey hym holde,—
1085 And radde it over, and gan the lettre folde.   *(he) read*

And with his salte teris gan he bathe   *tears*
The ruby in his signet, and it sette   *signet ring*
Upon the wex deliverliche and rathe.   *deftly and soon*
Therwith a thousand tymes, er he lette,   *ceased*
1090 He kiste tho the lettre that he shette,   *shut*
And seyde, "Lettre, a blisful destine
The shapyn is: my lady shal the see!"   *ordained*

This Pandare tok the lettre, and that bytyme   *early*
A-morwe, and to his neces paleis sterte,   *hurried*
1095 And faste he swor that it was passed prime,   *nine o'clock*
And gan to jape, and seyde, "Ywys, myn herte,   *joke, certainly*
So fressh it is, although it sore smerte,   *may hurt*
I may naught slepe nevere a Mayes morwe;
I have a °joly wo, a lusty sorwe."

1100 Criseyde, whan that she hire uncle herde,   *heard*
With dredful herte, and desirous to here
The cause of his comynge, thus answerde:
"Now, by youre fey, myn uncle," quod she, "dere,   *faith*
What manere wyndes gydeth yow now here?   *winds guide*
1105 Tel us youre joly wo and youre penaunce.   *penance*
How ferforth be ye put in °loves daunce?"   *how far have you got*

1080 Construe "that litel was" with "konnyng."
1099 Cf. 1. 420 and n.
1106 Cf. *CT, Gen. Prol.* A 476: "For she [the Wife of Bath] koude of that art the
olde daunce."

"By God," quod he, "I hoppe alwey byhynde!" *hop*
And she to-laugh, °it thoughte hire herte brest. *laughed heartily*
Quod Pandarus, "Loke alwey that ye fynde *see*
1110 °Game in myn hood; but herkneth, if yow lest! *it pleases you*
Ther is right now come into town a gest, *stranger*
A Greek espie, and telleth newe thinges, *spy*
For which I come to telle yow tydynges. *tidings*

"Into the gardyn go we, and ye shal here,
1115 Al pryvely, of this a long sermoun." *in private, account*
With that they wenten arm in arm yfeere *together*
Into the gardyn from the chaumbre down;
And whan that he so fer was that the sown *sound*
Of that he spak, no man heren myghte, *hear*
1120 He seyde hire thus, and out the lettre plighte: *plucked*

"Lo, he that is al holy youres free *wholly*
Hym recomaundeth lowely to youre grace, *commends himself*
And sent yow this lettre here by me. *sends*
Avyseth yow on it, whan ye han space, *consider it, leisure*
1125 And of som goodly answere yow purchace; *with, provide yourself*
Or, helpe me God, so pleynly for to seyne,
He may nat longe lyven for his peyne."

Ful dredfully tho gan she stonden stylle, *then*
And took °it naught, but al hire humble chere *demeanor*
1130 Gan for to chaunge, and seyde, "Scrit ne °bille, *writing, letter*
For love of God, that toucheth swich matere,
Ne brynge me noon; and also, uncle deere, *none*
To myn estat have more rewarde, I preye, *condition, regard*
Than to his lust! What sholde I more seye? *desire*

1108 it seemed to her her heart would burst
1110 a joke at my expense
1129 it (i.e., the letter)
1130 a "bille" may be any statement in writing

1135 "And loketh now if this be resonable,   *consider*
      And letteth nought, for favour ne for °slouthe,   *hesitate, sloth*
      To seyn a sooth; now were it covenable   *say, appropriate*
      To myn estat, by God and by youre trouthe,
      To taken it, or to han of hym routhe,   *pity*
1140 In harmyng of myself, or in repreve?   *reproof (of myself)*
      Ber it ayein, °for hym that ye on leve!"   *take it away*

      This Pandarus gan on hire for to stare,
      And seyde, "Now is this the grettest wondre
      That ever I seigh! Lat be this nyce fare!   *saw, foolish behavior*
1145 To dethe mot I smyten be with thondre,   *may I be struck*
      If for the citee which that stondeth yondre,
      Wold I a lettre unto yow brynge or take   *would*
      To harm of yow! °What list yow thus it make?

      "But thus ye faren, °wel neigh alle and some,   *behave*
1150 That he that most desireth yow to serve,
      Of hym ye recche leest wher he bycome,   *care, what becomes of him*
      And whethir that he lyve or elles sterve.   *dies*
      But for al that that ever I may deserve,
      Refuse it naught," quod he, and hente hire faste,   *grabbed her firmly*
1155 And in hire bosom the lettre down he thraste.   *thrust*

      And seyde hire, "Now cast it awey anon,
      That folk may seen and gauren on us tweye."   *gape at us two*
      Quod she, "I kan abyde til they be gon";   *hold off*
      And gan to smyle, and seyde hym, "Em, I preye,   *uncle*
1160 Swich answere as yow list youreself purveye,   *pleases you, provide*
      For trewely I nyl no lettre write."   *will not*
      "No? than wol I," quod he, "so ye endite."   *dictate*

1136 A possible modern equivalent would be "temporizing"—i.e., stalling to gain time.
1141 in behalf of him you believe in
1148 What's got into you to make it seem like this (i.e., that I would harm you)
1149 almost all you women

Therwith she lough, and seyde, °"Go we dyne." *laughed*
And he gan at hymself to jape faste, *poke fun at himself*
1165 And seyde, "Nece, I have so gret a pyne *sorrow*
For love, that everich other day I faste—" *every*
And gan his beste japes forth to caste, *jokes, play*
And made hire so to laughe at his folye, *foolery*
That she for laughter wende for to dye. *thought she'd die*

1170 And whan that she was comen into halle,
"Now, em," quod she, "we wol go dyne anon." *uncle, dine*
And gan some of hire wommen to hire calle,
And streght into hire chambre gan she gon; *straight, did she go*
But of hire besynesses this was on, *concerns, one*
1175 Amonges othere thynges, out of drede, *doubt*
Ful pryvely this lettre for to rede. *secretly*

Avysed word by word in every lyne, *having contemplated*
And fond no lakke, she thoughte °he koude good; *having found no fault*
And up it putte, and wente hire in to dyne. *dine*
1180 But Pandarus, that in a studye stood,
Er he was war, she took hym by the hood, *before, aware*
And seyde, "Ye were caught er that ye wiste." *realized (it)*
"I vouchesauf," quod he, "do what you liste." *grant (it), pleases*

Tho wesshen they, and sette hem down, and ete; *washed, ate*
1185 And after noon ful sleighly Pandarus *slyly*
Gan drawe hym to the wyndowe next the strete,
And seyde, "Nece, who hath araied thus *decorated*
The yonder hous, that stant aforyeyn us?" *stands opposite*
"Which hous?" quod she, and gan for to byholde,
1190 And knew it wel, and whos it was hym tolde;

1163 let's go dine
1178 she thought he knew how to do it—i.e., she thought he wrote politely

90

And fillen forth in speche of thynges smale,   *began to speak*
And seten in the windowe bothe tweye.   *two*
Whan Pandarus saugh tyme unto his tale,   *saw, opportunity, plot*
And saugh wel that hire folk were alle aweye,
1195 "Now, nece myn, tel on," quod he, "I seye,
How liketh yow the lettre that ye woot?   *you're aware of now*
°Kan he theron? For, by my trouthe, I noot."   *do not know*

Therwith al rosy hewed tho wex she,   *hued*
And gan to homme, and seyde, "So I trowe."   *hum, believe*
1200 "Aquite hym wel, for Goddes love," quod he;   *repay*
"Myself to medes wol the lettre sowe."   *as a reward, sew up*
And held his hondes up, and sat on knowe;   *knelt*
"Now, goode nece, be it nevere so lite,   *little*
Yif me the labour it to °sowe and plite."   *give, fold*

1205 "Ye, for I kan so writen," quod she tho;
"And ek I noot what I sholde to hym seye."   *do not know*
"Nay, nece," quod Pandare, "sey nat so.
Yet at the leeste thonketh hym, I preye,   *thank*
Of his good wille, and doth hym nat to deye.   *cause*
1210 Now, for the love of me, my nece deere,
Refuseth nat at this tyme my prayere!"

"Depardieux," quod she, "God leve al be wel!   *by God, grant*
God help me so, this is the firste lettre
That evere I wroot, ye, al or any del."   *part*
1215 And into a closet, for t'avise hire bettre,   *small room, consider*
She wente allone, and gan hire herte unfettre   *unfetter*
Out of desdaynes prison but a lite,
And sette hire down, and gan a lettre write,

1197 is he in the know about things
1204 sew up (i.e., seal)

Of which to telle in short is myn entente
1220 Th'effect, as fer as I kan understonde.
She thanked hym of al that he wel mente
Towardes hire, but holden hym in honde   *lead him on*
She nolde nought, ne make hireselven bonde   *would not, bound*
In love; but as his suster, hym to plese,   *sister*
1225 She wolde ay fayn, to doon his herte an ese.   *ever eagerly would wish*

She shette it, and in to Pandare gan goon,   *sealed, go*
Ther as he sat and loked into the strete,
And down she sette hire by hym on a stoon   *stone*
Of jaspre, upon a quysshyn °gold-ybete,   *cushion*
1230 And seyde, "As wisly help me God the grete,   *certainly*
I nevere dide thing with more peyne   *difficulty*
Than writen this, to which ye me constreyne";

And took it hym. He thonked hire and seyde,   *thanked*
"God woot, of thyng ful often looth bygonne
1235 Comth ende good; and nece myn, Criseyde,
That ye to hym of hard now ben ywonne   *with difficulty are now won*
°Oughte he be glad, by God and yonder sonne;
For-whi men seith, 'impressiounes lighte   *wherefore*
Ful lightly ben ay redy to the flighte.'   *ever*

1240 "But ye han played the tirant neigh to longe,   *nearly, too*
°And hard was it youre herte for to grave.   *make an impression on*
Now stynt, that ye no lenger on it honge,   *cease, remain undecided*
°Al wolde ye the forme of daunger save,
But hasteth yow to doon hym joye have;   *cause*
1245 For trusteth wel, °to longe ydoon hardnesse
Causeth despit ful often for destresse."   *despite*

1229 embroidered with gold
1236-7 "Oughte he be glad" governs "that ye to . . . ."
1241 Cf. 2. 47.
1243 even though you would preserve the appearance of haughtiness
1245 resistance too long maintained

"And right as they declamed this matere,   *discussed*
Lo, Troilus, right at the stretes ende,
Com rydyng °with his tenthe som yfere,
1250 Al softely, and thiderward gan bende   *turn*
Ther as they sete, as was his way to wende *sat, travel*
To paleis-ward; and Pandarus hym aspide, *saw*
And seyde, "Nece, ysee who comth here ride!

"O fle naught in (he seeth us, I suppose),
1255 Lest he may thynken that ye hym eschuwe." *are avoiding*
"Nay, nay," quod she, and wex as red as rose. *turned as red*
With that he gan hire humbly to saluwe, *salute*
With dredful chere, and oft °his hewes muwe; *respectful looks*
And up his look debonairly he caste,   *graciously*
1260 And bekked on Pandare, and forth he paste. *nodded to, passed*

God woot if he sat on his hors aright,   *knows*
Or goodly was biseyn, that ilke day! *looked his best, very*
God woot wher he was lik a manly knyght! *whether*
What sholde I drecche, or telle of his aray? *why, delay, array*
1265 Criseyde, which that alle thise thynges say, *saw*
To telle in short, hire liked al in-fere, *pleased, together*
His person, his aray, his look, his chere,

His goodly manere, and his gentilesse,
So wel that nevere, sith that she was born, *since*
1270 Ne hadde she swych routh of his destresse; *pity*
And how so she hath hard ben here-byforn, *insofar as, standoffish*
To God hope I, she hath now kaught a thorn, *devoutly I wish*
She shal nat pulle it out this nexte wyke. *week*
God sende mo swich thornes on to pike! *more of such, to pick out*

1249 together with his company of ten
1258 his complexion change

1275 Pandare, which that stood hire faste by,   *close*
     Felte iren hoot, and he bygan to smyte,   *iron, hot, strike*
     And seyde, "Nece, I pray yow hertely,
     Telle me that I shal axen yow a lite.   *ask, little*
     A womman, that were of his deth to wite,   *blame*
1280 Withouten his gilt, °but for hire lakked routhe,   *guilt*
     Were it wel doon?" Quod she, "Nay, by my trouthe!"

     "God help me so," quod he, "ye sey me soth.   *truth*
     Ye felen wel youreself that I nought lye.   *feel, lie*
     Lo, yond he rit!" "Ye," quod she, "so he doth!"   *rides*
1285 "Wel," quod Pandare, "as I have told yow thrie,   *thrice*
     Lat be youre nyce shame and youre folie,   *fastidious, foolishness*
     And spek with hym in esyng of his herte;   *easing*
     Lat nycete nat do yow bothe smerte."   *fastidiousness, harm*

     But theron was to heven and to doone.   *but this called for action*
1290 Considered al thing it may nat be;   *all things considered*
     And whi, for shame; and it were ek to soone   *too*
     To graunten hym so grete a libertee.   *grant*
     For pleynly hire entente, as seyde she,
     Was for to love hym unwist, if she myghte,   *without his knowing it*
1295 And guerdon hym with nothing but with sighte.   *reward*

     But Pandarus thought, "It shal nought be so,
     Yif that I may; this nyce opynyoun   *foolish opinion*
     Shall nought be holden fully yeres two."
     What sholde I make of this a long sermoun?
1300 He moste assente on that conclusioun,   *to*
     As for the tyme; and whan that it was eve,
     And al was wel, he roos and tok his leve.   *rose*

     And on his wey ful faste homward he spedde,
     And right for joye he felte his herte daunce;
1305 And Troilus he fond allone abedde,   *found*

_____

1280 but because pity was lacking in her

94

That lay, as do thise lovers, in a traunce
Bitwixen hope and derk disesperaunce.   *dark despair*
But Pandarus, right at his in-comynge,
He song, as who seyth, "Somwhat I brynge,"   *sang*

1310 And seyde, "Who is in his bed so soone
Iburied thus?" "It am I, frend," quod he.
"Who, Troilus? Nay, help me so the moone,"   *moon*
Quod Pandarus, "thow shalt arise and see
A charme that was sent right now to the,
1315 The which kan helen the of thyn accesse,   *heal, attack (of fever)*
If thow do forthwith al thi bisynesse."

"Ye, thorugh the myght of God," quod Troilus.
And Pandarus gan hym the lettre take,
And seyde, "Parde, God hath holpen us!   *indeed, helped*
1320 Have here a light, and loke on al this blake."   *black (ink)*
But ofte gan the herte glade and quake   *gladden*
Of Troilus, whil that he gan it rede,   *read*
So as the wordes yave hym hope or drede.   *gave, dread*

But finaly, he took al for the beste
1325 That she hym wroot, for somwhat he byheld,   *wrote*
On which hym thoughte he myghte his herte reste,   *it seemed to him*
Al °covered she the wordes under sheld.   *although, shield*
Thus to the more worthi part he held,
That, what for hope and Pandarus byheste,   *promise*
1330 His grete wo foryede he at the leste.   *he abandoned, least*

But as we may alday oureselven see,
Thorugh more wode or col, the more fir,   *wood, coal, fire*
Right so encrees of hope, of what it be,   *increase, whatever*
Therwith ful ofte encresseth ek desir;   *also*
1335 Or as an ook comth of a litel spir,   *oak, shoot*

1327 i.e., she wrote obliquely, circumspectly.

95

So thorugh this lettre, which that she hym sente,
Encressen gan desir, of which he brente.　　　　　　*with, burned*

Wherfore I seye alwey, that day and nyght　　　　　　*say*
This Troilus gan to desiren moore
1340 Thanne he did erst, thorugh hope, and did his myght　　*at first*
To preessen on, as by Pandarus loore,　　　　　　　*press*
And writen to hire of his sorwes soore.
Fro day to day he leet it nought refreyde,　　　　*let it not grow cold*
That by Pandare he wroot somwhat or seyde;　　　　*wrote*

1345 And dide also his other observaunces
　°That til a lovere longeth in this cas;
And °after that thise dees torned on chaunces,
So was he outher glade or seyde "allas!"　　　　　*either*
°And held after his gestes ay his pas;
1350 And after swiche answeres as he hadde,　　　　　*according to*
So were his dayes sory outher gladde.　　　　　　*or*

But to Pandare alwey was his recours,　　　　　　*recourse*
And pitously gan ay to hym to pleyne,　　　　　　*complain*
And hym bisoughte of reed and som socours;　　*guidance, succour*
1355 And Pandarus, that sey his woode peyne,　　　　*saw, mad pain*
°Wex wel neigh ded for routhe, sooth to seyne,　　*pity, truth*
And bisily with al his herte caste　　　　*busily, cast (for a way)*
Som of his wo to slen, and that as faste;　　　　*slay, quickly*

1346 that to a lover are appropriate in this condition
1347 as these dice turned by chance
1349 The line is vexed— "gestes" should perhaps read "gistes" ("stations or stages of a journey")—but the basic sense of the line is still fairly obvious: he proceeded in the conduct of his love in harmony with such developments in it as he achieved—i.e., he was not hot and hasty or dull and slow.
1356 almost fell dead

And seyde, "Lord, and frend, and brother dere,
1360 God woot that thi disese doth me wo.   *knows, distress*
But °wiltow stynten al this woful cheere,   *cease, behavior*
And, by my trouthe, er it be dayes two,
And God toforn, yet shal I shape it so,   *God as my witness*
That thow shalt come into a certeyn place,
1365 There as thow mayst thiself hire preye of grace.   *pray her for grace*

"And certeynly, I noot if thow it woost,   *do not know, know*
But tho that ben expert in love it seye,   *those who*
It is oon of the thynges °forthereth most,
A man to han a layser for to preye,   *have an opportunity*
1370 And siker place his wo for to bywreye;   *safe, reveal*
For in good herte it mot som routhe impresse,   *pity*
To here and see the giltlees in distresse.   *hear, guiltless*

"Peraunter thynkestow: though it be so,   *perhaps*
That Kynde wolde don hire to bygynne   *Nature, cause*
1375 To have a manere routhe upon my woo,   *a kind of pity, woe*
Seyth °Daunger, 'Nay, thow shalt me nevere wynne!'   *win*
So reulith hire hir hertes gost withinne,   *governs, heart's spirit*
That though she bende, yeet she stant on roote;   *firmly rooted*
What in effect is this unto my boote?   *remedy*

1380 °"Thenk here-ayeins: whan that the stordy ook,   *sturdy, oak*
On which men hakketh ofte, for the nones,   *back, for the occasion*
Receyved hath the happy fallyng strook,   *felling stroke*
The greete sweigh doth it come al at ones,   *sway (downward), once*
As don thise rokkes or thise milnestones;   *millstones*
1385 For swifter cours comth thyng that is of wighte,   *weight*
Whan it descendeth, than don thynges lighte.

1361-2 "Wiltow ... / And" is to be construed as "if you will ...."
1368 that most advances (one's case)
1376 See 2. 384 and n.
1380 consider in regard to this

97

"And reed that boweth down for every blast,
Ful lightly, cesse wynd, it wol aryse;   *if the wind cease*
But so nyl nought an ook, whan it is cast; *will not, cast (down)*
1390 It nedeth me nought °the longe to forbise.
Men shal rejoissen of a gret empryse   *undertaking*
Acheved wel, and °stant withouten doute,   *(it) stands*
Al han men ben the lenger theraboute. *though, have, longer at it*

"But, Troilus, yet telle me, if the lest,   *it please*
1395 A thing which that I shal now axen the: *ask*
Which is thi brother that thow lovest best,
As in thi verray hertes privitee?"   *heart's privacy*
"Iwis, my brother Deiphebus," quod he.   *indeed*
"Now," quod Pandare, "er houres twyes twelve, *twice*
1400 He shal the ese, unwist of it hymselve. *ease, not knowing*

"Now lat m'alone, and werken as I may,"   *work*
Quod he; and to °Deiphebus wente he tho,
Which hadde his lord and grete frend ben ay;
Save Troilus, no man he loved so.   *except for*
1405 To telle in short, withouten wordes mo,
Quod Pandarus, "I pray yow that ye be
Frend to a cause which that toucheth me." *that I am involved in*

"Yis, parde," quod Deiphebus, "wel thow woost, *know*
In al that evere I may, and God tofore,   *as my witness*
1410 °Al nere it but for man I love moost,   *unless it were*
My brother Troilus; but sey wherfore   *say*
It is; for sith that day that I was bore,   *since*
I nas, ne nevere mo to ben I thynke,   *was not, more*
Ayeins a thing, °that myghte the forthynke." *against*

1390 to instruct you by multiplying examples
1392 Cf. the modern idiom, "it stands to reason."
1402 The episode at the house of Deiphebus is Ch's invention.
1410 i.e., he would do as much for P as for anyone with the possible exception of T
1414 in such a way that might displease you

98

1415 Pandare gan hym thank, and to hym seyde,
"Lo, sire, I have a lady in this town,
That is my nece, and called is Criseyde,
Which some men wolden don oppressioun,   *to whom, would*
And wrongfully han hire possessioun;   *would have*
1420 Wherfore I of youre lordship yow biseche
To ben oure frend, withouten more speche."

Deiphebus hym answerde, "O, is nat this,
That thow spekest of to me thus straungely,   *distantly*
Criseyda, my frend?" He seyde, "Yis."
1425 "Than nedeth," quod Deiphebus, "hardyly,   *hardly*
Namore to speke, for trusteth wel that I
Wol be hire champioun with °spore and yerde;   *will*
I roughte nought though alle hire foos it herde.   *would care, foes*

"But telle me, thow that woost al this matere,   *matter*
1430 How I myght best avaylen." – "Now lat se,"   *help*
Quod Pandarus; "if ye, my lord so dere,
Wolden as now do this honour to me,
To preyen hire to-morwe, lo, that she
Come unto yow, hire pleyntes to devise,   *complaints, relate*
1435 Hire adversaries wolde of it agrise.   *tremble*

"And yif I more dorste preye yow as now,   *dared*
And chargen yow to han so grete travaille,   *trouble*
To han som of youre bretheren here with yow,
That myghten to hire cause bet availle,
1440 Than wot I wel she myghte nevere faille   *know*
For to ben holpen, what at youre instaunce,   *helped, urging*
What with hire other frendes governaunce."   *management*

Deiphebus, which that comen was of kynde   *who, naturally*
To alle honour and bounte to consente,   *(such as) to*

1427 with spur and staff—i.e., eagerly

1445 Answerd, "It shal be don; and I kan fynde
Yet grettere help to this, in myn entente.
What wiltow seyn, if I for Eleyne sente
To speke of this? I trowe it be the beste,   *believe*
For she may leden Paris as hire leste.   *lead, as it pleases her*

1450 "Of Ector, which that is my lord, my brother,
It nedeth naught to preye hym frend to be;
For I have herd hym, o tyme and ek oother,   *one*
Speke of Cryseyde swich honour, that he
May seyn no bet, °swich hap to hym hath she.   *say, better*
1455 It nedeth naught his helpes for to crave;
He shal be swich, right as we wol hym have.

"Spek thow thiself also to Troilus
On my byhalve, and prey hym with us dyne."
"Syre, al this shal be don," quod Pandarus,
1460 And took his leve, and nevere gan to fyne,   *began, stop*
But to his neces hous, as streyght as lyne,
He com; and fond hire fro the mete arise,   *rising from the meal*
And sette hym down, and spak right in this wise.

He seide, "O verray God, so have I ronne!   *run*
1465 Lo, nece myn, se ye nought how I swete?   *sweat*
I not wheither ye the more °thank me konne.   *do not know*
Be ye naught war how false °Poliphete   *aware*
Is now aboute eftsoones for to plete,   *immediately, bring suit*
And brynge on yow advocacies newe?"   *charges*
1470 "I? no," quod she, and chaunged al hire hewe.   *color*

1454 such favor with him has she
1466 are grateful to me
1467 Ch probably took the name Poliphete from the *Aen.* (6. 484) where it is the
name of a Trojan priest; it is not in Boccaccio.

100

°"What is he more aboute, me to drecche
And don me wrong? What shal I doon, allas?
Yet of hymself nothing ne wolde I recche,   *care*
Nere it for °Antenor and Eneas,   *were it not*
1475 That ben his frendes in swich manere cas.
But, for the love of God, myn uncle deere,
No fors of that, lat hym han al yfeere.   *matter about, together*

"Withouten that I have ynough for us."
"Nay," quod Pandare, "it shal nothing be so.   *in no way*
1480 For I have ben right now at Deiphebus,
At Ector, and myn oother lordes moo,
And shortly maked eche of hem his foo,   *each, foe*
That, by my thrift, he shal it nevere wynne,   *arrangements*
For aught he kan, whan that so he bygynne."   *can (do)*

1485 And as thei casten what was best to doone,   *cast about for*
Deiphebus, of his owen curtesie,
Com hire to preye, in his propre persone,   *ask, own*
To holde hym on the morwe compaignie
At dyner; which she nolde nought denye,
1490 But goodly gan to his preier obeye.   *request*
He thonked hire, and went upon his weye.

Whan this was don, this Pandare up anon,
To telle in short, and forth gan for to wende   *did go*
To Troilus, as stille as any ston;
1495 And al this thyng he tolde hym, word and ende,   *beginning and end*
And how that he Deiphebus gan to blende,   *hoodwink*

1471-2 why is he at it again, to cause me trouble and do me wrong
1474 Antenor is the Trojan taken prisoner by the Greeks for whom Criseyde will
be exchanged; later—this is a major irony of the Troy legend—he betrays Troy to the
Greeks. Aeneas is the hero of Virgil's *Aen.*, the Trojan who escapes the sack of Troy
to found Rome.

101

And seyde hym, "Now is tyme, if that thow konne,   *can*
To bere the wel tomorwe, and al is wonne.   *bear, won*

"Now spek, now prey, now pitously compleyne;
1500 °Lat nought for nyce shame, or drede, or slouthe!
Somtyme a man mot telle his owen peyne.   *must, pain*
Bileve it, and she shal han on the routhe;   *have on you pity*
°Thow shalt be saved by thi feyth, in trouthe.   *faith*
But wel woot I that thow are now in drede,
1505 And what it is, I leye, I kan arede.   *wager, conjecture*

"Thow thynkest now, 'How sholde I don al this?
For by my cheres mosten folk aspie   *looks must people discern*
That for hire love is that I fare amys;
Yet hadde I levere unwist for sorwe dye.'   *rather unperceived*
1510 Now thynk nat so, for thow dost gret folie;
For I right now have founden o manere   *one (a)*
Of sleyghte, for to coveren al thi cheere.   *strategem, appearance*

"Thow shalt gon over nyght, and that bylyve,   *quickly*
Unto Deiphebus hous, as the to pleye,   *as if to amuse yourself*
1515 Thi maladie awey the bet to dryve,—   *better*
For-whi thow semest sik, soth for to seye.   *because*
Soone after that, down in thi bed the leye,   *lay*
And sey, thow mayst no lenger up endure,   *longer*
And lye right there, and °bide thyn aventure.

1520 "Sey that thi fevre is wont the for to take,   *fever is accustomed*
The same tyme, and lasten til a-morwe;   *at this time (every day)*
And lat se now how wel thow kanst it make,   *let's, play your part*
For, parde, sik is he that is in sorwe.   *indeed*

1500 leave nothing undone for foolish shame, etc.
1503 Cf. Mark 16. 16; Luke 1. 45; 8. 12, 50; John 3. 15; Rom. 10. 11; Hebrews 4. 3.
1519 await what happens to you

Go now, farwel! and Venus here to borwe,   *as your surety*
1525 I hope, and thow this purpos holde ferme,   *if*
Thi grace she shal fully ther conferme."

Quod Troilus, "Iwis, thow nedeles   *unnecessarily*
Conseilest me that siklich I me feyne,   *counsel, pretend*
For I am sik in ernest, douteles,
1530 So that wel neigh I sterve for the peyne."   *die*
Quod Pandarus, "Thow shalt the bettre pleyne,   *moan*
And hast the lasse nede to countrefete,   *counterfeit*
For hym men demen hoot that men seen swete.   *judge hot, sweat*

"Lo, hold the at thi °triste cloos, and I   *station close*
1535 Shal wel the deer unto thi bowe dryve."
Therwith he took his leve al softely,
And Troilus to paleis wente blyve.   *soon*
So glad ne was he nevere in al his lyve,
And to Pandarus reed gan al assente,   *counsel*
1540 And to Deiphebus hous at nyght he wente.

What nedeth yow to tellen al the cheere   *comfort*
That Deiphebus unto his brother made,
Or his accesse, or his sikliche manere,   *(about) his attack of fever*
How men gan hym with clothes for to lade,   *bed-clothes, load*
1545 Whan he was leyd, and how men wolde hym glade?   *put to bed, gladden*
But al for nought; he held forth ay the wyse   *form of behavior*
That ye han herd Pandare er this devyse.

But certayn is, er Troilus hym leyde,   *lay down*
Deiphebus had hym preied over-nyght   *prayed the previous night*
1550 To ben a frend and helpyng to Criseyde.
God woot that he it graunted anon-right,   *immediately*
To ben hire fulle frend with al his myght;

1534 In medieval hunting the hunters stationed themselves at a suitable spot ("triste") while the huntsmen and dogs drove the deer in their direction.

But swich a nede was to preye hym thenne,
°As for to bidde a wood man for to renne.   *bid a mad man run*

1555 The morwen com, and neighen gan the tyme   *approach*
Of meeltide, that the faire queene Eleyne   *dinner-time*
Shoop hire to ben, an houre °after the prime,   *arranged*
With Deiphebus, to whom she nolde feyne;   *dissemble*
But as his suster, homly, soth to seyne,   *plainly, truth*
1560 She com to dyner in hire pleyne entente.   *innocent intent*
But God and Pandare wist al what this mente.   *knew*

Com ek Criseyde, al innocent of this,
°Antigone, hire suster Tarbe also.
But fle we now prolixitee best is,   *(that) we flee*
1565 For love of God, and lat us faste go
Right to th'effect, withouten tales mo,   *to the point, more*
Whi al this folk assembled in this place;
And lat us of hire saluynges pace.   *greetings skip over*

Gret honour did hem Deiphebus, certeyn,
1570 And fedde hem wel with al that myghte like;   *please (them)*
But evere mo "Allas!" was his refreyn,   *refrain*
"My goode brother Troilus, the syke,   *sick*
Lith yet"—and therwithal he gan to sike;   *lies, sigh*
And after that, he peyned hym to glade   *took pains to gladden*
1575 Hem as he myghte, and cheere good he made.

Compleyned ek Eleyne of his siknesse
So feythfully, that pite was to here,   *sincerely, pity, hear*
And every wight °gan waxen for accesse   *person*
A leche anon, and seyde, "In this manere   *physician*

1554 Cf. 4. 230.
1557 after the prime (i.e., 10 a.m.)
1563 C's nieces (See 2. 816.)
1578 began, on account of the fever, to turn into a physician

1580 Men curen folk."—"This charme I wol yow leere."   *teach*
But ther sat oon, °al list hire nought to teche,
That thoughte, "Best koude I yet ben his leche."   *could*

After compleynte, hym gonnen they to preyse,   *did they praise*
As folk don yet, whan some wight hath bygonne   *person*
1585 To preise a man, and up with pris hym reise   *praise, raise*
A thousand fold yet heigher than the sonne: *sun*
"He is, he kan, that fewe lordes konne."   *can (do) that (which)*
And Pandarus, of that they wolde afferme,   *that (which)*
°He naught forgat hire preisynge to conferme.

1590 Herde al this thyng Criseyde wel inough,
And every word gan for to notifie;   *take note of*
For which with sobre cheere hire herte lough.   *solemn, laughed*
For who is that ne wolde hire glorifie,   *is (it), wouldn't herself*
To mowen swich a knyght don lyve or dye?   *be able, to cause (to)*
1595 But al passe I, lest ye to longe dwelle;   *too*
For for o fyn is al that evere I telle.   *since, one purpose*

The tyme com fro dyner for to ryse,
And as hem aughte, arisen everichon.   *ought*
And gonne a while of this and that devise.   *talk*
1600 But Pandarus brak al this speche anon,   *interrupted*
And seide to Deiphebus, "Wol ye gon,   *start*
If it youre wille be, as I yow preyde,
To speke here of the nedes of Criseyde?"

Eleyne, which that by the hond hire held,   *hand*
1605 °Took first the tale, and seyde, "Go we blyve";   *let us begin*
And goodly on Criseyde she biheld,   *gazed*
And seyde, "Joves lat hym nevere thryve,   *prosper*

1581 although she chose not to teach
1589 i.e., he did not neglect to underscore the good they were saying of him
1605 was the first to speak

That doth yow harm, and brynge hym soone of lyve,　　　*out of life*

And yeve me sorwe, but he shal it rewe,　　　*give, unless, regret*

1610 °If that I may, and alle folk be trewe!"

"Telle thow thi neces cas," quod Deiphebus　　　*niece's case*

To Pandarus, "for thow kanst best it telle."

"My lordes and my ladys, it stant thus:　　　*stands*

What sholde I lenger," quod he, "do yow dwelle?"　　　*why*

1615 He rong hem out a °proces lik a belle　　　*rang, discourse*

Upon hire foo, that highte Poliphete,　　　*was called*

So heynous, that men myghte on it spete.　　　*hateful, spit regarding it*

Answerde of this ech werse of hem than other,　　　*responded to, worse*

And Poliphete they gonnen thus to warien:　　　*curse*

1620 "Anhonged be swich oon, were he my brother!　　　*hanged*

And so he shal, for it ne may nought varien!"　　　*be otherwise*

What shold I lenger in this tale tarien?　　　*tarry*

Pleynliche, alle at ones, they hire highten　　　*plainly, promised*

To ben hire helpe in al that evere they myghten.　　　*might be able to do*

1625 Spak than Eleyne, and seyde, "Pandarus,　　　*spoke*

Woot ought my lord, my brother, this matere,　　　*knows at all, matter*

I meene Ector? or woot it Troilus?"

He seyde, "Ye, but wole ye now me here?　　　*will*

Me thynketh this, sith that Troilus is here,

1630 It were good, if that ye wolde assente,

She tolde hireself hym al this, er she wente.　　　*before*

"For he wol have the more hir grief at herte,

By cause, lo, that she a lady is;

And, by youre leve, I wol but in right sterte　　　*I'll just pop in*

1635 And do yow wyte, and that anon, iwys,　　　*let you know, quickly*

1610 Cf. the modern colloquialism, "if I have anything to do with it."

1615 Cf. 2. 424; "proces" is "discourse" in the sense of a plea entered in court against a party.

If that he slepe, or wol ought here of this."	*bear*
And in he lepte, and seyde hym in his ere,	*leapt, ear*
°"God have thi soule, ibrought have I thi beere!"	*bier*

To smylen of this gan tho Troilus,	*smile, about*
1640 And Pandarus, withouten rekenynge,	*without further ado*
Out wente anon to Eleyne and Deiphebus,	
And seyde hem, "So ther be no taryinge,	*in order that, dawdling*
Ne moore prees, he wol wel that ye brynge	*crowd*
Criseÿda, my lady, that is here;	
1645 And as he may enduren, he wol here.	*bear up, hear*

"But wel ye woot, the chaumbre is but lite.	*small*
And fewe folk may lightly make it warm;	*easily*
°Now loketh ye (for I wol have no wite,	
To brynge in prees that myghte don hym harm,	
1650 Or hym disesen, for my bettre arm)	
Wher it be bet she bide til eftsonys;	
Now loketh ye, that knowen what to doon is.	*consider*

"I sey for me, best is, as I kan knowe,	
That no wight in ne went but ye tweye,	*person*
1655 But it were I, for I kan in a throwe	*moment*
Reherce hire cas °unlik that she kan seye;	
And after this, she may hym ones preye	*once*
To ben good lord, in short, and take hire leve.	
This may nought muchel of his ese hym reve.	*much, ease, deprive*

1638 The joke depends on the feigned fever: T is supposedly in peril of death; hence P has brought him a bier, namely Criseyde.

1648-51 now consider (for I will incur no blame for bringing in a crowd that might do him harm or discomfit him, not even if it cost me my right arm) whether it may be better that she wait until later

1656 differently from what she can say—i.e., more forcefully

1660 "And ek, for she is straunge, he wol forbere   *a stranger, forgo*
His ese, which that hym thar nought for yow;   *which he need not do*
Ek oother thing, that toucheth nought to here,   *her*
He wol yow telle—I woot it wel right now—
That secret is, and for the townes prow."   *benefit*
1665 And they, that nothyng knewe of his entente,
Withouten more, to Troilus in they wente.   *without more ado*

Eleyne, in al hire goodly softe wyse,   *manner*
Gan hym salue, and wommanly to pleye,   *greet, behave femininely*
And seyde, "Iwys, ye moste alweies arise!   *get up soon*
1670 Now, faire brother, beth al hool, I preye!"   *healed*
And gan hire arm right over his shulder leye,   *shoulder*
And hym with al hire wit to reconforte;
As she best koude, she gan hym to disporte.   *amuse*

So after this quod she, "We yow biseke,   *said, beseech*
1675 My deere brother, Deiphebus, and I,
For love of God—and so doth Pandare eke—   *also*
To ben good lord and frend, right hertely,
Unto Criseyde, which that certeynly
Receyveth wrong, as woot weel here Pandare,   *knows*
1680 That kan hire cas wel bet than I declare."   *better*

This Pandarus gan newe his tong affile,   *once more, file*
And al hire cas reherce, and that anon.   *right away*
Whan it was seyd, soone after in a while,
Quod Troilus, "As sone as I may gon,   *said, walk*
1685 I wol right fayn with al my myght ben oon,   *gladly, one*
Have God my trouthe, hire cause to sustene."   *sustain*
"Good thrift have ye!" quod Eleyne the queene.

Quod Pandarus, "And it youre wille be,   *if*
That she may take hire leve, er that she go?"   *say good-bye*
1690 "O, elles God forbede it," tho quod he,   *otherwise*
"If that she vouchesauf for to do so."   *grant*

And with that word quod Troilus, "Ye two,
Deiphebus and my suster lief and deere,   *beloved*
To yow have I to speke of o matere,   *one (a)*

1695 To ben avysed by youre reed the bettre—"   *advised, counsel*
And fond, as hap was, at his beddes hed,   *found, as it turned out*
The copie of a tretys and a lettre,   *treatise*
That Ector hadde hym sent to axen red   *ask (his) counsel*
If swych a man was worthi to ben ded,   *deserved*
1700 Woot I nought who; but in a grisly wise   *know, serious*
He preyede hem anon on it avyse.   *study*

Deiphebus gan this lettre for t'onfolde
In ernest greet; so did Eleyne the queene;   *in great earnest*
And romyng outward, °faste it gonne byholde,   *going outdoors*
1705 Downward a steire, into an herber greene.   *staircase, garden*
This ilke thing they redden hem bitwene,   *same object, read*
And largely the mountance of an houre   *fully, length*
Thei gonne on it to reden and to poure.   *pore (over it)*

Now lat hem rede, and torne we anon   *read, turn*
1710 To Pandarus, that gan ful faste prye   *look closely*
That al was wel, and out he gan to gon
Into the grete chaumbre, and that in hye,   *in haste*
And seyde, "God save al this compaynye!
Come, nece myn, my lady queene Eleyne
1715 Abideth yow, and ek my lordes tweyne.   *waits for, twain*

"Rys, take with yow youre nece Antigone,   *niece*
°Or whom yow list; or no fors; hardyly   *no matter, certainly*
The lesse prees, the bet; com forth with me,   *crowd, better*
And loke that ye thonken humblely   *look*
1720 Hem alle thre, and whan ye may goodly

1704 carefully began to consider it
1717 or whom it pleases you

Youre tyme se, taketh of hem youre leeve,
Lest we to longe his restes hym byreeve."   *deprive*

Al innocent of Pandarus entente,
Quod tho Criseyde, "Go we, uncle deere";   *said*
1725 And arm in arm inward with hym she wente,
°Avysed wel hire wordes and hire cheere;   *countenance*
And Pandarus, in ernestful manere,
Seyde, "Alle folk, for Godes love, I preye,
Stynteth right here, °and softely yow pleye.   *stop*

1730 "Aviseth yow what folk ben hire withinne,   *consider*
And in what plite oon is, God hym amende!"   *condition, heal*
And inward thus, "Ful softely bygynne,   *on the way in (he said)*
Nece, I conjure and °heighly yow defende,   *implore*
On °his half which that soule us alle sende,
1735 And °in the vertu of corones tweyne,   *by the strength of two crowns*
Sle naught this man, that hath for yow this peyne!   *slay, pain*

"Fy on the devel! thynk which one he is,   *who*
And in what plite he lith; com of anon!   *state he lies, come on now*
Thynk al °swich taried tyde but lost it nys.   *is but lost*
1740 That wol ye bothe seyn, whan ye ben oon.   *say, one*
Secoundely, ther yet devyneth noon   *secondly, guesses*
Upon yow two; come of now, if ye konne!   *about*
While folk is blent, lo, al the tyme is wonne.   *blinded*

1726 having considered carefully
1729 and amuse yourselves quietly
1733 strictly forbid you
1734 i.e., God's
1735 This is something of a notorious crux, with various solutions competing for consensus; the two crowns may signify Pity and Bounty, or Justice and Mercy, or nuptial crowns, or something else. None of the solutions proposed so far has gained wide acceptance.
1739 such time delayed

°"In titeryng, and pursuyte, and delayes,
1745 The folk devyne at waggyng of a stree;
And though ye wolde han after mirye dayes,
Than dar ye naught; and whi? for she, and she   *dare*
Spak swych a word; thus loked he, and he!   *spoke*
Allas tyme iloste! I dar nought with yow dele.   *deal (now)*
1750 Com of, therfore, and bryngeth hym to hele!"   *health*

But now to yow, ye loveres that ben here,
Was Troilus nought in a °kankedort,   *predicament*
That lay, and myghte whisprynge of hem here,   *hear*
And thoughte, "O Lord, right now renneth my sort   *falls out, fate*
1755 Fully to deye, or han anon comfort!"
And was the firste tyme he shulde hire preye   *(this) was, entreat.*
Of love; O myghty God, what shal he seye?

1744–6 in (cases of) vacillation and entreaty and delays, from the merest trifle, people will suspect something, and though you would like to have afterwards merry days
1752 The origin of the word is unknown and the meaning must be inferred from the context.

111

BOOK THREE

O blisful light, of which the bemes clere   *beams*
Adorneth al the °thridde heven faire!   *third heaven*
O sonnes lief, O Joves doughter deere,   *darling of the sun, dear*
Plesance of love, O goodly debonaire,   *gracious person*
5 In gentil hertes ay redy to repaire!   *hearts, reside*
O veray cause of heele and of gladnesse,   *true, well-being*
Iheryed be thy myght and thi goodnesse!   *praised*

In hevene and helle, in erthe and salte see   *sea*
Is felt thi myght, if that I wel descerne;   *discern*
10 As man, bird, best, fissh, herbe, and grene tree   *beast*
°Thee fele in tymes with vapour eterne.
God loveth, and to love wol nought werne;   *will deny nothing to love*
And in this world no lyves creature   *living*
Withouten love is worth, or may endure.   *of value*

15 Ye °Joves first to thilk effectes glade,   *those same*
Thorugh which that thynges lyven alle and be,
°Comeveden, and amorous him made   *urged*
On mortal thyng, and as yow list, ay ye   *for, it pleased you, ever*
Yeve hym in love ese or adversitee;   *gave, ease*
20 And in a thousand formes down hym sente
For love in erthe, and whom yow liste, he hente.   *to, seized*

---

2 the third sphere, in which the planet Venus (the "blisful light") was supposed to dwell
11 feel your influence at various seasons through eternal emanation
15,17 Construe "Joves" as object of "comeveden."

112

Ye fierse Mars apaisen of his ire,   *appease*
And as yow list, ye maken hertes digne;   *worthy*
Algates hem that ye wol sette a-fyre,   *nevertheless*
25 They dreden shame, and vices they resygne;   *dread*
Ye do hem corteys be, fresshe and benigne;   *courteous, vigorous*
And heighe or lowe, °after a wight entendeth,
The joies that he hath, youre myght him sendeth.

°Ye holden regne and hous in unitee;   *kingdom*
30 Ye sothfast cause of frendshipe ben also;   *trustworthy*
Ye knowe al thilke °covered qualitee   *that same, obscure*
Of thynges, which that folk on wondren so,   *wonder at*
Whan they kan nought construe how it may °jo   *jibe*
She loveth hym, or whi he loveth here,
35 As whi this fissh, and naught that, comth to were.   *trap*

Ye folk a lawe han set in universe,   *for folk*
And this knowe I by hem that lovers be,
That whoso stryveth with yow hath the werse.   *worse*
Now, lady bryght, for thi benignite,
40 At reverence of hem that serven the,   *out of respect for*
Whos clerc I am, so techeth me devyse   *clerk, (to) relate*
Som joye of that is felt in thi servyse.   *that (which)*

Ye in my naked herte sentement   *ill-provided*
Inhielde, and do me shewe of thy swetnesse.   *pour in, cause me to show*

---

27 according to the way a person inclines

29 The sense of the line is that Venus holds all the world together in unity, which is what Boccaccio says (*F*, III. 78).

31 "covered" in the sense of the hidden, obscure motives compelling amorous joining

33 A word otherwise unknown, "jo," it has been suggested, is related to OF "joer," "to play," in which case the sense here would be something like "to happen"; the gloss offered here suggests that the sense of the line asks for a notion of "congruence" or "harmony" and thus offers a modern colloquialism with that sense as a possible equivalent for the ME.

45 °Caliope, thi vois be now present,   *voice*
    For now is nede; sestow nought my destresse,   *do you not see*
    How I mot telle anon-right the gladnesse   *must, soon now*
    Of Troilus, to Venus heryinge?   *in Venus's praise*
    To which gladnesse, who nede hath, God hym brynge!   *has need of it*

50 Lay al this mene while Troilus,
    Recordyng his lesson in this manere: *rehearsing*
    "Mafay," thoughte he, "thus wol I sey, and thus;   *upon my faith*
    Thus wol I pleyne unto my lady dere;   *complain*
    That word is good, and this shal be my cheere;
55 This nyl I nought foryeten in no wise."   *forget*
    God leve hym °werken as he kan devyse!   *grant*

    And, Lord, so that his herte gan to quappe,   *flutter*
    Heryng hire come, and °shorte for to sike!   *hearing*
    And Pandarus, that ledde hire by the lappe,   *flap of her garment*
60 Com ner, and gan in at the curtyn pike,   *near, peek*
    And seyde, "God do boot on alle syke!   *send remedy to all (the) sick*
    Se who is here yow comen to visite;   *see*
    Lo, here is she that is youre deth to wite."   *to blame for*

    Therwith it semed as he wepte almost.   *as (if)*
65 "A-ha," quod Troilus so reufully,
    "Wher me be wo, O myghty God, thow woost!   *whether, woe, know*
    Who is al ther? I se nought trewely."   *exactly*
    "Sire," quod Criseyde, "it is Pandare and I."
    "Ye, swete herte? allas, I may nought rise,
70 To knele and do yow honour in som wyse."   *kneel*

    And dressed hym upward, and she right tho   *raised himself, then*
    Gan bothe hire hondes softe upon hym leye.   *lay*

---

45 Calliope, muse of epic poetry and chief of the muses
56 to perform it as he can arrange it
58 and (with) short (breaths he began) to sigh

"O, for the love of God, do ye nought so
To me," quod she, "I! what is this to seye?   *what does this mean*
75 Sire, comen am I to yow for causes tweye: *two*
First, yow to thonke, and of youre lordshipe eke   *patronage*
Continuance I wolde yow biseke."   *beseech*

This Troilus, that herde his lady preye
Of lordshipe hym, wax neither quyk ne ded,   *became, alive*
80 Ne myghte o word for shame to it seye,   *modesty (in response) to*
Although men sholde smyten of his hed.   *smite off*
But, Lord, so he wex sodeynliche red,   *suddenly*
And sire, his lessoun, that he °wende konne   *rehearsed speech*
To preyen hire, is thorugh his wit ironne.   *pray (to), run*

85 Criseyde al this aspied wel ynough,   *observed*
For she was wis, and loved hym nevere the lasse,   *shrewd*
°Al nere he malapert, or made it tough,
Or was to bold, to synge a fool a masse.   *too*
But whan his shame gan somewhat to passe,
90 His resons, as I may my rymes holde,
I wol yow telle, as techen bokes olde.   *teach*

In chaunged vois, right for his verray drede,   *voice, pure dread*
Which vois ek quook, and therto his manere   *quavered*
Goodly abaist, and now his °hewes rede,   *becomingly abashed*
95 Now pale, unto Criseyde, his lady dere,
With look down cast and °humble iyolden chere,   *submissive*

---

83 assumed he would be able
87–8 The lines are vexed; their meaning remains uncertain. Baugh expands thus: "all the more because he did not behave insolently, or haughtily, or overboldly to accomplish no useful purpose" (as would someone, in other words, who sang a mass to a fool).
94 complexion red
96 humbly submissive appearance

115

Lo, the alderfirste word that hym asterte   *very first, escaped*
Was, twyes, "Mercy, mercy, swete herte!"   *twice*

And °stynte a while, and whan he myghte outbrynge,   *utter (a word)*
100 The nexte word was, "God woot, for I have,   *knows*
As ferforthly as I have had konnynge,   *far, wit*
Ben youres al, God so my soule save,
And shal, til that I, woful wight, be grave!   *shall (be), buried*
And though I ne dar, ne kan, unto yow pleyne,   *not, dare, complain*
105 Iwis, I suffre nought the lasse peyne.   *certainly, pain*

"Thus muche as now, O wommanliche wif,   *now, pattern of womanhood*
I may out-brynge, and if this yow displese,   *express*
That shal I wreke upon myn owen lif   *avenge*
Right soone, I trowe, and do youre herte an ese,   *ease*
110 If with my deth youre wreththe I may apese.   *wrath, appease*
But syn that ye han herd me somwhat seye,   *since*
Now recche I nevere how soone that I deye."   *care, die*

Therwith his manly sorwe to biholde,
It myghte han mad an herte of stoon to rewe;   *feel pity*
115 And Pandare wep as he to water wolde,   *wept as if he would (turn)*
And poked evere his nece new and newe,
And seyde, "Wo bygon ben hertes trewe!   *with woe beset are hearts*
For love of God, make of this thing an ende,
Or sle us both at ones, er ye wende."   *slay, before, depart*

120 "I! what?," quod she, "by God and by my trouthe,
I not nat what ye wilne that I seye."   *know not, you want me to say*
"I! what?" quod he, "that ye han on hym routhe,   *pity*
For Goddes love, and doth hym nought to deye."   *die*
"Now thanne thus," quod she, "I wolde hym preye
125 To telle me the fyn of his entente.   *purpose*
Yet wist I nevere wel what that he mente."   *knew*

---

99 and (he) ceased

"What that I mene, O swete herte deere?" *mean*
Quod Troilus, "O goodly, fresshe free, *gracious (lady)*
That with the stremes of youre eyen cleere *streams*
130 Ye wolde somtyme frendly on me see, *in a friendly way look on me*
And thanne agreen that I may ben he,
Withouten braunche of vice on any wise, *species, in, manner*
In trouthe alwey to don yow my servise,

"As to my lady right and chief resort, *proper, source of help*
135 With al my wit and al my diligence;
And I to han, right as yow list, comfort, *it pleases you*
Under yowre yerde, egal to myn offence, *correction, equal*
As deth, if that I breke youre defence; *break your prohibition*
And that ye deigne me so muche honoure,
140 Me to comanden aught in any houre; *anything*

"And I to ben youre verray humble trewe, *true (servant)*
Secret, and in my paynes pacient,
And evere mo desiren fresshly newe
To serve, and ben ay ylike diligent, *everywhere in the same way*
145 And with good herte al holly youre °talent *desire*
Receyven wel, how sore that me smerte,— *however sorely, pains*
Lo, this mene I, myn owen swete herte." *mean*

Quod Pandarus, "Lo, here an hard requeste,
And resonable, a lady for to werne! *refuse*
150 Now, nece myn, °by natal Joves feste,
Were I a god, ye sholden sterve as yerne, *die quickly*
That heren wel this man wol nothing yerne *desire*

---

145 The word *talent* does mean "desire," "wish," or something like that. Perhaps its most famous use in medieval poetry is in the Paolo and Francesca episode of Dante's *Inf.* (5. 39), where it clearly means "desire." However, it descends through Old French from the Scriptural *talent* (Matt 25. 15) and thus forms a crucial element in the economic vocabulary that forms an important sub-text in *T&C*.

150 by the feast of Jupiter as the god who presides over nativities (i.e., beginnings)

But youre honour, and sen hym almost sterve,   *die*
And ben so loth to suffren hym yow serve."

155 With that she gan hire eyen on hym caste
Ful esily and ful debonairly,   *gently*
Avysyng hire, and hied nought to faste   *reflecting, hastened, too*
With nevere a word, but seyde hym softely,
"Myn honour sauf, I wol wel trewely,
160 And in swich forme as he gan now devyse,   *did now set forth*
Receyven hym fully to my servyse,

"Bysechyng hym, for Goddes love, that he   *beseeching*
Wolde, in honour of trouthe and gentilesse,
As I wel mene, eke mene wel to me,   *also*
165 And myn honour with wit and bisynesse   *mindfully and diligently*
Ay kepe; and if I may don hym gladnesse,   *ever, keep*
From hennesforth, iwys, I nyl nought feyne.   *play at it*
Now beth al hool; no lenger ye ne pleyne.   *whole, complain*

"But natheles, this warne I yow," quod she,
170 "A kynges sone although ye be, ywys,   *indeed*
Ye shal namore han °sovereignete
Of me in love, °than right in that cas is;
N'y nyl forbere, if that ye don amys,   *I will not*
To wratthe yow; and whil that ye me serve,   *to get angry with*
175 Chericen yow right after ye disserve.   *cherish, as*

"And shortly, deere herte and al my knyght,
Beth glad, and draweth yow to lustinesse,   *(renewed) enjoyment of life*
And I shal trewely, with al my myght,
Youre bittre tornen al into swetenesse;   *turn*
180 If I be she that may yow do gladnesse,

---

171 Cf. *CT, Franklin's Tale* V F 751.
172 than is right in that case

118

For every wo ye shal recovere a blisse."
And hym in armes took, and gan hym kisse.

Fil Pandarus on knees, and up his eyen   *fell, eyes*
To heven threw, and held his hondes highe,
185 "Immortal god," quod he, "that mayst nought deyen,   *die*
Cupide I mene, of this mayst glorifie;   *in this you may glory*
And Venus, thow mayst maken melodie!
°Withouten hond, me semeth that in towne,   *hand*
For this merveille, ich here ech belle sowne.   *marvel, hear, sound*

190 "But ho! namore as now of this matere;
For-whi this folk wol comen up anon,   *because*
That han the lettre red; lo, I hem here.   *read, hear*
But I conjure the, Criseyde, °and oon,
And two, thow Troilus, whan thow mayst goon,   *are able to go*
195 That at myn hous ye ben at my warnynge,   *notice*
For I ful well shal shape youre comynge;

"And eseth there youre hertes right ynough;   *ease*
And lat se which of yow shal °bere the belle,   *be the first*
To speke of love aright!"—therwith he lough—   *laughed*
200 "For ther have ye a leiser for to telle."   *leisure*
Quod Troilus, "How longe shal I dwelle,
Er this be don?" Quod he, "Whan thow mayst ryse,   *before*
This thyng shal be right as I yow devyse."   *explain*

With that Eleyne and also Deiphebus
205 Tho comen upward, right at the steires ende;   *staircase's*
And Lord, so thanne gan gronen Troilus,   *groan*
His brother and his suster for to blende.   *deceive*

---

188 i.e., spontaneously
193-4 both one and the other, you too, T
198 bear the bell like the bellwether sheep (i.e., be first). S. Barney notes there is
evidence for the meaning "take the prize" in a race—*ad loc.*

Quod Pandarus, "It tyme is that we wende.   *depart*
Tak, nece myn, youre leve at alle thre,
210 And lat hem speke, and cometh forth with me."

She took hire leve at hem ful thriftily,   *in a becoming manner*
As she wel koude, and they hire °reverence
Unto the fulle diden, hardyly,   *assuredly*
And wonder wel speken, in hire absence,   *spoke (they)*
215 Of hire, in preysing of hire excellence,
Hire governaunce, hire wit; and hire manere   *composure, good sense*
Comendeden, it joie was to here.   *commended (they), hear*

Now lat hire wende unto hire owen place,   *go*
And torne we to Troilus ayein,   *again*
220 That gan ful lightly of the lettre pace   *quickly, treat*
That Deiphebus hadde in the gardyn seyn;   *seen*
And of Eleyne and hym he wolde feyn   *gladly*
Delivered ben, and seyde that hym leste   *it pleased him*
To slepe, and after tales have reste.   *talks*

225 Eleyne hym kiste, and took hire leve blyve,   *kissed, quickly*
Deiphebus ek, and hom wente every wight;   *person*
And Pandarus, as faste as he may dryve,   *hasten*
To Troilus tho com, as lyne right,   *directly*
And on a paillet al that glade nyght   *pallet*
230 By Troilus he lay, with mery chere,   *demeanor*
To tale; and °wel was hem they were yfeere.   *to discuss everything*

Whan every wight was voided but they two,   *departed*
And alle the dores weren faste yshette,   *shut*
To telle in short, withouten wordes mo,
235 This Pandarus, withouten any lette,   *delay*
Up roos, and on his beddes syde hym sette,   *rose*

211-12 paid her reverence unto the full (i.e., they very much admired her)
231 and it was good for them that they were together

120

And gan to speken in a sobre wyse   *manner*
To Troilus, as I shal yow devyse: *relate*

"Myn alderlevest lord, and brother deere,   *dearest, dear*
240 God woot, and thow, that it sat me so soore,   *knows, it pained me*
When I the saugh so langwisshyng to-yere   *saw, this year*
For love, of which thi wo wax alwey moore,   *woe, grew*
That I, with al my myght and al my loore,   *know-how*
Have evere sithen don my bisynesse   *since, business*
245 To brynge the to joye out of distresse,

"And have it brought to swich plit as thow woost,   *a state, you know*
So that thorugh me thow stondest now in weye   *are in such a shape as*
To faren wel; I sey it for no bost,   *boast*
And wostow whi? for °shame it is to seye: *do you know why*
250 For the have I bigonne a gamen pleye,   *game*
Which that I nevere do shal eft for other,   *again*
Although he were a thousand fold my brother.

"That is to seye, for the am I bicomen,
Bitwixen game and ernest, swich a meene   *between, go-between*
255 As maken wommen unto men to comen;
Al sey I nought, thow wost wel what I meene.   *although, say*
For the have I my nece, of vices cleene,   *clean*
So fully maad thi °gentilesse triste,   *trust*
That al shal ben right as thiselven liste.   *pleases you*

260 "But God, that al woot, take I to witnesse,   *knows*
That nevere I this for coveitise wroughte,   *covetousness did*
But oonly for t'abregge that distresse   *shorten*
For which wel neigh thow deidest, °as me thoughte.   *died*
But, goode brother, do now as the oughte,   *you ought*

---

249 I'm ashamed to say it
258 "Gentilesse" is the object of "triste."
263 so it seemed to me

265 For Goddes love, and kep hire out of blame,
Syn thow art wys, and save alwey hire name. *prudent, reputation*

"For wel thow woost, the name as yet of here *you know, her*
Among the peeple, as who seyth, halwed is; *as one says, reverenced*
For that man is unbore, I dar wel swere, *unborn*
270 That evere wiste that she dide amys. *knew, wrong*
But wo is me, that I, that cause al this,
May thynken that she is my nece deere,
And I hire em, and traitour eke yfeere! *uncle, also mixed together*

"And were it wist that I, thorugh myn °engyn, *known, machinations*
275 Hadde in my nece yput this fantasie,
To doon thi lust and holly to ben thyn, *pleasure, wholly*
Whi, al the world upon it wolde crie, *cry out*
And seyn that I the werste trecherie *worst*
Dide in this cas that evere was bigonne,
280 And she forlost, and thow °right nought ywonne. *(was) utterly lost*

"Wherfore, er I wol ferther gon a pas, *before, step*
Yet eft I the biseche and fully seye, *again*
That privete go with us in this cas, *privacy (secrecy)*
That is to seyn, that thow us nevere wreye; *betray*
285 And be nought wroth, though I the ofte preye *angry*
To holden secree swich an heigh matere, *secret, profound matter*
For skilfull is, thow woost wel, my praiere. *prudent, know*

"And thynk what wo ther hath bitid er this, *befallen, before*
For makyng of avantes, as men rede; *boasts, read*
290 And what meschaunce in this world yet ther is,
Fro day to day, right for that wikked dede;
For which thise wise clerkes that ben dede *dead*

---

274 See 2. 565 and n.
280 nothing (had) won

122

Han evere thus proverbed to us yonge,   *young (folk)*
That 'firste vertu is to kepe tonge.'   *hold one's tongue*

295 "And nere it that I wilne as now t'abregge   *were it not, abbreviate*
Diffusioun of speche, I koude almoost   *prolixity*
A thousand olde stories the allegge   *adduce*
Of wommen lost through fals and foles bost.   *foolish boast*
°Proverbes kanst thiself ynowe and woost,
300 Ayeins that vice, for to ben a labbe,
Al seyde men soth as often as thei gabbe.   *though, truth, boasted*

"O tonge, allas! so often here-byforn   *one*
Hath mad ful many a lady bright of hewe
Seyd 'weilaway, the day that I was born!'   *to have said, alas*
305 And many a maydes sorwe for to newe;   *to be renewed*
And for the more part, al is untrewe
That men of yelpe, °and it were brought to preve.   *boast about*
°Of kynde non avauntour is to leve.

"Avauntour and a lyere, al is on;   *boaster, liar, the same thing*
310 As thus; I pose, a womman graunte me   *hypothesize*
Hire love, and seith that other wol she non,   *another she won't have*
And I am sworn to holden it secree,   *secret*
And after I go telle it two or thre;
Iwis, I am avauntour at the leeste,   *least*
315 And lyere, for I breke my biheste.   *promise*

"Now loke thanne, if they be nought to blame,
Swich manere folk—what shal I clepe hem? what?   *call them*
That hem avaunte of wommen, and by name,   *boast, (do so) by name*
That nevere yet bihyghte hem this ne that,   *promised*

299-300 you're aware of proverbs enough yourself and you know enough against
that vice to become a tell-tale
307 if it were brought to the test
308 by nature no boaster is such as to be believed

320 Ne knewe hem more than myn olde hat!   *(they, the women) did not know*
No wonder is, so God me sende hele,   *well-being*
Though wommen dreden with us men to dele.   *dread, deal*

"I sey nought this for no mistrust of yow,   *because of any*
Ne for no wise men, but for foles nyce,   *silly fools*
325 And for the harm that in the werld is now,   *world*
°As wel for folie ofte as for malice;   *foolishness*
For wel woot I, in wise folk that vice   *know*
No womman drat, if she be wel avised;   *dreads, has considered well*
°For wyse ben by foles harm chastised.   *wise (men), punished*

330 "But now to purpos; leve brother deere,   *beloved*
Have al this thyng that I have seyd in mynde,
And kep the clos, and be now of good cheere,   *be discreet*
For at thi day thow shalt me trewe fynde.   *at the proper time*
I shal thi proces set in swych a °kynde,   *case arrange, nature*
335 And God toforn, that it shal the suffise,   *God as my witness*
For it shal be right as thow wolt devyse.   *arrange it*

"For wel I woot, thow menest wel, parde;   *certainly*
Therfore I dar this fully undertake.
Thow woost ek what thi lady graunted the,   *also*
340 °And day is set, the chartres up to make.
Have now good nyght, I may no lenger wake;
And bid for me, syn thow art now in blysse,   *pray*
That God me sende deth or soone lisse."   *death, joy*

---

326 harm . . . resulting as well from foolishness often as from malice
329 for wise men learn their lesson ("ben chastised") from the harm done by fools
334 "nature" in the sense that a "way" or "mode" has its own internal "nature," i.e.,
structure or arrangement, appropriate to it
340 A time is appointed for making matters definite, as in signing charters to some
effect.

Who myghte tellen half the joie or °feste
345 Whiche that the soule of Troilus tho felte,
Heryng th'effect of Pandarus byheste?   *hearing, promise*
His olde wo, that made his herte swelte,   *woe, perish*
Gan tho for joie wasten and tomelte,   *diminish, melt*
And al the richesse of his sikes sore   *his abundant sighs*
350 At ones fledde; he felte of hem namore.   *once, felt*

But right so as thise holtes and thise hayis,   *woods and hedges*
That han in wynter dede ben and dreye,   *dead, dry*
Revesten hem in grene, when that May is,   *reclothe*
Whan every lusty liketh best to pleye;   *person full of life's joy*
355 Right in that selve wise, soth to seye,   *same way, truth*
Wax sodeynliche his herte ful of joie,   *grew suddenly*
That gladder was ther nevere man in Troie.

And gan his look on Pandarus up caste
Ful sobrely, and frendly for to se,   *in an observably friendly manner*
360 And seyde, "Frend, in Aperil the laste,—
As wel thow woost, if it remembre the,—   *if you recall*
How neigh the deth for wo thow fownde me,   *near to*
And how thow dedest al thi bisynesse   *performed, solicitude*
To knowe of me the cause of my destresse.

365 "Thow woost how longe ich it forbar to seye   *refrained*
To the, that art the man that I best triste;   *trust*
And peril non was it to the bywreye,   *it to disclose to you*
That wist I wel, but telle me, if the liste,   *knew, please you*
Sith I so loth was that thiself it wiste,   *since, know*
370 How dorst I mo tellen of this matere,   *would I dare others*
That quake now, and no wight may us here?   *person, hear*

---

344 "delight" in the sense of the pleasure associated with feasting (See 2. 361 and n.)

125

°"But natheles, by that God I the swere,
That, as hym list, may al this world governe, —
And, if I lye, Achilles with his spere
375 Myn herte cleve, al were my lif eterne,
As I am mortal, if I late or yerne
Wolde it bewreye, or dorst, or sholde konne,
For al the good that God made under sonne—

"That rather deye I wolde, and determyne,
380 As thynketh me, now stokked in prisoun,   *it seems to, set in stocks*
In wrecchidnesse, in filthe, and in vermyne,   *vermin*
Caytif to cruel kyng °Agamenoun;   *captive*
And this in all the temples of this town
Upon the goddes alle, I wol the swere
385 To-morwe day, °if that it liketh the here.   *tomorrow daybreak*

"And that thow hast so muche ido for me   *done*
That I ne may it nevere more diserve,
This know I wel, al myghte I now for the   *even though*
A thousand tymes on a morwe sterve.   *die*
390 I kan namore, but that I wol the serve   *can (do)*
Right as thi sclave, whider so thow wende,   *slave, wherever you go*
For evere more, unto my lyves ende.

"But here, with al myn herte, I the biseche
That nevere in me thow deme swich folie   *reckon*

372-79 But nevertheless, by that God who, as he pleases, may all this world govern,
I swear to you (and if I lie, may Achilles with his spear cleave my heart in two, even
though my life were eternal, as I am mortal) I swear to you that, if I, early or late,
would betray it, or would dare to, or would even be able to (for all the good that
God made under the sun)—I would rather die than do that, and come to an end.
(Note that in this paraphrase I have attempted to capture the "nervousness" and "haste"
of T's "breathless" syntax.)
382 Agamemnon, king of Mycenae and leader of the Greek host at Troy
385 if it pleases you to hear me take this oath

126

395 As I shal seyn; me thoughte by thi speche
That this which thow me dost for compaignie,   *friendship*
I sholde wene it were a bauderye.   *assume, pimping*
I am nought wood, al-if I lewed be!   *mad, even though, ignorant*
It is nought so, that woot I wel, parde!   *know, indeed*

400 "But he that gooth, for gold or for richesse,   *goes*
On swich message, calle hym what the list;   *an errand, pleases you*
And this that thow doost, calle it gentilesse,
Compassioun, and felawship, and trist.   *trust*
°Departe it so, for wyde-wher is wist   *everywhere is known*
405 How that ther is diversite requered   *required*
Bytwixen thynges like, as I have lered.   *between, learned*

"And, that thow knowe I thynke nought, ne wene,   *assume*
That this servise a shame be or jape,   *trick*
I have my faire suster Polixene,
410 Cassandre, Eleyne, or any of the frape,   *group*
Be she nevere so faire or wel yshape,   *shaped*
Tel me which thow wilt of everychone,
To han for thyn, and lat me thanne allone.   *leave the rest to me*

"But sith thow hast idon me this servyse,   *done*
415 My lif to save, and for non hope of mede,   *reward*
So, for the love of God, this grete emprise   *undertaking*
Perfourme it out, for now is moste nede;
For heigh and lough, withouten any drede,   *high, low*
I wol alwey thyn hestes alle kepe.   *commands, obey*
420 Have now good nyght, and lat us bothe slepe."

Thus held hym ech of other wel apayed,   *each, satisfied with*
That al the world ne myghte it bet amende;   *improve upon the situation*
And on the morwe, whan they were arayed,   *up and dressed*
Ech to his owen nedes gan entende.   *busy himself*

---

404 make this distinction (Cf. 1. 637; 645.)

127

425 But Troilus, though as the fir he brende
For sharp desir of hope and of plesaunce,
He nought forgat his gode governaunce.

But in hymself with manhod gan restreyne
Ech racle dede and ech unbridled chere,   *rash, uncontrolled look*
430 That alle tho that lyven, soth to seyne,   *those, truth*
Ne sholde han wist, by word or by manere,   *known*
What that he mente, as touchyng this matere.
From every wight as fer as is the cloude   *person*
He was, so wel dissimulen he koude.   *dissemble*

435 And al the while which that I yow devyse,   *tell about*
This was his lif: with all his fulle myght,
By day, he was in Martes heigh servyse,   *Mars's*
This is to seyn, in armes as a knyght;
And for the more part, the longe nyght
440 He lay and thoughte how that he myghte serve
His lady best, hire thonk for to deserve.   *gratitude*

Nil I naught swere, although he lay ful softe,   *I will not*
That in his thought he nas somwhat disesed,   *was not, troubled*
Ne that he torned on his pilwes ofte,
445 °And wold of that hym missed han ben sesed.
But in swich cas man is nought alwey plesed,
For aught I woot, namore than was he;   *know*
That kan I deme of possibilitee.   *assume, from hypothesis*

But certeyn is, to purpos for to go,
450 That in this while, as writen is in geeste,   *the source*
He say his lady somtyme, and also   *saw*
She with hym spak, whan that she dorst and °leste;   *dared, liked*
And by hire bothe avys, as was the beste,   *in the judgment of both*

---

445 and wished to be in possession of what he lacked

°Apoynteden full warly in this nede, *carefully, need*
455 So as they durste, how they wolde procede. *dared*

But it was spoken in so short a wise,
In swich await alwey, and in swich feere, *such watchfulness, fear*
Lest any wight devynen or devyse *guess, conjecture*
Wolde of hem two, or to it laye an ere, *ear*
460 °That al this world so leef to hem ne were *dear, was not*
As that Cupide wolde hem grace sende
To maken of hire speche aright an ende. *quickly*

But thilke litel that they spake or wroughte, *that same*
His wise goost took ay of al swych heede, *spirit*
465 It semed hire he wiste what she thoughte *knew*
Withouten word, so that it was no nede
To bidde hym ought to doon, or ought forbeede; *pray*
For which she thought that love, al come it late, *although*
Of alle joie hadde opned hire the yate. *gate*

470 And shortly of this proces for to pace, *pass*
So wel his werk and wordes he bisette, *work, arranged*
That he so ful stood in his lady grace,
That twenty thousand tymes, er she lette, *ceased*
She thonked God that evere she with hym mette. *had met*
475 So koude he hym governe in swich servyse,
That al the world ne myght it bet devyse. *imagine it better*

For whi she fond hym so discret in al, *wherefore*
So secret, and of swich obëisaunce,
That wel she felte he was to hire a wal
480 Of stiel, and sheld from every displesaunce; *steel, shield*
That to ben in his goode governaunce, *(such) that*

---

454 (they) decided
460-1 all this world was not so dear to them as [their desire] that, etc.

129

So wis he was, she was namore afered,—   *prudent, afraid*
I mene, as fer as oughte ben requered.   *expected in such a matter*

And Pandarus, to quike alwey the fir,   *quicken, fire*
485 Was evere ylike prest and diligent;   *uniformly, ready*
To ese his frend was set al his desir.   *ease*
He shof ay on, he to and fro was sent;   *thrust*
He lettres bar whan Troilus was absent;   *bore*
That nevere man, as in his frendes nede,
490 Ne bar hym bet than he, withouten drede.   *doubt*

But now, paraunter, som man wayten wolde   *perhaps, expect*
That every word, or soonde, or look, or cheere   *sound*
Of Troilus that I rehercen sholde,
In al this while unto his lady deere.
495 I trowe it were a long thyng for to here;   *I guess, hear*
Or of what wight that stant °in swich disjoynte,   *man, stands*
His wordes alle, or every look, °to poynte.   *narrate*

For sothe, I have naught herd it don er this
In story non, °ne no man here, I wene;   *none, assume*
500 And though I wolde, I koude nought, ywys;
For ther was som epistel hem bitwene,   *letter*
That wolde, as seyth myn autour, wel contene   *occupy*
Neigh half this book, of which hym liste nought write.   *it pleases him*
How sholde I thanne a lyne of it endite?   *compose*

505 But to the grete effect. Than sey I thus,   *main point*
That stondyng in concord and in quiete,
Thise ilke two, Criseyde and Troilus,   *same*
As I have told, and °in this tyme swete,—   *sweet*

---

496 in such a plight
497 Construe "to poynte" as a complement of "it were a long thyng" (495), too.
499 here in the audience either
508-9 the time was sweet except that often they could not meet, etc.

Save only often myghte they nought mete,
510 Ne leiser have hire speches to fulfelle,— *fulfill*
That it bifel right as I shal yow telle:

That Pandarus, that evere dide his myght
Right for the fyn that I shal speke of here, *goal*
As for to bryngen to his hows som nyght *house*
515 His faire nece and Troilus yfere, *together*
Wher as at leiser al this heighe matere, *leisure*
Touchyng here love, °were at the fulle upbounde,
Hadde out of doute a tyme to it founde.

For he with gret deliberacioun
520 Hadde every thing that herto myght availle
Forncast and put in execucioun,
And neither left for cost ne for travaile. *omitted nothing, trouble*
°Come if hem list, hem sholde no thyng faille;
And for to ben in ought aspied there, *discovered*
525 That, wiste he wel, an impossible were. *knew, impossibility*

°Dredeles, it clere was in the wynd
From every pie and every lette-game;
Now al is wel, for al the world is blynd
In this matere, bothe °fremed and tame.
530 This tymbur is al redy up to frame; *timber, cut and set in place*
°Us lakketh nought but that we witen wolde *should know*
A certeyn houre, in which she comen sholde.

---

517 might be bound up (completed) at their leisure
523 if it pleased them to come, they would find nothing lacking to them
526-7 doubtless, the wind was blowing directly away from every magpie (a tell-tale bird) and spoil-sport
529 both wild and tame—i.e., everyone
531 nothing is lacking to us

And Troilus, that al this purveiaunce   *preparation*
Knew at the fulle, and waited on it ay,   *observed, ever*
535 Hadde hereupon ek made gret ordinaunce,   *plans*
And found his cause, and therto his aray,   *arrangement*
If that he were missed, nyght or day,
Ther-while he was aboute this servyse,—
That he was gon to don his sacrifise,   *(namely) that*

540 And moste at swich a temple allone wake,   *wake and watch*
Answered of Apollo for to be;
And first to sen the holy °laurer quake,   *see*
Er that Apollo spake out of the tree,
To telle hym next whan Grekes sholde flee,—
545 And forthy lette hym no man, God forbede,   *therefore, hinder*
But prey Apollo helpen in this nede.   *pray*

Now is ther litel more for to doone,
But Pandare up, and shortly for to seyne,
Right sone upon the chaungynge of the moone,   *soon*
550 Whan lightles is the world a nyght or tweyne,   *two*
And that the wolken shop hym for to reyne,   *sky prepared itself*
He streght o morwe unto his nece wente;   *on the morrow*
Ye han wel herd the fyn of his entente.   *goal*

Whan he was come, he gan anon to pleye
555 As he was wont, and of hymself to jape;   *make fun of himself*
And finaly he swor and gan hire seye,
By this and that, she sholde hym nought escape,
Ne lenger don hym after hire to gape;   *wish for her (presence)*
But certeynly she moste, by hire leve,   *must*
560 Come soupen in his hous with hym at eve.   *dine*

At which she lough, and gan hire faste excuse,   *laughed*
And seyde, "It reyneth; lo, how sholde I gon?"   *is raining*

---

542 The laurel tree was sacred to Apollo; see 3. 726 and n.

"Lat be," quod he, "ne stond nought thus to muse.   *ponder what to do*
This moot be don! Ye shal be ther anon."   *must*
565 So at the laste herof they fille aton,   *reached an agreement*
Or elles, softe he swor hire in hire ere,
He nolde nevere comen ther she were.   *would*

Soone after this, she to hym gan to rowne,   *whisper*
And axed hym if Troilus were there.
570 He swor hire nay, for he was out of towne,
And seyde, "Nece, I pose that he were;   *suppose he was*
Yow thurste nevere han the more fere;   *you would need, fear*
For rather than men myghte hym ther aspie,
Me were levere a thousand fold to dye."   *I'd prefer*

575 Nought list myn auctour fully to declare   *it does not please*
What that she thoughte whan he seyde so,
That Troilus was out of towne yfare,   *gone*
As if he seyde therof soth or no;   *truth*
But that, withowten °await, with hym to go,   *delay*
580 She graunted hym, sith he hire that bisoughte,   *requested*
And, as his nece, obeyed as hire oughte.

But natheles, yet gan she hym biseche,   *nevertheless*
Although with hym to gon it was no fere,   *she was not afraid*
For to ben war of goosish poeples speche,   *silly*
585 That dremen thynges whiche that nevere were,   *dream*
And wel avyse hym whom he broughte there;   *consider*
And seyde hym, "Em, syn I moste on yow triste,   *uncle, most, trust*
Loke al be wel, and do now as yow liste."   *pleases you*

He swor hire yis, °by stokkes and by stones,
590 And by the goddes that in hevene dwelle,

---

579 We should also note the possible senses "watchfulness" or "caution" usual in the word at this time.

589 "stokkes," "stones": sacred images or idols, often used contemptuously of such objects because made of wood and stone

133

Or elles were hym levere, fel and bones, *preferable, skin*
With Pluto kyng as depe ben in helle *to be*
As Tantalus!—what sholde I more telle?
Whan al was wel, he roos and took his leve, *rose*
595 And she to soper com, whan it was eve,

With a certein of hire owen men, *certain number*
And with hire faire nece Antigone, *niece*
And other of hire wommen nyne or ten.
But who was glad now, who, as trowe ye, *you may believe*
600 But Troilus, that stood and myght it se *see*
Thorughout a litel wyndow in a °stuwe,
Ther he bishet syn mydnyght was in °mewe, *shut up, coop*

Unwist of every wight but of Pandare? *unbeknownst to*
But to the point; now whan that she was come,
605 With alle joie and alle frendes fare, *friendly behavior*
Hire em anon in armes hath hire nome, *embraced*
And after to the soper, alle and some,
Whan tyme was, ful softe they hem sette.
God woot, ther was no deynte for to fette! *delicacy to be fetched*

610 And after soper gonnen they to rise,
At ese wel, with hertes fresshe and glade,
And wel was hym that koude best devyse *it was well with, arrange*
To liken hire, or that hire laughen made. *please*
He song; she pleyde; he tolde tale of °Wade.
615 But at the laste, as every thyng hath ende,
She took hire leve, and nedes wolde wende. *necessarily, depart*

---

601 a small heated room, generally for bathing (But see also *CT* VI C 465.)
602 a cage or coop where hawks are placed to molt
614 Wade is a hero of romance; it is possible that the phrase *tale of Wade* here means simply a tall story.

But O Fortune, executrice of wyrdes!	*fates*
O influences of thise hevens hye!	*high*
Soth is, that under God ye ben oure hierdes,	*shepherds*
620 Though to us bestes ben the causes wrie.	*beasts, hidden*
This mene I now, for she gan homward hye,	*go*
But execut was al bisyde hire leve	*performed, without her leave*
The goddes wil; for which she moste bleve.	*must remain*

°The bente moone with hire hornes pale,	*curved*
625 Saturne, and Jove, in Cancro joyned were,	
That swych a reyn from heven gan avale,	*rain, descend*
That every maner womman that was there	
Hadde of that smoky reyn a verray feere;	*fear*
At which Pandare tho lough, and seyde thenne,	*laughed*
630 "Now were it tyme a lady to gon henne!	*go away*

"But goode nece, if I myghte evere plese	
Yow any thyng, than prey ich yow," quod he,	*pray*
"To don myn herte as now so grete an ese	
As for to dwelle here al this nyght with me,	
635 For-whi this is youre owen hous, parde.	*because, certainly*
For, by my trouthe, I sey it nought a-game,	*in jest*
To wende as now, it were to me a shame."	*depart*

Criseyde, °which that koude as muche good	
As half a world, took hede of his preyere;	
640 And syn it ron, and al was on a flod,	*rained, flooding*
She thoughte, "°As good chepe may I dwellen here,	*easily*
And graunte it gladly with a frendes chere,	*in a friendly manner*

624-5 The astronomical conjunction here referred to (Jupiter and Saturn in the sign Cancer) is a rare one, occurring only once in roughly 600 years. The conditions described obtained in May or, possibly, June, 1385. For its bearing on the date of the poem see the very informative note by Barney, *Riverside Chaucer, ad loc.*

638 who had as much common sense and native intelligence

641 "as cheaply"–hence "as easily," "without undue expense"

135

And have a thonk, as grucche and thanne abide;   *thanks, complain*
For hom to gon, it may nought wel bitide."   *take place*

645 "I wol," quod she, "myn uncle lief and deere;   *beloved*
Syn that yow list, it skile is to be so.   *it pleases, reasonable*
I am right glad with yow to dwellen here;
I seyde but a-game, I wolde go."   *in jest*
"Iwys, graunt mercy, nece," quod he tho,   *thank you, then*
650 "Were it a-game or no, soth for to telle,
Now am I glad, syn that yow list to dwelle."

Thus al is wel; but tho bigan aright
The newe joie and al the feste agayn.   *celebration*
But Pandarus, if goodly hadde he myght,   *had he been able fittingly*
655 He wolde han hyed hire to bedde fayn,   *hastened, gladly*
And seyde, "Lord, this is an huge rayn!
This were a weder for to slepen inne;   *weather*
And that I rede us soone to bygynne.   *advise*

"And, nece, woot ye wher I wol yow leye,   *know, will have you lie*
660 For that we shul nat liggen far asonder,   *lie*
And for ye neither shullen, dar I seye,   *so that, shall*
Heren noyse of reynes nor of thonder?
By God, right in my litel °closet yonder.
And I wol in that outer hous allone
665 Be wardein of youre wommen everichone.   *warden, everyone*

"And in this myddel chaumbre that ye se
Shul youre wommen slepen, wel and softe;
And there I seyde shal youreselven be;   *there (where)*
And if ye liggen wel to-nyght, com ofte,   *lie*

---

663 The "closet" is a small room, probably adjoining the main hall. The supper was in the hall. Afterwards, in preparation for the night, we must suppose that a curtain (*travers*) was drawn across the hall dividing it into what P calls the *myddel chaumbre*, where C's women will sleep, and the *outer hous*, which he will occupy.

670 And careth nought what weder is alofte.	*weather*
°The wyn anon, and whan so that yow leste,	*it pleases you*
So go we slepe; I trowe it be the beste."	*reckon*
Ther nys no more, but hereafter soone,	*isn't any more*
The voidë dronke, and travers drawe anon,	*wine, curtain*
675 Gan every wight that hadde nought to done	
More in the place out of the chaumbre gon.	
And evere mo so sterneliche it ron,	*it rained so hard*
And blew therwith so wondirliche loude,	
That wel neigh no man heren other koude.	*hear*
680 Tho Pandarus, hire em, right as hym oughte,	*uncle*
With wommen swiche as were hire most aboute,	
Ful glad unto hire beddes syde hire broughte,	
And took his leve, and gan ful lowe loute,	*bow*
And seyde, "Here at this closet dore withoute,	
685 Right overthwart, youre wommen liggen alle,	*opposite, lie*
That, whom yow list of hem, ye may here calle."	*it pleases you*
So whan that she was in the closet leyd,	*comfortably placed*
And alle hire wommen forth by ordinaunce	
Abedde weren, ther as I have seyd,	
690 °There was nomore to skippen nor to traunce,	
But boden go to bedde, with meschaunce,	
If any wight was steryng anywhere,	
And lat hem slepen that abedde were.	
But Pandarus, that wel koude eche a deel	*knew in each detail*
695 °The olde daunce, and every point therinne,	*dance (of love)*

---

671 Wine was drunk before retiring in the Middle Ages, accompanied by spices and often cakes, dates, figs, raisins, etc. The little repast was called the *voidee* (see 3. 674).

690 There was to be no more skipping and tramping around (by the servants), but they were bidden to go to bed, with a malediction upon any who stirred

695 See *T&C* 2.1106 and also *CT* I A 476.

137

Whan that he sey that alle thyng was wel,   *saw*
He thought he wolde upon his werk bigynne,   *work*
And gan the stuwe doore al softe unpynne, *small room's*
And stille as stoon, withouten lenger lette,   *delay*
700 By Troilus adown right he hym sette.

And, shortly to the point right for to gon,
Of al this werk he tolde hym word and ende, *from beginning to end*
And seyde, "Make the redy right anon,   *ready*
For thow shalt into hevene blisse wende." *heavenly, go*
705 "Now, blisful Venus, thow me grace sende!"
Quod Troilus, "For nevere yet no nede
Hadde ich er now, ne halvendel the drede."   *half*

Quod Pandarus, "Ne drede the nevere a deel, *fear, bit*
For it shal be right as thow wolt desire;
710 So thryve I, this nyght shal I make it weel, *may I prosper, well*
°Or casten al the gruwel in the fire."
"Yet, blisful Venus, this nyght thow me enspire,"
Quod Troilus, "As wys as I the serve,   *certainly*
And evere bet and bet shal, til I sterve.   *better, die*

715 "And if ich hadde, O Venus ful of myrthe,
°Aspectes badde of Mars or of Saturne,
Or thow °combust or let were in my birthe,
Thy fader prey al thilke harm disturne *father (Jupiter), turn aside*
Of grace, and that I glad ayein may turne, *graciously, again*
720 For love of hym thow lovedest in the shawe, *wood*
I meene °Adoun, that with the boor was slawe. *slain*

---

711 The sense is "or chuck it all in."
716 Mars and Saturn in certain relative positions were baleful planets.
717 The word "combust" (lit., "burnt up") indicates the position of a planet within 8.5° of the sun. The influence of Venus for good was destroyed under these circumstances. Her influence could also be hindered ("let") by other astronomical conditions.
721 Ovid tells the story of Adonis at *Metam.* 10. 708ff. Venus loved Adonis so

"O Jove ek, for the love of faire °Europe,   *bull, fetched*
The which in forme of bole awey thow fette,
Now help! O Mars, thow with thi °blody cope,   *blood-stained cloak*
725 For love of Cipris, thow me nought ne lette!   *Venus, hinder*
O Phebus, thynk whan °Dane hireselven shette
Under the bark, and °laurer wax for drede,
Yet for hire love, O help now at this nede!

°"Mercurie, for the love of Hierse eke,
730 For which Pallas was with Aglawros wroth,   *angry*
Now help! and ek °Diane, I the biseke,
That this viage be nought to the looth.   *undertaking, angry*
°O fatal sustren, which, er any cloth   *sisters*
Me shapen was, my destine me sponne,   *spun*
735 So helpeth to this werk that is bygonne!"   *work*

Quod Pandarus, "Thow wrecched mouses herte,
Artow agast so that she wol the bite?   *that*
Why, don this furred cloke upon thy sherte,   *over your shirt*
And folwe me, for I wol have the wite.   *blame*

---

greatly that after he had been killed hunting a wild boar she persuaded Pluto, with the help of Jupiter, to let him return to earth for the spring and summer of each year.

722 Jupiter, to obtain Europa, assumed the form of a bull and carried her off on his back—see *Metam.* 10. 833ff.

724 The description is appropriate to the god of war.

726 With the help of her father, the river-god, Daphne became a laurel to escape from the pursuit of Apollo—see *Metam.* 1. 452ff.

727 and became a laurel tree on account of fear

729 Pallas (Minerva), displeased by Aglauros, made her envious of her sister Herse. When Aglauros tried to thwart Mercury in his love for Herse, he turned her to stone— see *Metam.* 2. 708ff.

731 T beseeches Diana, the chaste goddess, that his undertaking may not be displeasing to her.

733 the Fates, who spun the web of his destiny before any cloth was woven for him (See 5. 1 and n.)

139

740 But bide, and lat me gon biforn a lite." *little*
And with that word he gan °undon a trappe, *unfasten a trapdoor*
And Troilus he brought in by the lappe. *corner (of his cloak)*

The sterne wynd so loude gan to route *roar*
That no wight oother noise myghte heere; *person*
745 And they that layen at the dore withoute,
Ful sikerly they slepten alle yfere; *together*
And Pandarus, with a ful sobre cheere, *countenance*
Goth to the dore anon, withouten lette, *hindrance*
There as they laye, and softely it shette. *shut*

750 And as he com ayeynward pryvely, *back (to Criseyde)*
His nece awook, and axed, "Who goth there?" *awoke*
"My dere nece," quod he, "it am I.
Ne wondreth nought, ne have of it no fere."
And ner he com, and seyde hire in hire ere,
755 "No word, for love of God, I yow bPeseche!
Lat no wight risen and heren of oure speche." *person*

"What! which wey be ye comen, *benedicite?*" *bless us*
Quod she, "and how thus unwist of hem alle?" *unbeknownst to*
"Here at this secre trappe-dore," quod he.
760 Quod tho Criseyde, "Lat me som wight calle!"
"I! God forbede that it sholde falle," *happen*
Quod Pandarus, "that ye swich folye wroughte! *committed*
They myghte demen thyng they nevere er thoughte. *suspect, imagined*

"It is nought good a slepyng hound to wake,
765 Ne yeve a wight a cause to devyne. *give, conjecture*
Youre wommen slepen alle, I undertake,
So that, for hem, the hous men myghte myne, *mine*

---

741 The *stuwe* where T had been concealed was presumably above (or below) the room in which C was sleeping, maybe in the wall. If above or below, stairs (possibly in the wall) would have connected the two rooms.

140

And slepen wollen til the sonne shyne.		*they will*
And whan my tale brought is to an ende,		
770 Unwist, right as I com, so wol I wende.		*unsuspected, go*

"Now, nece myn, ye shul wel understonde,"	
Quod he, "so as ye wommen demen alle,	*judge (it)*
That for °to holde in love a man in honde,	
And hym hire lief and deere herte calle,	*beloved*
775 °And maken hym an howve above a calle,	
I meene, as love another in this while,	*during this time*
She doth hireself a shame, and hym a gyle.	*deceit*

"Now, wherby that I telle yow al this:	*why*
Ye woot youreself, as wel as any wight,	*know, person*
780 How that youre love al fully graunted is	
To Troilus, °the worthieste knyght	
Oon of this world, and therto trouthe yplight,	*(your) truth promised*
That, °but it were on hym along, ye nolde	*unless*
Hym nevere °falsen while ye lyven sholde.	*live*

785 "Now stant it thus, that sith I fro yow wente,	*since*
This Troilus, right platly for to seyn,	*plainly*
Is thorugh a goter, by a pryve wente,	*gutter, passage*
Into my chaumbre come in al this reyn,	
Unwist of every manere wight, certeyn,	*unbeknownst to, person*
790 Save of myself, as wisly have I joye,	*certainly*
And by that feith I shal Priam of Troie.	*owe to*

---

773 lead a man on with false hopes
775 The idiom means "to engage in double dealing," such as loving another at the same time (line 776). A *calle* (caul) is a close-fitting cap; a *howve* is a hood.
781 a variation in word order of *oon the worthieste knyght*
783 unless it were he who was to blame
784 Cf. 4. 1537; 5. 1845.

"And he is come in swich peyne and distresse
That, but he be al fully wood by this,   *mad*
He sodeynly mot falle into wodnesse,   *must, madness*
795 But if God helpe; and cause whi this is,   *unless*
He seith hym told is of a frend of his,   *by a friend*
How that ye sholden love oon hatte °Horaste;   *are said to, one named*
For sorwe of which this nyght shal ben his laste."

Criseyde, which that al this wonder herde,
800 Gan sodeynly aboute hire herte colde,   *grow cold*
And with a sik she sorwfully answerde,   *sigh*
"Allas! I wende, whoso tales tolde,   *assumed, whoever*
My deere herte wolde me nought holde
So lightly fals! Allas! conceytes wronge,
805 What harm they don, for now lyve I to longe!   *too*

"Horaste! allas, and falsen Troilus?
I knowe hym nought, God helpe me so," quod she.
"Allas, what wikked spirit tolde hym thus?
Now certes, em, tomorwe, and I hym se,
810 I shal therof as ful excusen me,   *fully*
As evere dide womman, if hym like."
And with that word she gan ful soore sike.   *sigh*

°"O God!" quod she, "so worldly selynesse,   *happiness*
Which clerkes callen fals felicitee,
815 Imedled is with many a bitternesse!   *mixed*
Ful angwissous than is, God woot," quod she,   *anguished, knows*
"Condicioun of veyn prosperitee;   *vain*
For either joies comen nought yfeere,   *together*
Or elles no wight hath hem alwey here.

---

797 Ch adopts a well-known name (Orestes) for P's invented story.
813ff. C's philosophical musing is based on Boethius, *CP* 2. pr. 4.

820 "O brotel wele of mannes joie unstable!   *brittle, fortune*
    With what wight so thow be, or how thow pleye,   *whatever, however*
    Either he woot that thow, joie, art muable,   *knows, changeable*
    Or woot it nought; it mot ben oon of tweye.   *must, (the) two*
    Now if he woot it nought, how may he seye
825 That he hath verray joie and selynesse,   *happiness*
    That is of ignoraunce ay in derknesse?

    "Now if he woot that joie is transitorie,
    As every joie of worldly thyng mot flee,
    Than every tyme he °that hath in memorie,
830 The drede of lesyng maketh hym that he   *losing*
    May in no perfit selynesse be;
    And if to lese his joie he sette a myte,   *lose, cares (only) a bean*
    Than semeth it that joie is worth ful lite.   *little*

    "Wherfore I wol diffyne in this matere,   *conclude*
835 That trewely, for aught I kan espie,   *discern*
    Ther is no verray weele in this world heere.   *joy*
    But O thow wikked serpent, jalousie,
    Thow mysbyleved and envyous folie,   *misbelieving*
    Why hastow Troilus mad to me untriste,   *made distrustful toward me*
840 That nevere yet agylt hym, that I wiste?"   *wronged, know*

    Quod Pandarus, "Thus fallen is this cas—"   *that is how matters stand*
    "Why, uncle myn," quod she, "who tolde hym this?
    Why doth my deere herte thus, allas?"
    "Ye woot, ye, nece myn," quod he, "what is.   *know*
845 I hope al shal be wel that is amys;
    For ye may quenche al this, if that yow leste.   *it please you*
    And doth right so, for I holde it the beste."

    "So shal I do to-morwe, ywys," quod she,
    And God toforn, so that it shal suffise."   *I swear*

---

829 Construe as "has that," i.e., the knowledge that joy is fleeting.

850 "To-morwe? allas, that were a fair!" quod he. *a fine thing to do*
"Nay, nay, it may nat stonden in this wise. *way*
For, nece myn, thus writen clerkes wise,
That peril is with drecchyng in ydrawe; *danger is introduced by delay*
Nay, swiche abodes ben nought worth an °hawe. *delays*

855 "Nece, alle thyng hath tyme, I dar avowe,
For whan a chaumbre afire is, or an halle,
Wel more nede is, it sodeynly rescowe *rescue*
Than to dispute and axe amonges alle *ask*
How is this candele in the straw i-falle. *fallen*
860 A, *benedicite*! for al among that fare *bless me, during that time*
The harm is don, and °farewel feldefare!

"And nece myn—ne take it naught agrief—
If that ye suffre hym al nyght in this wo, *(to remain)*
God help me so, ye hadde hym nevere lief,— *you never held him dear*
865 That dar I seyn, now ther is but we two.
But wel I woot that ye wol nat do so;
Ye ben to wys to doon so gret folie,
To putte his lif al nyght in jupertie." *jeopardy*

"Hadde I hym nevere lief? by God, I weene *guess*
870 Ye hadde nevere thyng so lief!" quod she.
"Now by my thrift," quod he, "that shal be seene! *let me prosper*
For syn ye make this ensaumple of me, *example*
If ich al nyght wolde hym in sorwe se,
For al the tresour in the town of Troie,
875 I bidde God I nevere mote have joie. *pray, may*

"Now loke thanne, if ye that ben his love
Shul putte his lif al night in jupertie
For thyng of nought, now, by that God above,

---

854 "fruit of hawthorn"—i.e., thing of no value
861 a proverbial expression signifying "the bird has flown," "it's too late"

144

°Naught oonly this delay comth of folie,

880 But of malice, if that I shal naught lie.

What! platly, and ye suffre hym in destresse,   *plainly*

Ye neyther bounte don ne gentilesse."

Quod tho Criseyde, "Wol ye don o thyng,

And ye therwith shal stynte al his disese?   *put an end to*

885 Have heere, and bereth hym this blewe ryng,   *blue*

For ther is nothyng myghte hym bettre plese,

Save I myself, ne more hys herte apese;   *assuage*

And sey my deere herte, that his sorwe   *say (to)*

Is causeles, that shal be sene to-morwe."   *seen*

890 "A ryng?" quod he, "ye, °haselwodes shaken!

Ye, nece myn, that ryng moste han a °stoon   *have*

That myhte dede men alyve maken;   *might*

And swich a ryng trowe I that ye have non.   *suspect*

Discrecioun out of youre hed is gon;   *good sense*

895 That fele I now," quod he, "and that is routhe.   *feel, pity*

O tyme ilost, wel maistow corsen slouthe!   *curse*

°"Woot ye not wel that noble and heigh corage

Ne sorweth nought, ne stynteth ek, for lite?

But if a fool were in a jalous rage,   *if it were only a fool who*

900 °I nolde setten at his sorwe a myte,

But feffe hym with a fewe °wordes white   *grant him, specious words*

---

879 this delay comes not only of folly but . . . etc.

890 a form of exclamation whose sense is something like "what a waste of time!"

891 Various stones were supposed to have magical properties and were described in medieval lapidaries.

897 don't you know that a noble heart neither sorrows nor ceases to sorrow because of little things

900 I wouldn't care a fig for his sorrow

901 Cf. 3. 1567.

Anothir day, whan that I myghte hym fynde;
°But this thyng stant al in another kynde.

"This is so gentil and so tendre of herte,   *this (man)*
905 That with his deth he wol his sorwes wreke;   *make up for*
For trusteth wel, how sore that hym smerte,   *it pains*
He wol to yow no jalous wordes speke.
And forthi, nece, er that his herte breke,   *therefore*
So speke youreself to hym of this matere;
910 For with o word ye may his herte stere.   *one, govern*

"Now have I told what peril he is inne,
And his comynge unwist is to every wight;   *unknown*
Ne, parde, harm may ther be non, ne synne;   *indeed*
I wol myself be with yow al this nyght.
915 Ye knowe ek how it is youre owen knyght,
And that bi right ye moste upon hym triste,   *trust*
And I al prest to fecche hym whan yow liste."   *ready, it pleases you*

This accident so pitous was to here,
And ek so like a sooth, at prime face,   *at first appearance*
920 And Troilus hire knyght to hir so deere,
His prive comyng, and the siker place,   *secret, safe*
That, though that she did hym as thanne a grace,
Considered alle thynges as they stoode,
No wonder is, syn she did al for goode.

925 Criseyde answerde, "As wisly God at reste   *certainly*
My soule brynge, as me is for hym wo!   *I am sorry for him*
And, em, iwis, fayn wolde I don the beste,   *uncle, prefer*
If that ich hadde grace to do so.
But whether that ye dwelle or for hym go,   *stay here*

---

903 this matter is altogether different

146

930 I am, til God me bettre mynde sende,
    At °dulcarnoun, right at my wittes ende."   *perplexed*

Quod Pandarus, "Yee, nece, wol ye here?   *bear*
Dulcarnoun called is °'flemyng of wrecches.'
It semeth hard, for wrecches wol nought lere,   *learn*
935 For verray slouthe or other wilfull tecches;   *real, faults*
°This seyd by hem that ben nought worth two fecches.
But ye ben wis, and that we han on honde   *have*
Nis neither hard, ne skilful to withstonde."   *reasonable*

"Than, em," quod she, "doth herof as yow list.   *pleases you*
940 But er he come, I wil up first arise,
And, for the love of God, syn al my trist   *trust*
Is on yow two, and ye ben bothe wise,
So werketh now in so discret a wise   *discrete*
That I honour may have, and he plesaunce;
945 For I am here al in youre governaunce."

"That is wel seyd," quod he, "my nece deere.
Ther good thrift on that wise gentil herte!   *(let) there (be), luck*
But liggeth still, and taketh hym right here;   *lie*
It nedeth nought no ferther for hym sterte.   *(for you to) move*
950 And ech of yow ese otheres sorwes smerte,   *bitter*
For love of God; and Venus, I the herye;   *praise*
For soone, hope I, we shul ben alle merye."

---

931 The expression comes from an Arabic epithet meaning "two-horned." It was also the name of the 47th proposition of Euclid's geometry.

933 "Flemyng of wrecches" is a translation of *fuga miserorum*, corresponding to *Eleufuga*, a name for Euclid's 5th proposition (also a difficult one). The phrase means "banishment of the miserable." It would appear that P is confusing terms, but perhaps he does so on purpose.

936 this is said of them that are not worth two beans

This Troilus ful soone on knees hym sette
Ful sobrely, right be hyre beddes hed,
955 And in his beste wyse his lady grette.   *greeted*
But, Lord, so she wex sodeynliche red!   *suddenly*
Ne though men sholde smyten of hire hed,   *head*
She kouthe nought a word aright out-brynge   *could*
So sodeynly, for his sodeyn comynge.

960 But Pandarus, that so wel koude feele   *empathize*
In every thyng, to pleye anon bigan,
And seyde, "Nece, se how this lord kan knele!
Now, for youre trouthe, se this gentil man!"   *see*
And with that word he for a quysshen ran,   *cushion*
965 And seyde, "Kneleth now, while that yow leste,   *it pleases you*
There God youre hertes brynge soone at reste!"

Kan I naught seyn, for she bad hym nought rise,   *because, asked*
If sorwe it putte out of hire remembraunce,
Or elles that she took it in the wise   *manner*
970 Of dewete, as for his observaunce;   *duty, from his respect (for her)*
But wel fynde I she dede hym this pleasaunce,
That she hym kiste, although she siked sore,   *sighed*
And bad hym sitte adown withouten more.   *more (ado)*

Quod Pandarus, "Now wol ye wel bigynne.
975 Now doth hym sitte, goode nece deere,   *have*
Upon youre beddes syde al ther withinne,   *inside the curtains*
That ech of yow the bet may other heere."
And with that word he drow hym to the feere,   *drew, fire*
And took a light, and °fond his contenaunce   *contrived a posture*
980 As for to loke upon an old romaunce.   *look*

---

979 A fuller expansion would be: "invented as a pretence (*fond*) the appearance of,"
where *fond* suggests the notion of *inventio* ("invention"), in classical and medieval rhetoric
the first step in the composition of a discourse (i.e., the "finding" of the topic of the
discourse).

148

Criseyde, that was Troilus lady right,
And cler stood on a ground of sikernesse,   *security*
Al thoughte she hire servant and hire knyght   *although*
Ne sholde of right non untrouthe in hire gesse,   *guess*
985 Yet natheles, considered his distresse,
And that love is in cause of swich folie,   *responsible for*
Thus to hym spak she of his jalousie:

"Lo, herte myn, as wolde the excellence   *would (suggest)*
Of love, ayeins the which that no man may
990 Ne oughte ek goodly make resistence;
And ek bycause I felte wel and say   *saw*
Youre grete trouthe and servise every day,
And that youre herte al myn was, soth to seyne,–   *truth*
This drof me for to rewe upon youre peyne.   *compelled*

995 "And youre goodnesse have I founde alwey yit,
Of which, my deere herte and al my knyght,
I thonke it yow, as fer as I have wit,
Al kan I nought as muche as it were right;   *even though*
And I, emforth my connyng and my myght,   *to the extent of my wit*
1000 Have and ay shal, how sore that me smerte,   *however, pains*
Ben to yow trewe and hool with al myn herte;

"And dredeles, that shal be founde at preve.   *proof*
But, herte myn, what al this is to seyne
Shal wel be told, so that ye nought yow greve,   *grieve*
1005 Though I to yow right on youreself compleyne.
For therwith mene I fynaly the peyne   *pain*
That halt youre herte and myn in hevynesse   *holds*
Fully to slen, and every wrong redresse.   *slay*

"My goode myn, noot I for-why ne how   *do not know*
1010 That jalousie, allas! that wikked wyvere,   *viper*
Thus causeles is cropen into yow,   *has crept*
The harm of which I wolde fayn delyvere.   *eliminate*

149

Allas, that he, al hool, or of hym slyvere,   *(a) sliver*

Shuld han his refut in so digne a place,   *refuge, worthy*

1015 Ther Jove hym soone out of youre herte arace!   *root out*

"But O, thow Jove, O auctour of nature,

Is this an honour to thi deyte,   *deity*

That folk ungiltif suffren hire injure,   *not guilty, injury*

And who that giltif is, al °quyt goth he?   *free*

1020 O, were it leful for to pleyn on the,   *lawful to complain against you*

°That undeserved suffrest jalousie,

Of that I wolde upon the pleyne and crie!

"Ek al my wo is this, that folk now usen

To seyn right thus, 'Ye, jalousie is love!'

1025 And wolde a busshel venym al excusen,

For that o greyn of love is on it shove.   *one*

But that woot heighe God that sit above,   *knows*

If it be likkere love, or hate, or grame;   *more like, sorrow*

And after that, it oughte bere his name.   *in keeping with, to bear*

1030 "But certeyn is, som manere jalousie

Is excusable more than som, iwys;   *some (other)*

As whan cause is, and °som swich fantasie

With piete so wel repressed is

That it unnethe doth or seyth amys,

1035 But goodly drynketh up al his distresse;

And that excuse I, for the gentilesse.

"And som so ful of furie is and despit

That it sourmounteth his repressioun.   *overwhelms, restraint*

But, herte myn, ye be nat in that plit,   *condition*

1019 Cf. *CT* IV D 425.

1021 that tolerate jealousy where it is undeserved

1032-5 and some imagining of this kind is so well repressed through a sense of duty that it scarcely does or says anything amiss, but patiently drinks up its (cup of) distress

1040 That thonke I God; for which youre passioun
    I wol nought calle it but illusioun,   *nothing*
    Of habundaunce of love and besy cure,   *zeal*
    That doth youre herte this disese endure.   *causes*

    "Of which I am right sory, but nought wroth;   *angry*
1045 But, for my devoir and youre hertes reste,   *duty*
    Wherso yow list, °by ordal or by oth,   *wherever it pleases you*
    By sort, or in what wise so yow leste,   *divination, pleases you*
    For love of God, lat preve it for the beste;   *prove*
    And if that I be giltif, do me deye!   *guilty, die*
1050 Allas, what myght I more don or seye?"

    With that a fewe brighte teris newe   *tears*
    Owt of hire eighen fille, and thus she seyde,   *eyes, fell*
    "Now God, thow woost, in thought ne dede untrewe   *you know, deed*
    To Troilus was nevere yet Criseyde."
1055 With that here heed down in the bed she leyde,
    And with the sheete it wreigh, and sighte soore,   *covered, sighed*
    And held hire pees; nought o word spak she more.   *peace, one*

    But now help God to quenchen al this sorwe!
    So hope I that he shal, for he best may.
1060 °For I have seyn, of a ful misty morwe   *seen*
    Folowen ful ofte a myrie someris day;   *merry*
    And after wynter foloweth grene May.
    Men sen alday, and reden ek in stories,   *seen*
    That after sharpe shoures ben victories.   *battles*

1065 This Troilus, whan he hire wordes herde,
    Have ye no care, °hym liste nought to slepe;   *rest assured*

1046 by ordeal or by judicial oath
1060 Cf. similar weather imagery elsewhere in the poem—e.g., 1. 175.
1066 he had no desire to sleep

°For it thought hym no strokes of a yerde   *rod*
To heere or seen Criseyde, his lady, wepe;   *weep*
But wel he felt about his herte crepe,   *creep*
1070 For everi tere which that Criseyde asterte,   *escaped from*
The crampe of deth, to streyne hym by the herte.   *constrict*

And in his mynde he gan the tyme acorse   *cursed*
That he com there, and that he was born;
For now is wikke torned into worse,   *wicked*
1075 And al that labour he hath don byforn,
He wende it lost; he thoughte he nas but lorn.   *considered, undone*
"O Pandarus," thoughte he, "allas, thi wile   *trickery*
Serveth of nought, so weylaway, the while!"   *not at all, alas*

And therwithal he heng adown the heed,
1080 And fil on knees, and sorwfully he sighte.   *sighed*
What myghte he seyn? He felte he nas but deed,   *dead*
For wroth was she that sholde his sorwes lighte.   *alleviate*
But natheles, whan that he speken myghte,
Than seyde he thus, "God woot that of this game,
1085 Whan al is wist, than am I nought to blame."   *known*

Therwith the sorwe so his herte shette,   *shut (down)*
That from his eyen fil ther nought a tere,   *fell*
°And every spirit his vigour in-knette,
So they astoned or oppressed were.   *astonished*
1090 The felyng of his sorwe, or of his fere,
Or of aught elles, fled was out of towne;
And down he fel al sodeynly aswowne.   *in a faint*

1067 the blows of a rod seemed to him no pain at all compared to the pain of seeing his lady weep

1088-9 The three spirits of the human creature are the vital, in the heart; the natural, in the liver; and the animal, in the brain; each of these contracted its vigor ("vigour in-knette")—i.e., shut down its functioning.

152

This was no litel sorwe for to se;
But al was hust, and Pandare up as faste,— *silent*
1095 "O nece, pes, or we be lost!" quod he, *peace*
"Beth naught agast!" but certeyn, at the laste,
For this or that, he into bed hym caste,
And seyde, "O thef, is this a mannes herte?" *thief*
And of he rente al to his bare sherte; *he tore away, shirt*

1100 And seyde, "Nece, but ye helpe us now,
Allas, youre owen Troilus is lorn!" *lost*
"Iwis, so wolde I, and I wiste how, *if, knew*
Ful fayn," quod she; "Allas, that I was born!" *gladly*
"Yee, nece, wol ye pullen out the thorn
1105 That stiketh in his herte," quod Pandare,
"Sey °'al foryeve,' and stynt is al this fare!" *finished, business*

"Ye, that to me," quod she, "ful levere were *preferable*
Than al the good the sonne aboute gooth." *goes around*
And therwithal she swor hym in his ere,
1110 "Iwys, my deere herte, I am nought wroth, *angry*
Have here my trouthe!" and many an other oth; *oath*
"Now speke to me, for it am I, Criseyde!"
But al for nought; yit myght he nought abreyde. *come to*

Therwith his pous and paumes of his hondes *pulse, palms*
1115 They gan to frote, and wete his temples tweyne; *rub, wet*
And to deliveren hym fro bittre bondes,
She ofte hym kiste; and shortly for to seyne,
Hym to revoken she did al hire peyne. *restore to consciousness*
And at the laste, he gan his breth to drawe,
1120 And of his swough sone after that adawe, *faint, awaken*

And gan bet mynde and reson to hym take, *better*
But wonder soore he was abayst, iwis. *dismayed*

1106 all is forgiven

And with a sik, whan he gan bet awake,   *sigh*
He seyde, "O mercy, God, what thyng is this?"
1125 "Why do ye with youreselven thus amys?"   *behave so strangely*
Quod tho Criseyde; "Is this a mannes game?"   *manly behavior*
What, Troilus, wol ye do thus for shame?"

And therwithal hire arm over hym she leyde,
And al foryaf, and ofte tyme hym keste.   *kissed*
1130 He thonked hire, and to hire spak, and seyde
As fil to purpos for his hertes reste;   *what was to the point*
And she to that answerde hym as hire leste,   *it pleased her*
And with hire goodly wordes hym disporte   *cheer up*
She gan, and ofte his sorwes to comforte.

1135 Quod Pandarus, "For aught I kan aspien,   *see*
This light, nor I, ne serven here of nought.   *are of no use here*
Light is nought good for sike folkes yën!   *sick, eyes*
But, for the love of God, syn ye ben brought
In thus good plit, lat now no hevy thought   *state*
1140 Ben hangyng in the hertes of yow tweye"–
And bar the candele to the chymeneye.   *fireplace*

Soone after this, though it no nede were,
Whan she swiche othes as hire leste devyse   *it pleased her, compose*
Hadde of hym take, hire thoughte tho no fere,   *it seemed to, fear*
1145 Ne cause ek non to bidde hym thennes rise.   *thence*
Yet lasse thyng than othes may suffise
In many a cas; for every wyght, I gesse,
That loveth wel, meneth but gentilesse.   *means*

But in effect she wolde wite anon   *know*
1150 Of what man, and ek wheer, and also why
He jalous was, syn ther was cause non;
And ek the sygne that he took it by,   *sign*
She badde hym that to telle hire bisily;   *earnestly*

Or elles, certeyn, she bar hym on honde	*accused him*
1155 That this was don of malice, hire to fonde.	*test*
Withouten more, shortly for to seyne,	
He most obeye unto his lady heste;	*must, command*
And for the lasse harm, he moste feyne.	*dissemble*
He seyde hire, whan she was at swiche a feste,	*festival*
1160 She myght on hym han loked at the leste,—	*him*
°Noot I nought what, al deere ynough a rysshe,	
As he that nedes most a cause fisshe.	*needs, fish for*
And she answerde, "Swete, al were it so,	*sweetheart, even if*
What harm was that, syn I non yvel mene?	*intend*
1165 °For, by that God that bought us bothe two,	
In alle thyng is myn entente cleene.	
Swiche argumentes ne ben naught worth a beene.	
Wol ye the childissh jalous contrefete?	*imitate*
Now were it worthi that ye were ybete."	*beaten*
1170 This Troilus gan sorwfully to sike —	*sigh*
Lest she be wroth, hym thoughte his herte deyde —	*it seemed to him*
And seyde, "Allas, upon my sorwes sike	*sick*
Have mercy, swete herte myn, Criseyde!	
And if that in tho wordes that I seyde	
1175 Be any wrong, I wol no more trespace.	
Doth what yow list, I am al in youre grace."	*pleases*
And she answerde, "Of gilt misericorde!	*for (your) guilt, mercy*
That is to seyn, that I foryeve al this.	
And evere more on this nyght yow recorde,	*always remember this night*
1180 And beth wel war ye do namore amys."	
"Nay, dere herte myn," quod he, "iwys!"	

1161 I don't know what, at any rate a worthless fable
1165 See 1. 694 and n.

"And now," quod she, "that I have don yow smerte,   *caused you pain*
Foryeve it me, myn owene swete herte."

This Troilus, with blisse of that supprised,   *seized*
1185 Putte al in Goddes hand, as he that mente
Nothyng but wel; and sodeynly avysed,   *by a sudden resolution*
He hire in armes faste to hym hente.   *caught*
And Pandarus, with a ful good entente,
Leyde hym to slepe, and seyde, "If ye be wise,   *went to bed*
1190 Swouneth nought now, lest more folk arise!"   *faint*

°What myghte or may the sely larke seye,   *hapless*
Whan that the sperhauk hath it in his foot?
I kan namore, but of thise ilke tweye,—
°To whom this tale sucre be or soot,—
1195 Though that I tarie a yer, somtyme I moot,   *linger, must*
After myn auctour, tellen hire gladnesse,   *following*
As wel as I have told hire hevynesse.

Criseyde, which that felte hire thus itake,   *taken*
As writen clerkes in hire bokes olde,
1200 Right as an aspes leef she gan to quake,   *aspen leaf*
Whan she hym felte hire in his armes folde.
But Troilus, al hool of cares colde,   *whole*
Gan thanken tho the blisful goddes sevene.   *i. e., the planets*
°Thus sondry peynes bryngen folk to hevene.

1205 This Troilus in armes gan hire streyne,   *press*
And seyde, "O swete, as evere mot I gon,   *may I thrive*
Now be ye kaught, now is ther but we tweyne!
Now yeldeth yow, for other bote is non!"   *remedy*

1191 Cf. 2. 683 and 1. 35 and n.
1194 no matter to whom this tale be sugar or soot (in the MA often referred to as bitter)
1204 Cf. 3. 1599–1600.

To that Criseyde answerde thus anon,
1210 "Ne hadde I er now, my swete herte deere,   *before*
Ben yold, ywis, I were now nought heere!"   *yielded*

O, sooth is seyd, that heled for to be   *it is truly said, healed*
As of a fevre, or other gret siknesse,
Men moste drynke, as men may ofte se,
1215 °Ful bittre drynke; and for to han gladnesse,
Men drynken ofte peyne and gret distresse;
I mene it here, as for this aventure,
That thorugh a peyne hath founden al his cure.   *regarding someone who*

And now swetnesse semeth more swete,
1220 That bitternesse assaied was byforn;   *since, experienced*
For out of wo in blisse now they flete;   *float*
Non swich they felten syn that they were born.
Now is this bet than bothe two be lorn.   *lost*
For love of God, take every womman heede   *let every woman take*
1225 To werken thus, if it comth to the neede.

Criseyde, al quyt from every drede and tene,   *delivered, sorrow*
As she that juste cause hadde hym to triste,   *trust*
°Made hym swich feste, it joye was to seene,   *celebrated him so*
Whan she his trouthe and clene entente wiste;   *knew*
1230 And as aboute a tree, with many a twiste,
°Bytrent and writh the swote wodebynde,   *sweet*
Gan eche of hem in armes other wynde.

And as the newe abaysed nyghtyngale,   *just startled*
That stynteth first whan she bygynneth to synge,   *ceases suddenly*
1235 Whan that she hereth any herde tale,   *any shepherd speak*

1215 Cf. 2. 651 and n.
1215–18 Cf. 1. 637.
1228 Cf. 2. 361 and n.
1231 encircles and twines about

157

Or in the hegges any wyght stirynge,   *hedges, person*
And after siker doth hire vois out rynge,   *afterwards confident again*
Right so Criseyde, whan hire drede stente,   *stopped*
Opned hire herte, and tolde hym hire entente.

1240 And right as he that seth his °deth yshapen,   *sees*
And dyen mot, °in ought that he may gesse,   *must*
And sodeynly rescous doth hym escapen,   *rescue, enables him to*
And from his deth is brought in sykernesse,   *(he) is, into security*
For al this world, in swych present gladnesse   *similar*
1245 Was Troilus, and hath his lady swete.
With worse hap God lat us nevere mete!   *fortune*

Hire armes smale, hire streghte bak and softe,
Hire sydes longe, flesshly, smothe, and white
He gan to stroke, and °good thrift bad ful ofte   *fortune*
1250 Hire snowisshe throte, hire brestes rounde and lite.   *small*
°Thus in this hevene he gan hym to delite,
And therwithal a thousand tyme hire kiste,
That what to don, for joie unnethe he wiste.   *hardly, knew*

Than seyde he thus, °"O Love, O Charite!
1255 Thi moder ek, Citherea the swete,   *Venus*
After thiself next heried be she,   *praised*
Venus mene I, the wel-willy planete!   *mean, beneficent*
And next that, °Imeneus, I the grete;   *salute*
For nevere man was to yow goddes holde   *beholden*
1260 As I, which ye han brought fro cares colde.

1240 death shaped (by destiny)
1241 so far as he can see (guess)
1249-50 many a blessing he invoked on her snowy throat and her small, round breasts
1251 Cf. 3. 1204.
1254ff. Ch is here drawing on Boethius, *CP* 3. prose 11, 170ff.
1258 Hymen (god of marriage)

°"Benigne Love, thow holy bond of thynges,
Whoso wol grace, and °list the nought honouren,   *will (have)*
Lo, his desir wol fle withouten wynges.   *fly*
For noldestow of bownte hem socouren   *if you would not, aid*
1265 °That serven best and most alwey labouren,   *must*
Yet were al lost, that dar I wel seyn certes,
But if thi grace passed oure desertes.   *unless, exceeded*

°"And for thow me, that leest koude disserve   *inasmuch as*
Of hem that noumbred ben unto thi grace,   *accounted are in*
1270 Hast holpen, ther I likly was to sterve,   *helped, where*
And me bistowed in so heigh a place
That thilke boundes may no blisse pace,   *those same, pass*
I kan namore; but laude and reverence   *praise*
Be to thy bounte and thyn excellence!"

1275 And therwithal Criseyde anon he kiste,   *kissed*
Of which certein she felte no disese.
And thus seyde he, "Now wolde God I wiste,   *knew*
Myn herte swete, how I yow myght plese!
What man," quod he, "was evere thus at ese
1280 As I, on which the faireste and the beste
That evere I say, °deyneth hire herte reste?   *saw*

"Here may men seen that mercy passeth right;   *exceeds*
Th'experience of that is felt in me,   *proof*
That am unworthi to so swete a wight.   *person*
1285 But herte myn, of youre benignite,
So thynketh, though that I unworthi be,

1261ff. Ch draws in T's speech here on Dante, *Para.* 33. 13–18.
1262 is not pleased to honor you
1265 "That serven, etc." complements "hem."
1268-73 This is one thought, five and a half lines long in expression, culminating in "I kan namore."
1281 condescends to rest her heart

Yet mot I nede amenden in som wyse,   *must*
Right thorugh °the vertu of youre heigh servyse.

"And for the love of God, my lady deere,
1290 Syn God hath wrought me °for I shall yow serve,—
As thus I mene, he wol ye be my steere,   *will (that), pilot*
To do me lyve, if that yow liste, or sterve,—   *cause, die*
So techeth me how that I may disserve
Youre thonk, so that I thorugh myn ignoraunce,
1295 Ne do no thing that yow be displesaunce.   *(to) you (may)*

"For certes, fresshe wommanliche wif,   *woman*
This dar I seye, that trouth and diligence,
That shal ye fynden in me al my lif;
N'y wol nat, certein, °breken youre defence;   *I will not*
1300 And if I do, present or in absence,
For love of God, °lat sle me with the dede,
If that it like unto youre wommanhede."   *that should be pleasing*

"Iwys," quod she, "myn owen hertes list,   *pleasure*
My ground of ese, and al myn herte deere,
1305 Gramercy, for on that is al my trist!   *trust*
But lat us falle awey fro this matere,
For it suffiseth, this that seyd is heere,   *suffices*
And at o word, withouten repentaunce,   *regrets*
Welcome, my knyght, my pees, my suffisaunce!"   *peace*

1310 Of hire delit, or joies oon the leeste,   *the least of their joys*
Were impossible to my wit to seye;
But juggeth ye that han ben at the °feste   *feast*

1288 the powerful effects of being in your exalted service
1290 for (the purpose that)
1299 do what you forbid
1301 let me be slain in that very instant
1312 Cf. 3. 1228 and 2. 361 and n.

Of swich gladnesse, if that hem liste pleye!   *it pleased them, play*
I kan namore, but thus thise ilke tweye,
1315 That nyght, bitwixen drede and sikernesse,   *doubt and security*
Felten in love the grete worthynesse.

O blisful nyght, of hem so longe isought,
How blithe unto hem bothe two thow weere!
Why nad I swich oon with my soule ybought,   *had I not*
1320 Ye, or the leeste joie that was theere?
Awey, thow foule °daunger and thow feere,   *haughtiness, fear*
And lat hem in this hevene blisse dwelle,
That is so heigh that al ne kan I telle!

But soth is, though I kan nat tellen al,
1325 As kan myn auctour, of his excellence,   *(out) of*
Yet have I seyd, and God toforn, and shal   *in God's sight*
In every thyng the grete of his sentence;   *essential*
And if that ich, at Loves reverence,
Have any word in eched for the beste,   *added*
1330 Doth therwithal right as youreselven leste.   *it pleases you*

For myne wordes, heere and every part,   *where*
I speke hem alle under correccioun
Of yow that felyng han in loves art,   *feeling have*
And putte it al in youre discrecioun   *judgment*
1335 T'encresse or maken dymynucioun
Of my langage, and that I yow biseche.
But now to purpos of my rather speche.   *earlier*

Thise ilke two, that ben in armes laft,   *left*
°So loth to hem asonder gon it were,   *to go asunder*
1340 That ech from other wenden ben biraft,   *from the other felt taken away*

1321 See 2. 384 and n.
1339-40 The expanded sense would be roughly "so loath were they to separate that even the thought of it made them feel bereft of each other."

Or elles, lo, this was hir mooste feere,   *greatest*
That al this thyng but nyce dremes were;   *fond dreams*
For which ful ofte ech of hem seyde, "O swete,
Clippe ich yow thus, or elles I it meete?"   *embrace, do I dream it*

1345 And Lord! so he gan goodly on hire se,
That nevere his look ne bleynte from hire face,   *turned away*
And seyde, "O deere herte, may it be
That it be soth, that ye ben in this place?"   *true*
"Yee, herte myn, God thank I of his grace,"
1350 Quod tho Criseyde, and therwithal hym kiste,   *kissed*
That where his spirit was, for joie he nyste.   *did not know*

This Troilus ful ofte hire eyen two
Gan for to kisse, and seyde, "O eyen clere,
It weren ye that wroughte me swich wo,
1355 Ye humble nettes of my lady deere!   *nets*
Though ther be mercy writen in youre cheere,   *countenance*
God woot, the text ful hard is, soth, to fynde!   *knows*
How koude ye withouten bond me bynde?"

Therwith he gan hire faste in armes take,
1360 And wel an hondred tymes gan he syke,   *sigh*
Naught swiche sorwfull sikes as men make
For wo, or elles when that folk ben sike,   *sick*
But esy sykes, swiche as ben to like,   *to be liked*
That shewed his affeccioun withinne;
1365 Of swiche sikes koude he nought bilynne.   *cease*

Soone after this they spake of sondry thynges,
As fel to purpos of this aventure,   *were related to*
And pleyinge entrechaungeden hire rynges,
Of which I kan nought tellen no °scripture;   *inscription*

1369 The inscriptions were engraved on the outside of the shanks of rings.

1370 But wel I woot, a broche, gold and °asure,
In which a ruby set was lik an herte,
Criseyde hym yaf, and stak it on his sherte. *gave, shirt*

Lord, trowe ye a coveytous or a wrecche, *do you imagine, miser*
That blameth love, and halt of it despit,
1375 That of tho pens that he kan mokre and crecche *board and grab*
Was evere yit yyeven hym swich delit *given (to)*
As is in love, in o poynt, in som plit? *one, situation*
Nay, douteles, for also God me save,
So perfit joie may no nygard have.

1380 They wol seyn "yis," but Lord! so that they lye, *how*
Tho besy wrecches, ful of wo and drede! *anxious*
Thei callen love a woodnesse or folie, *madness*
But it shall falle hem as I shal yow rede; *befall*
They shal forgon the white and ek the rede, *silver, gold*
1385 And lyve in wo, ther God yeve hem meschaunce,
And every lovere in his trouthe avaunce!

As wolde God tho wrecches that dispise *those*
Servise of love hadde erys also longe *ears, as*
As hadde Mida, ful of coveytise, *Midas*
1390 And therto dronken hadde as hoot and stronge *hot*
As °Crassus dide for his affectis wronge, *desires*
To techen hem that coveytise is vice, *teach*
And love is vertu, though men holde it nyce. *foolish*

Thise ilke two, of whom that I yow seye, *same*
1395 Whan that hire hertes wel assured were,
Tho gonne they to speken and to pleye, *then*
And ek rehercen how, and whan, and where

1370 lapis lazuli, probably, though possibly blue enamel
1391 Crassus was slain in battle by the king of Parthia and had molten gold poured
into his mouth because in life he had been so greedy for wealth.

Thei knewe hem first, and every wo and feere   *each other*
That passed was; but al swich hevynesse,
1400 I thank it God, was torned to gladnesse.

And evere mo, when that hem fel to speke   *they happened*
Of any wo of swich a tyme agoon,   *passed*
With kissyng al that tale sholde breke,   *be interrupted*
And fallen in a newe joye anoon;   *(they would) fall*
1405 And diden al hire myght, syn they were oon,
For to recoveren blisse and ben at eise,   *ease*
And passed wo with joie contrepeise.   *past, counterbalance*

Resoun wol nought that I speke of slep,
For it acordeth nought to my matere.
1410 God woot, they °took of that ful litel kep!
°But lest this nyght, that was to hem so deere,
Ne sholde in veyn escape in no manere,
It was byset in joie and bisynesse   *employed*
Of al that souneth into gentilesse.   *conduces to*

1415 But whan the cok, comune astrologer,   *rooster*
Gan on his brest to bete and after crowe,   *beat*
And °Lucyfer, the dayes messager,
Gan for to rise, and out hire bemes throwe,
And estward roos, to hym that koude it knowe,
1420 °*Fortuna Major*, °that anoon Criseyde,
With herte soor, to Troilus thus seyde:

1410 paid little attention to that
1411 "lest ... ne ... no": so that ... not ... any
1417 the morning star (the planet Venus)
1420 *Fortuna Major* is a designation (probably) for Jupiter, but the allusion is supposed to be to a group of six stars in the constellations Aquarius and Pegasus; see also *Purg.* 19.4–7.
1420 an elliptical construction—"it was then that"

°"Myn hertes lif, my trist, and my plesaunce,   *trust*

That I was born, allas, what me is wo,   *what woe is it to me*

That day of us moot make disseveraunce!

1425 For tyme it is to ryse and hennes go,

Or ellis I am lost for evere mo!

O nyght, allas! why nyltow over us hove,   *hover*

As longe as whan °Almena lay by Jove?

"O blake nyght, as folk in bokes rede,   *books*

1430 That shapen art by God this world to hide

At certeyn tymes wyth thi derke wede,   *cloak*

That under that men myghte in reste abide,

Wel oughten bestes pleyne, and folk the chide,   *beasts*

That there as day wyth labour wolde us breste,   *overcome*

1435 That thow thus fleest, and deynest us nought reste.   *flee, grant*

"Thow doost, allas, to shortly thyn office,   *duty*

Thow rakle nyght, °ther God, maker of kynde,   *hasty, Nature*

The, for thyn haste and thyn unkynde vice,

So faste ay to oure hemysperie bynde,   *tightly*

1440 That nevere more under the ground thow wynde!   *revolve*

For now, for thow so hiest out of Troie,   *hasten*

Have I forgon thus hastili my joie!"   *lost*

This Troilus, that with tho wordes °felte,

As thoughte hym tho, for pietous distresse,   *seemed (to), piteous*

1445 The blody teris from his herte melte,   *tears*

As he that nevere yet swich hevynesse

Assayed hadde, out of so gret gladnesse,   *experienced*

1422-8 This and the following stanzas represent the *aube* or *aubade* (Provençal *alba*) or dawn song, in which lovers lament the coming of day when they must part.

1428 Alcmena was the mother of Hercules by Jove; the night of their intercourse was three times longer than normal.

1437 introducing a curse—"wherefore God, etc."

1443 Construe as governing the infinitive phrase "(to) melt" in line 1445.

Gan therwithal Criseyde, his lady deere,
In armes streyne, and seyde in this manere: *embrace*

1450 "O cruel day, accusour of the joie   *betrayer*
That nyght and love han stole and faste iwryen,   *hidden*
Acorsed be thi comyng into Troye,   *cursed*
For every bore hath oon of thi bryghte yën!   *chink, eyes*
Envyous day, what list the so to spien?   *why does it please*
1455 What hastow lost, why sekestow this place?
°Ther God thi light so quenche, for his grace!

"Allas! what have thise loveris the agylt,   *how, offended*
Dispitous day? Thyn be the peyne of helle!   *(let) thine be*
For many a lovere hastow slayn, and wilt;
1460 Thy pourynge in wol nowher lat hem dwelle.
What profrestow thi light here for to selle?   *why do you offer*
Go selle it hem °that smale selys grave;
We wol the nought, us nedeth no day have."

And ek the sonne, °Titan, gan he chide,
1465 And seyde, "O fool, wel may men the dispise,
That hast the Dawyng al nyght by thi syde,   *Dawn (Aurora, the dawn)*
And suffrest hire so soone up fro the rise,
For to disese loveris in this wyse.   *in order to*
What! holde youre bed ther, thow, and ek thi Morwe!   *Morwe (Aurora)*
1470 I bidde God, so yeve yow bothe sorwe!"   *pray*

Therwith ful soore he syghte, and thus he seyde: *sighed*
"My lady right, and of my wele or wo
The welle and roote, O goodly myn, Criseyde,
And shal I rise, allas, and shal I so?
1475 Now fele I that myn herte moot a-two.   *must (break)*

1456 Cf. 3. 1437 and n.
1462 who engrave small seals and therefore need a good light
1464 the sun, confused with Tithonus, the husband of Aurora, the dawn

For how sholde I my lif an houre save,
Syn that with yow is al the lyf ich have?

"What shal I don? For, certes, I not how,   *do not know*
Ne whan, allas! I shal the tyme see
1480 That in this plit I may ben eft with yow.   *situation*
And of my lif, God woot how that shal be,   *knows*
Syn that desir right now so biteth me,   *bites*
That I am ded anon, but I retourne.   *unless*
How sholde I longe, allas, fro yow sojourne?

1485 "But natheles, myn owen lady bright,
Yit were it so that I wiste outrely   *knew completely*
That I, youre humble servant and youre knyght,
Were in youre herte iset as fermely   *fixed as firmly*
As ye in myn, the which thyng, trewely,
1490 Me levere were than °thise worldes tweyne,   *preferable*
Yet sholde I bet enduren al my peyne."   *better*

To that Criseyde answerde right anon,
And with a sik she seyde, "O herte deere,   *sigh*
The game, ywys, so ferforth now is gon,   *so far advanced is now*
1495 That first shal Phebus fallen fro his spere,   *sphere*
And everich egle ben the dowves feere,   *eagle, companion*
And everi roche out of his place sterte,   *rock*
Er Troilus out of Criseydes herte.

"Ye ben so depe in-with myn herte grave,   *engraved*
1500 That, though I wolde it torne out of my thought,
As wisly verray God my soule save,   *certainly*
°To dyen in the peyne, I koude nought.
And, for the love of God that us hath wrought,

_____

1490 two worlds such as this one
1502 even if I were tortured to death, I could not erase you from my heart

Lat in youre brayn non other fantasie
1505 So crepe, that it cause me to dye!   *creep*

"And that ye me wolde han as faste in mynde
As I have yow, that wolde I yow biseche;
°And if I wiste sothly that to fynde,
God myghte nought a poynt my joies eche.   *increase*
1510 But herte myn, withouten more speche,
Beth to me trewe, or ellis were it routhe;   *a shame*
For I am thyn, by God and by my trouthe!

"Beth glad, forthy, and lyve in sikernesse!   *therefore, certainty*
Thus seyde I nevere er this, ne shal to mo;   *any others*
1515 And if to yow it were a gret gladnesse
To torne ayeyn soone after that ye go,   *return*
As fayn wolde I as ye that it were so,   *gladly*
As wisly God myn herte brynge at reste!"   *certainly*
And hym in armes tok, and ofte keste.   *kissed*

1520 Agayns his wil, sith it mot nedes be,   *must*
This Troilus up ros, and faste hym cledde,   *dressed*
And in his armes took his lady °free   *noble*
An hondred tyme, and on his wey hym spedde;   *hundred*
And with swiche voys as though his herte bledde,
1525 He seyde, "Farewel, dere herte swete,
Ther God us graunte sownde and soone to mete!"   *health, meet again*

To which no word for sorwe she answerde,
So soore gan his partyng hire distreyne;   *distress*
And Troilus unto his paleys ferde,   *went*
1530 As wo-bygon as she was, soth to seyne.   *truth*
So harde hym wrong °of sharp desir the peyne,   *wrung*

1508 and if I could be sure that I would find that to be true
1522 Cf. 2. 161 and n.
1531 the pain of sharp desire to be again there where he had been, etc.

For to ben eft there he was in plesaunce,
That it may nevere out of his remembraunce. *memory*

Retorned to his real paleys soone, *royal*
1535 He softe into his bed gan for to slynke, *creep*
To slepe longe, as he was wont to doone. *accustomed*
But al for nought; he may wel ligge and wynke, *lie, close his eyes*
But slep ne may ther in his herte synke,
Thynkyng how she, for whom desir hym brende, *burned*
1540 A thousand fold was worth more than he wende. *supposed*

And in his thought gan up and down to wynde *revolve*
Hire wordes alle, and every countenaunce, *look*
And fermely impressen in his mynde
The leeste point that to him was plesaunce; *least*
1545 And verraylich, of thilke remembraunce, *truly*
Desir al newe hym brende, and lust to brede *burned, desire, grow*
Gan more than erst, and yet °took he non hede. *before*

Criseyde also, right in the same wyse, *manner*
Of Troilus gan in hire herte shette *enclose (to preserve)*
1550 His worthynesse, his lust, his dedes wise, *energy, deeds*
His gentilesse, and how she with hym mette,
Thonkynge Love he so wel hire bisette; *laid siege to her*
Desirying eft to han hire herte deere *again*
In swich a plit, °she dorste make hym cheere. *situation*

1555 Pandare, o-morwe which that comen was *who in the morning had come*
Unto his nece and gan hire faire grete,
Seyde, "Al this nyght so reyned it, allas, *rained*
That al my drede is that ye, nece swete,
Han litel laiser had to slepe and mete. *leisure, dream*

1547 he remained oblivious
1554 (where) she dared

1560 Al nyght," quod he "hath reyn so do me wake,   *caused me (to)*
That som of us, I trowe, hire hedes ake."   *ache*

And ner he come, and seyde, "How stant it now   *near, stands*
This mury morwe? Nece, how kan ye fare?"   *merry*
Criseyde answerde, "Nevere the bet for yow,   *better*
1565 Fox that ye ben! God yeve youre herte kare!   *anxiety*
God help me so, ye caused al this fare,   *all this business*
Trowe I," quod she, "for al youre °wordes white.   *specious words*
O, whoso seeth yow, knoweth yow ful lite."   *little*

With that she gan hire face for to wrye   *cover*
1570 With the shete, and wax for shame al reed;
And Pandarus gan under for to prie,   *peek*
And seyde, "Nece, if that I shal be ded,   *dead*
Have here a swerd and smyteth of myn hed!"   *head*
With that his arm al sodeynly he thriste   *thrust*
1575 Under hire nekke, and at the laste hire kyste.   *kissed*

°I passe al that which chargeth nought to seye.
What! °God foryaf his deth, and she al so
Foryaf, and with here uncle gan to pleye,
For other cause was ther noon than so.
1580 But of this thing right to the effect to go,   *essential point*
Whan tyme was, hom to here hous she wente,
And Pandarus hath fully his entente.

Now torne we ayeyn to Troilus,   *return we*
That resteles ful longe abedde lay,
1585 And pryvely sente after Pandarus,
To hym to com in al the haste he may.
He com anon, nought ones seyde he nay;   *once*

1567 Cf. 3. 901.
1576 I skip over all that which is not important to say
1577 God forgave those responsible for his crucifixion

And Troilus ful sobrely he grette,   *greeted*
And down upon his beddes syde hym sette.

1590 This Troilus, with al th'affeccioun
Of frendes love that herte may devyse,   *conceive*
To Pandarus on knowes fil adown,   *knees fell*
And er that he wolde of the place arise,
He gan hym thonken in his beste wise   *manner*
1595 An hondred sythe, and gan the tyme blesse   *times*
That he was born, to brynge hym fro destresse.   *he (Pandarus)*

He seyde, "O frend of frendes the alderbeste   *very best*
That evere was, the sothe for to telle,   *truth*
Thow hast in hevene ybrought my soule at reste
1600 Fro °Flegetoun, the fery flood of helle;   *fiery*
That, though I myght a thousand tymes selle,
Upon a day, my lif in thi servise,
It myghte naught a moote in that suffise.   *particle*

"The sonne, which that al the world may se,
1605 Saugh nevere yet my lif, that dar I leye,   *in my life, wager*
So inly fair and goodly as is she,
Whos I am al, and shal, tyl that I deye.
And that I thus am hires, dar I seye,
That thanked be the heighe worthynesse
1610 Of Love, and ek thi kynde bysynesse.

"Thus hastow me no litel thing yyive,   *given*
For which to the obliged be for ay   *forever*
My lif, and whi? For thorugh thyn help I lyve,
Or elles ded hadde I ben many a day."   *dead*
1615 And with that word down in his bed he lay,
And Pandarus ful sobrely hym herde
Til al was seyd, and than he thus answerde:

1600 Phlegethon, the fiery river of Hades (See *Aen.* 6. 550–1 and *Inf.* 12. 47ff.)

"My deere frend, if I have don for the   *served you*
In any cas, God wot, it is me lief;   *knows, gratifying*
1620 And am as glad as man may of it be,
God help me so; but tak it nat a-grief   *do not take it wrongly*
That I shal seyn, be war of this meschief,   *possible misfortune*
That, there as thow now brought art in thy blisse,   *whereas*
That thow thiself ne cause it nat to misse.   *be lost*

1625 °"For of fortunes sharpe adversitee
The worste kynde of infortune is this,
A man to han ben in prosperitee,
And it remembren, whan it passed is.
Th'art wis ynough, forthi do nat amys: *you are, therefore*
1630 Be naught to rakel, theigh thow sitte warme;   *too rash, though*
For if thow be, certeyn, it wol the harme.

"Thow art at ese, and hold the wel therinne;   *ease*
For also seur as reed is every fir,   *sure, red*
As gret a craft is kepe wel as wynne.   *skill, is (it) win*
1635 Bridle alwey wel thi speche and thi desir,
For worldly joie halt nought but by a wir.   *wire*
°That preveth wel it brest alday so ofte;
°Forthi nede is to werken with it softe."   *work, carefully*

Quod Troilus, "I hope, and God toforn,   *as my help*
1640 My deere frend, that I shal so me beere,   *conduct*
That in my gylt ther shal nothyng be lorn,   *through my fault, lost*
°N'y nyl nought rakle as for to greven heere.
It nedeth naught this matere ofte stere;   *urge*
For wystestow myn herte wel, Pandare,   *if you knew*
1645 God woot, of this thow woldest litel care."   *knows*

1625-8 Cf. Boethius, *CP* 2. prose 4, 5-9 and Dante, *Inf.* 5. 121-3.
1637 the fact that it constantly falls apart certainly proves as much
1638 hence it is necessary
1642 I will not act rashly so as to annoy her

Tho gan he telle hym of his glade nyght,
And wherof first his herte dred, and how,   *felt dread*
And seyde, "Frend, as I am trewe knyght,
And by that feyth I shal to God and yow,   *owe*
1650 I hadde it nevere half so hote as now;   *hot*
And ay the more that desir me biteth   *bites*
To love hire best, the more it me deliteth.

"I not myself naught wisly what it is;   *I do not know myself for sure*
But now I feele a newe qualitee,
1655 Yee, al another than I dide er this."
Pandare answerd, and seyde thus, that he
That ones may in hevene blisse be,—   *once*
"He feleth other weyes, dar I leye,   *wager*
Than thilke tyme he first herde of it seye."   *at that time*

1660 This is o word for al; this Troilus   *This is it in a nutshell*
Was nevere ful to speke of this matere,   *satiated*
And for to preisen unto Pandarus   *praise*
The bounte of his righte lady deere,
And Pandarus to thanke and maken cheere.   *be pleasant (to)*
1665 This tale was ay span-newe to bygynne,   *brand-new*
Til that the nyght °departed hem atwynne.

Soon after this, for that Fortune it wolde,   *would have it happen*
Icomen was the blisful tyme swete
That Troilus was warned that he sholde,
1670 There he was erst, Criseyde his lady mete;   *before, meet*
For which he felte his herte in joie flete,   *swim*
And feithfully gan alle the goddes herie;   *praise*
And lat se now if that he kan be merie!

1666 departed them each his own separate way

°And holden was the forme and al the wise
1675 Of hire commyng, and ek of his also,
    As it was erst, which nedeth nought devyse. *go into again*
    But pleynly to th'effect right for to go, *essential*
    In joie and suerte Pandarus hem two *security*
    Abedde brought, whan that hem bothe leste, *it pleased them both*
1680 And thus they ben in quyete and in reste. *quiet*

    Nought nedeth it to yow, syn they ben met, *since*
    To axe at me if that they blithe were; *ask*
    For if it erst was wel, tho was it bet *earlier, better*
    A thousand fold; this nedeth nought enquere. *inquire about*
1685 Agon was every sorwe and every feere; *gone*
    And bothe, ywys, they hadde, and so they wende, *thought*
    As muche joie as herte may comprende. *contain*

    This is no litel thyng of for to seye; *to talk about*
    This passeth every wit for to devyse; *exceeds, express*
1690 For eche of hem gan otheres lust obeye. *wish*
    Felicite, which that thise clerkes wise
    Comenden so, ne may nought here suffise; *commend*
    This joie may nought writen be with inke;
    This passeth al that herte may bythynke.

1695 But cruel day, so wailaway the stounde! *alas the time*
    Gan for t'aproche, as they by sygnes knewe; *signs*
    For which hem thoughte feelen dethis wownde. *they thought they felt*
    So wo was hem that changen gan hire hewe, *countenances*
    And day they gonnen to despise al newe, *did despise*
1700 Callyng it traitour, envyous, and worse,
    And bitterly the dayes light thei corse.

    Quod Troilus, "Allas, now am I war *aware*
    That °Pirous and tho swifte steedes thre, *those*

1674–6 Construe "and holden" with "as it was . . . ."
1703 Pyroïs, one of the four horses of the sun (Ovid names them at *Metam.* 2. 153–4)

174

Which that drawen forth the sonnes char, *chariot*
1705 °Han gon som bi-path in dispit of me;
That maketh it so soone day to be;
And, for the sonne hym hasteth thus to rise, *because*
Ne shal I nevere don him sacrifise."

But nedes day departe hem moste soone, *needs must day separate them*
1710 And whan hire speche don was and hire cheere, *mutual joy*
They twynne anon, as they were wont to doone, *separate*
And setten tyme of metyng eft yfeere. *meeting, again together*
And many a nyght they wroughte in this manere, *arranged*
And thus Fortune a tyme ledde in joie
1715 Criseyde, and ek this kynges sone of Troie.

In suffisaunce, in blisse, and in singynges,
This Troilus gan al his lif to lede. *lead*
He spendeth, jousteth, maketh festeynges; *festivities*
He yeveth frely ofte, and chaungeth wede, *gives, clothes*
1720 And held aboute hym alwey, out of drede, *without doubt*
A world of folk, as com hym wel of kynde, *was quite natural for him*
The fresshest and the beste he koude fynde;

That swich a vois was of hym and a stevene *fame*
Thorughout the world, of honour and largesse,
1725 That it up rong unto the yate of hevene. *gate*
And, as in love, he was in swich gladnesse,
That in his herte he demed, as I gesse, *judged*
That ther nys lovere in this world at ese *is not*
So wel as he; and thus gan love hym plese.

1730 The goodlihede or beaute which that kynde *excellence, Nature*
In any other lady hadde yset
°Kan nought the montance of a knotte unbynde,

1705 have taken a shortcut to spite me
1732-3 can not the extent of a single knot of C's whole net unbind from around his heart

Aboute his herte, of al Criseydes net.
He was so narwe ymasked and yknet,   *closely enmeshed and knit up*
1735 That it undon on any manere syde,—   *to undo in any way*
That nyl naught ben, °for aught that may bitide.

And by the hond ful ofte he wolde take
This Pandarus, and into gardyn lede,   *lead (him)*
°And swich a feste and swich a proces make
1740 Hym of Criseyde, and of hire womanhede,
And of hire beaute, that, withouten drede,   *doubt*
It was an hevene his wordes for to here;
And thanne he wolde synge in this manere:

°"Love, that of erthe and se hath governaunce,
1745 Love, that his hestes hath in hevenes hye,   *commands*
Love, that with an holsom alliaunce
Halt peples joyned, °as hym lest hem gye,   *holds*
Love, that knetteth lawe of compaignie,   *knits up, companionship*
And couples doth in vertu for to dwelle,   *causes*
1750 Bynd this acord, that I have told and telle.

"That that the world with feith, which that is stable,   *the fact that*
°Diverseth so his stowndes concordynge,
That elementz that ben so discordable   *(so) that*
Holden a bond perpetuely durynge,   *enduring*
1755 That Phebus mote his rosy day forth brynge,   *the fact that, may*
And that the mone hath lordshipe over the nyghtes,—
Al this doth Love, ay heried be his myghtes!   *causes, praised*

1736 no matter what may happen
1739–40 and he would talk so much ("swich a proces make") and make such a celebration of C to him
1744ff. Ch in this and the following three stanzas is drawing on Boethius, *CP* 2. meter 8.
1747 it pleases him to guide them
1752 so varies its harmonious seasons (i.e., varies its seasons harmoniously)

"That that the se, that gredy is to flowen,   *the fact that, greedy*
Constreyneth to a certeyn ende so   *constrains*
1760 His flodes that so fiersly they ne growen   *floods*
To drenchen erthe and al for evere mo;   *drown*
And if that Love aught lete his bridel go,   *bridle*
Al that now loveth asondre sholde lepe,   *leap*
And lost were al that Love halt now to-hepe.   *together*

1765 "So wolde God, that auctour is of kynde,   *author, Nature*
°That with his bond Love of his vertu liste
To cerclen hertes alle, and faste bynde,
That from his bond no wight the wey out wiste;   *creature, know*
And hertes colde, hem wolde I that he twiste   *them, would constrain*
1770 To make hem love, and °that hem liste ay rewe
On hertes sore, and kepe hem that ben trewe!"–   *sorrowing, sustain*

In alle nedes, for the townes werre,   *war*
He was, and ay, the first in armes dyght,   *ever, the first one armed*
And certeynly, but if that bokes erre,   *unless*
1775 Save Ector most ydred of any wight;   *dreaded, man*
And this encres of hardynesse and myght   *increase*
Com hym of love, his ladies thank to wynne,   *came to him from*
That altered his spirit so withinne.

In tyme of trewe, °on haukyng wolde he ride,   *truce*
1780 Or elles honte boor, beer, or lyoun;   *hunt, bear, lion*
The smale bestes leet he gon biside.   *be disregarded*
And whan that he com ridyng into town,
Ful ofte his lady from hire wyndow down,
As fressh as faukoun comen out of muwe,   *falcon, mew (molting cage)*
1785 Ful redy was hym goodly to saluwe.   *greet*

1766-7 that Love by his power be pleased to circle with his bond all hearts
1770 (I would that he would make it) that it please them ever to have pity
1779 he would ride for the hunt with hawks

And moost of love and vertu was his speche,
And in despit hadde alle wrecchednesse;   *had (he), meanness*
And douteles, no nede was hym biseche
To honouren hem that hadde worthynesse,
1790 And esen hem that weren in destresse.
And glad was he if any wyght wel ferde,   *person, fared*
That lovere was, whan he it wiste or herde.   *knew*

For, soth to seyne, he °lost held every wyght,   *truth, say*
But if he were in Loves heigh servise,—   *unless*
1795 I mene folk that oughte it ben of right.   *ought rightfully to be in it*
And over al this, so wel koude he devyse   *compose*
Of sentement, and in so unkouth wise,   *from, marvelous a manner*
Al his array, that every lovere thoughte   *complete behavior*
That al was wel, what so he seyde or wroughte.

1800 And though that he be come of blood roial,
°Hym liste of pride at no wight for to chace;
Benigne he was to ech in general,
For which he gat hym thank in every place.   *received gratitude*
Thus wolde Love, yheried be his grace,   *praised*
1805 That pride, envye, and ire, and avarice
He gan to fle, and everich other vice.   *flee*

Thow lady bryght, the doughter to Dyone,   *Venus*
Thy blynde and wynged sone ek, daun Cupide,   *lord Cupid*
Yee sustren nyne ek, that by Elicone   *sisters (i.e., the Muses)*
1810 In hil Pernaso listen for t'abide,   *Mount Parnassus, are pleased*
That ye thus fer han deyned me to gyde,   *condescended to guide me*
I kan namore, but syn that ye wol wende,   *can no more (say), depart*
Ye heried ben for ay withouten ende!   *may you be praised forever*

1793 considered everyone lost
1801 it pleased him to accost no one pridefully

Thorugh yow have I seyd fully in my song
1815 Th'effect and joie of Troilus servise,   *the essential part*
     Al be that ther was som disese among,   *unhappiness all the while*
     As to myn auctour listeth to devise.   *has been pleasing to compose*
     My thridde bok now ende ich in this wyse,   *third*
     And Troilus in luste and in quiete   *pleasure*
1820 Is with Criseyde, his owen herte swete.

BOOK FOUR

But al to litel, weylaway the whyle,   *alas*
Lasteth swich joie, ythonked be Fortune,   *thanks be to*
That semeth trewest whan she wol bygyle,   *beguile*
And kan to fooles so hire song entune,
5 That she hem hent and blent, traitour comune!   *catches and blinds*
And whan a wight is from hire whiel ythrowe,   *person, wheel*
Than laugheth she, and maketh hym the mowe.   *makes a face at him*

From Troilus she gan hire brighte face
Awey to writhe, and tok of hym non heede,   *turn*
10 But caste hym clene out of his lady grace,
And on hire whiel she sette up Diomede;
For which right now myn herte gynneth blede,   *bleed*
And now my penne, allas! with which I write,
Quaketh for drede of that I moste endite.   *dread, report*

15 For how Criseyde Troilus forsook,
Or at the leeste, how that she was unkynde,   *least*
Moot hennesforth ben matere of my book,   *must*
As writen folk thorugh which it is in mynde.
Allas! that they sholde evere cause fynde
20 To speke hire harm, and if they on hire lye,   *lie*
Iwis, hemself sholde han the vilanye.   *indeed, reproach*

O ye Herynes, Nyghtes doughtren thre,   *Furies, daughters*
That endeles compleignen evere in pyne,   *complain, sorrow*
Megera, Alete, and ek Thesiphone;
25 Thow cruel Mars ek, fader to °Quyryne,

---

25 another name for Romulus who, like Remus, was a son of Mars (Ovid, *Fasti* 2. 419, 476)

This ilke ferthe book me helpeth fyne, *conclude*
So that the losse of lyf and love yfeere *together*
Of Troilus be fully shewed heere.

Liggyng in oost, as I have seyd er this, *lying in a host, as an army*
30 The Grekys stronge aboute Troie town,
Byfel that, whan that Phebus shynyng is
Upon the brest of Hercules °lyoun,
That Ector, with ful many a bold baroun,
Caste on a day with Grekes for to fighte, *resolved*
35 As he was wont, to greve hem what he myghte. *grieve*

Not I how longe or short it was bitwene *I do not know*
This purpos and that day they fighten mente; *meant to fight*
But on a day wel armed, brighte and shene, *shining*
Ector and many a worthi wight out wente, *individual*
40 With spere in honde and bigge bowes bente;
And in the berd, withouten lenger lette, *face to face, delay*
Hire fomen in the feld anon hem mette. *foes*

The longe day, with speres sharpe igrounde,
With arwes, dartes, swerdes, maces felle, *terrible*
45 They fighte and bringen hors and man to grounde,
And with hire axes out the braynes quelle. *dash*
But in the laste shour, soth for to telle, *attack, truth*
The folk of Troie °hemselven so mysledden
That with the wors at nyght homward they fledden.

50 At whiche day was taken Antenore,
Maugre Polydamas or Monesteo, *in spite of*
Santippe, Sarpedon, Polynestore,

---

32 Since one of the labors of Hercules was the killing of the Nemaean lion, the lion was a symbol of the hero. The sun was in the sign Leo in late July and early August. The purpose is to indicate the time of the year.
48 conducted themselves so badly

Polite, or ek the Trojan daun Rupheo,
And other lasse folk as Phebuseo;   *lesser*
55 So that, for harm, that day the folk of Troie
Dredden to lese a gret part of hire joie.   *feared*

Of Priamus was yeve, at Grekes requeste,   *by, given*
A tyme of trewe, and tho they gonnen trete,   *truce, negotiate*
Hire prisoners to chaungen, meste and leste,   *exchange, greatest*
60 And for the surplus yeven sommes grete.   *sums*
This thing anon was couth in every strete,   *announced*
Bothe in th'assege, in town and everywhere,   *in the besieging force*
And with the firste it com to Calkas ere.   *ear*

Whan Calkas knew this tretis sholde holde,   *treaty*
65 In consistorie, among the Grekes soone   *council*
He gan in thringe forth with lordes olde,   *press*
And sette hym there as he was wont to doone;
And °with a chaunged face hem bad a boone,   *requested, favor*
For love of God, to don that reverence,
70 To stynte noyse, and yeve hym audience.   *cease, give*

Than seyde he thus, "Lo, lordes myn, ich was
Troian, as it is knowen out of drede;   *doubt*
And, if that yow remembre, I am Calkas,
That alderfirst yaf comfort to youre nede,   *first of all*
75 And tolde wel how that ye shulden spede.   *should prosper*
For dredeles, thorugh yow shal in a stownde   *doubtless, moment*
Ben Troie ybrend, and beten down to grownde.   *burned*

"And in what forme, or in what manere wise,
This town to shende, and al youre lust t'acheve,   *destroy, pleasure*
80 Ye han er this wel herd me yow devyse.   *relate to you*
This knowe ye, my lordes, as I leve.   *believe*
And, for the Grekis weren me so leeve,   *because, so special to me*

---

68 The phrase usually connotes a change of color.

I com myself, in my propre persone,   *came, own*
To teche in this how yow was best to doone, *it was best for you*

85 "Havyng unto my tresor ne my rente   *income*
Right no resport, °to respect of youre ese.   *regard*
Thus al my good I lefte and to yow wente,
Wenyng in this yow, lordes, for to plese.   *expecting*
But al that los ne doth me no disese.   *regret*
90 I vouchesauf, as wisly have I joie,   *I am willing, certainly*
For yow to lese al that I have in Troie,   *lose*

"Save of a doughter that I lefte, allas!   *except for*
Slepyng at hom, whanne out of Troie I sterte. *departed*
O sterne, O cruel fader that I was!
95 How myghte I have in that so harde an herte?
Allas, °I ne hadde ibrought hire in hire sherte! *shirt*
For sorwe of which I wol nought lyve tomorwe,
But if ye lordes rewe upon my sorwe.   *unless, have pity*

"For, by that cause I say no tyme er now *because, saw*
100 Hire to delivere, ich holden have my pees;   *peace*
But now or nevere, if that it like yow,   *pleases*
I may hire have right soone, douteles.
O help and grace! amonges al this prees,   *throng*
Rewe on this olde caytyf in destresse,   *wretch*
105 Syn I thorugh yow have al this hevynesse.   *since*

"Ye have now kaught and fetered in prisoun
Troians ynowe; and if youre willes be,   *enough*
My child with oon may han redempcioun,
Now, for the love of God and of bounte,
110 °Oon of so fele, allas, so yive hym me!   *many*

---

86 in comparison with
96 that I did not bring
110 give me one of so many, alas, as an exchange (for my daughter)

What nede were it this preiere for to werne,   *deny*
Syn ye shul bothe han folk and town as yerne?   *very soon*

"On peril of my lif, I shal nat lye,
Appollo hath me told it feithfully;
115 I have ek founde it be astronomye,   *by astrology*
By sort, and by augurye ek, trewely,   *lots, divination*
And dar wel say, the tyme is faste by   *near at hand*
That fire and flaumbe on al the town shal sprede,
And thus shal Troie torne to asshen dede.   *dead*

120 "For certein, °Phebus and Neptunus bothe,
That makeden the walles of the town,
Ben with the folk of Troie alwey so wrothe,   *angry*
That they wol brynge it to confusioun,
Right in despit of kyng Lameadoun.
125 Bycause he nolde payen hem here hire,   *wages*
The town of Troie shal ben set on-fire."

Tellyng his tale alwey, this olde greye,   *gray(beard)*
Humble in his speche, and in his lokyng eke,   *countenance*
The salte teris from his eyen tweye   *tears*
130 Ful faste ronnen down by either cheke.
So longe he gan of socour hem biseke
That, for to hele hym of his sorwes soore,   *heal*
They yave hym Antenor, withouten moore.   *more (ado)*

But who was glad ynough but Calkas tho?
135 And of this thyng ful soone his nedes leyde   *(be) laid*
On °hem that sholden for the tretis go,

---

120 According to Benoît de Sainte-Maure (*Roman de Troye* 25, 921ff.) Neptune built the walls and Apollo dedicated them, but he merely says they were badly deceived. Ovid and others relate that when Neptune and Apollo were for a time condemned to serve Laomedon the latter refused them their wages.
136 them that should go for the truce (negotiations)

And hem for Antenor ful ofte preyde
To bryngen hom kyng °Toas and Criseyde.
And whan Priam his save-garde sente,   *safe-conduct*
140 Th'embassadours to Troie streight they wente.

The cause itold of hire comyng, the olde
Priam, the kyng, ful soone in general
Let her-upon his parlement to holde,   *to be held*
Of which th'effect rehercen yow I shal.   *essential*
145 Th'embassadours ben answered for fynal,   *finally*
Th'eschaunge of prisoners and al this nede   *everything necessary*
Hem liketh wel, and forth in they procede.   *pleases*

This Troilus was present in the place,
Whan axed was for Antenor Criseyde;
150 For which ful soone chaungen gan his face,
As he that with tho wordes wel neigh deyde.   *died*
But natheles he no word to it seyde,   *nevertheless*
Lest men sholde his affeccioun espye;   *discern*
With mannes herte he gan his sorwes drye,   *endure*

155 And ful of angwissh and of grisly drede
Abod what lordes wolde unto it seye;   *waited for*
And if they wolde graunte, as God forbede,
Th'eschaunge of hire, than thoughte he thynges tweye,   *then*
First, how to save hire honour, and what weye   *way*
160 He myghte best th'eschaunge of hire withstonde;
Ful faste he caste how al this myghte stonde.   *considered*

Love hym made al prest to don hire byde,   *ready, have her remain*
And rather dyen than she sholde go;
But resoun seyde hym, on that other syde,
165 "Withouten assent of hire ne do nat so,
Lest for thi werk she wolde be thy fo,   *work, foe*

---

138 Thoas was king of Calydon and with C was to be exchanged for Antenor.

And seyn that thorugh thy medlynge is iblowe   *rumored abroad*
°Youre bother love, ther it was erst unknowe."   *earlier*

For which he gan deliberen, for the beste,   *deliberate*
170 That though the lordes wolde that she wente,
He wolde lat hem graunte what hem leste,   *pleased them*
And telle his lady first what that they mente;
And whan that she hadde seyd hym hire entente,
Therafter wolde he werken also blyve,   *very quickly*
175 Theigh al the world ayeyn it wolde stryve.   *though*

Ector, which that wel the Grekis herde,
For Antenor how they wolde han Criseyde,
Gan it withstonde, and sobrely answerde:
"Syres, she nys no prisonere," he seyde;
180 "I not on yow who that this charge leyde,   *do not know*
But, on my part, ye may eftsone hem telle,   *immediately*
We usen here no wommen for to selle."

The noyse of peple up stirte thanne at ones,   *rose*
As breme as blase of straw iset on-fire;   *fierce*
185 For infortune it wolde, for the nones,   *ill fortune*
They sholden hire confusioun desire.   *ruin*
"Ector," quod they, "what goost may yow enspyre,   *spectre*
This womman thus to shilde, and don us leese   *shield, lose*
Daun Antenor—a wrong wey now ye chese—   *choose*

190 "That is so wys and ek so bold baroun?   *a baron*
And we han nede of folk, as men may se.
He is ek oon the grettest of this town.
O Ector, lat tho fantasies be!
O kyng Priam," quod they, "thus sygge we,   *declare*
195 That al oure vois is to forgon Criseyde."   *give up*
And to deliveren Antenor they preyde.

---

168 the love of you both

186

°O Juvenal, lord! trewe is thy sentence,
That litel wyten folk what is to yerne   *know, to be desired*
That they ne fynde in hire desire offence;   *(such) that*
200 For cloude of errour lat hem nat discerne   *lets*
What best is. And lo, here ensample as yerne: *very soon*
This folk desiren now deliveraunce
Of Antenor, that brought hem to meschaunce.   *disaster*

For he was after traitour to the town
205 Of Troye; allas, they quytte hym out to rathe!   *released him too soon*
O nyce world, lo, thy discrecioun!
Criseyde, which that nevere dide hem scathe,   *harm*
Shal now no lenger in hire blisse bathe;
But Antenor, he shal com hom to towne,
210 And she shal out; thus seyden here and howne.   *all and sundry*

For which delibered was by parlement,   *decided*
For Antenor to yelden out Criseyde,   *surrender*
And it pronounced by the president,
Altheigh that Ector "nay" ful ofte preyde.   *although*
215 And fynaly, what wight that it withseyde,   *whoever spoke against it*
It was for nought; it moste ben and sholde,   *must, would have to be*
For substaunce of the parlement it wolde.   *majority, wished*

Departed out of parlement echone,   *each one*
This Troilus, withouten wordes mo,
220 Unto his chambre spedde hym faste allone,
But if it were a man of his or two,   *unless*
The which he bad out faste for to go,
Bycause he wolde slepen, as he seyde,
And hastily upon his bed hym leyde.

---

197 See Juvenal's *Satires* 10. 2–4: "Few are able to distinguish true good from what is very different, separated by a cloud of error."

187

225 And as in wynter leves ben biraft,   *taken away*
    Ech after other, til the tree be bare,
    So that ther nys but bark and braunche ilaft,
    Lith Troilus, byraft of ech welfare,
    Ibounden in the blake bark of care,   *black*
230 Disposed wood out of his wit to breyde,   *mad, go suddenly*
    So sore hym sat the chaungynge of Criseyde.   *weighed upon him*

    He rist hym up, and every dore he shette   *rose, shut*
    And wyndow ek, and tho this sorwful man
    Upon his beddes syde adown hym sette,
235 Ful lik a ded ymage, pale and wan;   *dead*
    And in his brest the heped wo bygan   *heaped-up*
    Out breste, and he to werken in this wise   *behave*
    In his woodnesse, as I shal yow devyse.   *crazed state, relate*

    °Right as the wylde bole bygynneth sprynge,   *bull, lunge*
240 Now her, now ther, idarted to the herte,   *pierced with a dart*
    And of his deth roreth in compleynynge,
    Right so gan he aboute the chaumbre sterte,   *rush*
    Smytyng his brest ay with his fistes smerte;   *ever cruelly*
    His hed to the wal, his body to the grounde
245 Ful ofte he swapte, hymselven to confounde.   *struck*

    His eyen two, for piete of herte,   *compassion*
    Out stremeden as swifte welles tweye;   *streamed*
    The heighe sobbes of his sorwes smerte   *cruel*
    His speche hym refte; unnethes myghte he seye,   *took away, hardly*
250 "O deth, allas! why nyltow do me deye?
    Acorsed be that day which that Nature
    Shop me to ben a lyves creature!"   *living*

    But after, whan the furie and al the rage
    Which that his herte twiste and faste threste,   *wrung and pierced*

239ff. See, e.g., Virgil, *Aen*. 2. 222–4.

255 By lengthe of tyme somwhat gan aswage,   *to be assuaged*
    Upon his bed he leyde hym down to reste.
    But tho bygonne his teeris more out breste,   *began, burst*
    That wonder is the body may suffise   *be adequate*
    To half this wo, which that I yow devyse.   *to (bear), describe*

260 Than seyde he thus, "Fortune, allas the while!
    What have I don? What have I thus agylt?   *done wrong*
    How myghtestow for rowthe me bygile?   *pity*
    Is ther no grace, and shal I thus be spilt?   *destroyed*
    Shal thus Criseyde awey, for that thow wilt?
265 Allas! how maistow in thyn herte fynde
    To ben to me thus cruwel and unkynde?

    "Have I the nought honoured al my lyve,   *life*
    As thow wel woost, above the goddes alle?   *know*
    Whi wiltow me fro joie thus deprive?
270 O Troilus, what may men now the calle
    But °wrecche of wrecches, out of honour falle   *fallen*
    Into miserie, in which I wol bewaille
    Criseyde, allas! til that the breth me faille?

    "Allas, Fortune! if that my life in joie
275 Displesed hadde unto thi foule envye,
    Why ne haddestow my fader, kyng of Troye,
    Byraft the lif, or don my bretheren dye,   *taken away, brothers*
    Or slayn myself, that thus compleyne and crye,
    I, °combre-world, that may of nothyng serve,
280 But °evere dye and nevere fulli sterve?   *die, cease to be*

    "If that Criseyde allone were me laft,   *left*
    Nought roughte I whider thow woldest me steere;   *wouldn't care, send*

271-2 Cf. *CT* VII B2 3166-7.
279 an encumbrance to the world
280 Cf. 1. 420 and n.

And hire, allas! than hastow me biraft.
But everemore, lo, this is thi manere,
285 To reve a wight that most is to hym deere, *take away from, what*
To preve in that thi gerful violence. *changeable*
Thus am I lost, ther helpeth no diffence.

"O verrey lord, O Love! O god, allas!
That knowest best myn herte and al my thought,
290 What shal my sorwful lif don in this cas,
If I forgo that I so deere have bought? *that (which)*
Syn ye Criseyde and me han fully brought
Into youre grace, and bothe oure hertes seled, *sealed*
How may ye suffre, allas! it be repeled? *repealed*

295 "What shal I don? I shal, while I may dure *endure*
On lyve in torment and in cruwel peyne, *alive*
This infortune of this disaventure, *misfortune, catastrophe*
Allone as I was born, iwys, °compleyne;
Ne nevere wol I seen it shyne or reyne,
300 But ende I wol, as Edippe, in derknesse *Edippe (Oedipus)*
My sorwful lif, and dyen in distresse.

"O wery goost, that errest to and fro, *weary spirit, wanders*
Why nyltow fleen out of the wofulleste *fly*
Body that evere myghte on grounde go?
305 O soule, lyrkynge in this wo, unneste, *biding, leave the nest*
Fle forth out of myn herte, and lat it breste,
And folowe alwey Criseyde, thi lady dere.
Thi righte place is now no lenger here.

"O woful eyen two, syn youre disport *recreation*
310 Was al to sen Criseydes eyen brighte, *see*
What shal ye don but, for my discomfort,
Stonden for naught, and wepen out youre sighte,

---

298 Construe with "I shal" of 295.

Syn she is queynt, that °wont was yow to lighte? *quenched*

In vayn fro this forth have ich eyen tweye *two*

315 Ifourmed, syn youre vertu is aweye. *formed, (source of) power*

"O my Criseyde, O lady sovereigne

Of thilke woful soule that thus crieth, *this same*

Who shal now yeven comfort to the peyne? *give*

Allas! no wight; but whan myn herte dieth, *no one*

320 My spirit, which that so unto yow hieth, *hastens*

Receyve in gree, for that shal ay yow serve; *favorably*

Forthi °no fors is, though the body sterve. *hence, die*

"O ye loveris, that heigh upon the whiel *high*

Ben set of Fortune, in good aventure,

325 God leve that ye fynde ay love of °stiel, *grant, steel*

And longe mote youre lif in joie endure!

But whan ye comen by my sepulture,

Remembreth that youre felawe resteth there;

For I loved ek, though ich unworthi were.

330 "O oold, unholsom, and myslyved man, *corrupt, of evil life*

Calkas I mene, allas! what eileth the, *ails*

To ben a Grek, syn thow art born Troian?

O Calkas, which that wolt my bane be, *death*

In corsed tyme was thow born for me!

335 As wolde blisful Jove, for his joie, *so would (grant it)*

That I the hadde where I wolde, in Troie!" *want (you)*

A thousand sikes, hotter than the gleede, *sighs, glowing coal*

Out of his brest ech after other wente,

Medled with pleyntes new, his wo to feede, *inmixed, complaints*

340 For which his woful teris nevere stente; *ceased*

---

313 that was accustomed to illumine you

322 it does not matter

325 Cf. 5. 831.

191

And shortly, so his peynes hym torente,   *tore asunder*
And °wex so mat, that joie nor penaunce   *dejected, sorrow*
He feleth non, but lith forth in a traunce.   *continually*

Pandare, which that in the parlement
345 Hadde herd what every lord and burgeys seyde,   *citizen*
And how ful graunted was by oon assent   *fully, common*
For Antenor to yelden so Criseyde,   *yield*
Gan wel neigh wood out of his wit to breyde,   *mad, go*
So that, for wo, he nyste what he mente,   *did not know*
350 But in a rees to Troilus he wente.   *rush*

A certeyn knyght, that for the tyme kepte
The chambre door, undide it hym anon;   *for him instantly*
And Pandare, that ful tendreliche wepte,
Into the derke chambre, as stille as ston,
355 Toward the bed gan softely to gon,
So confus that he nyste what to seye;
For verray wo his wit was neigh aweye.   *very, nearly gone*

And with his chiere and lokyng al totorn,   *countenance, distraught*
For sorwe of this, and with his armes folden,
360 He stood this woful Troilus byforn,
And on his pitous face he gan byholden.   *pitiful*
But, Lord, so ofte gan his herte colden,   *grow cold*
Seyng his frend in wo, whos hevynesse   *seeing*
His herte slough, °as thoughte hym, for destresse.   *slew*

365 This woful wight, this Troilus, that felte
His frende Pandare ycomen hym to se,
Gan as the snow ayeyn the sonne melte;   *beneath*
For which this sorwful Pandare, of pitee,
Gan for to wepe as tendreliche as he;

---

342 (he) became
364 as it seemed to him

370 And specheles thus ben thise ilke tweye, *same two*
That neither myghte o word for sorwe seye. *one word on account of*

But at the laste this woful Troilus,
Neigh ded for smert, gan bresten out to rore, *nearly, pain, burst*
And with a sorwful noise he seyde thus,
375 Among hise sobbes and his sikes sore: *sighs*
"Lo, Pandare, I am ded, withouten more. *more (ado)*
Hastow nat herd at parlement," he seyde,
"For Antenor how lost is my Criseyde?"

This Pandarus, ful dede and pale of hewe, *deathly looking*
380 Ful pitously answerde and seyde, "Yis!
As wisly were it fals as it is trewe, *certainly would it were ·*
That I have herd, and woot al how it is. *know*
O mercy, God, who wolde have trowed this? *believed*
Who wolde have wend that in so litel a throwe *space of time*
385 Fortune oure joie wold han overthrowe?

"For in this world ther is no creature,
As to my dom, that ever saw ruyne *judgment, ruin*
Straunger than this, thorugh cas or aventure. *chance, happenstance*
But who may al eschue, or al devyne. *foresee*
390 Swich is this world! forthi I thus diffyne: *hence, conclude*
Ne trust no wight to fynden in Fortune
Ay propretee; hire yiftes ben °comune. *appropriateness (to himself)*

"But telle me this, whi thow art now so mad
To sorwen thus? Whi listow in this wise, *do you lie*
395 Syn thi desire al holly hastow had, *wholly*
So that, by right, it oughte ynough suffise?
But I, that nevere felte in my servyse
A frendly cheere, or lokyng of an eye,
Lat me thus wepe and wailen til I deye.

_____

392 common (to all)

400 "And over al this, as thow wel woost thiselve,   *moreover, know*
This town is ful of ladys al aboute;
And, to my doom, °fairer than swiche twelve   *judgment*
As evere she was, shal I fynde in som route,   *crowd*
Yee, on or two, withouten any doute.
405 Forthi be glad, myn own deere brother!   *hence*
If she be lost, we shal recovere an other.

"What! God forbede alwey that ech plesaunce
In o thyng were, and in non other wight!   *one, creature*
If oon kan synge, an other kan wel daunce;
410 If this be goodly, she is glad and light;   *(another) she*
And this is fair, and that kan good aright.   *understands*
Ech for his vertu holden is for deere,   *valuable*
°Both heroner and faucoun for ryvere.

"And ek, as writ °Zanzis, that was ful wys,
415 'The newe love out chaceth ofte the olde;'
°And upon newe cas lith newe avys.
Thenk ek, thi lif to saven artow holde.   *obligated*
Swich fir, by proces, shal of kynde colde;   *grow cold*
For syn it is but °casuel plesaunce,
420 Som cas shal putte it out of remembraunce.   *chance occurrence*

"For also seur as day comth after nyght,   *sure*
The newe love, labour, or oother wo,
Or elles selde seynge of a wight,   *seldom seeing a person*
Don olde affecciouns alle overgo.   *causes, to pass from memory*

---

402 twelve times as fair
413 both the falcon trained to hunt herons and the falcon trained to hunt water-
fowl (Cf. 3. 1784.)
414 Zanzis is probably, like Lollius (1. 394), Ch's invention.
416 a new situation requires new consideration
419 casual pleasure (but also "pleasure that is the result of chance")

425 And, for thi part, thow shalt have °oon of tho   *abbreviate*
    T'abregge with thi bittre peynes smerte;
    Absence of hire shal dryve hire out of herte."

    Thise wordes seyde he for the nones alle,   *for the time being*
    To help his frend, lest he for sorwe deyde;
430 For douteles, to don his wo to falle,   *cause, cease*
    He roughte nought what unthrift that he seyde.   *cared, impropriety*
    But Troilus, that neigh for sorwe deyde,   *nearly*
    Took litel heede of al that evere he mente;
    Oon ere it herde, at the other out it wente.

435 But at the laste he answerde, and seyde, "Frend,
    This lechecraft, or heeled thus to be,   *medicine, healed*
    Were wel sittyng, if that I were a fend,   *appropriate, fiend*
    To traysen hir that trewe is unto me!   *betray*
    I pray God lat this conseil nevere ythe;   *prosper*
440 But do me rather sterve anon-right here,   *die immediately*
    Er I thus do as thow me woldest leere!   *teach*

    "She that I serve, iwis, what so thow seye,   *whatever*
    To whom myn herte enhabit is by right,   *devoted*
    Shal han me holly hires til that I deye.   *wholly*
445 For, Pandarus, syn I have trouthe hire hight,   *promised*
    I wol nat ben untrewe for no wight;   *creature*
    But as hire man I wol ay lyve and sterve,   *die*
    And nevere other creature serve.

    "And ther thow seist thow shalt as faire fynde   *say*
450 As she, lat be, make no comparisoun
    To creature yformed here by kynde!   *nature*
    O leve Pandare, in conclusioun,
    I wol nat ben of thyn opynyoun,

---

425 one of those experiences

Touchyng al this; for which I the biseche,
455 So hold thi pees; thow sleest me with thi speche!   *peace, slay*

"Thow biddest me I shulde love another
Al fresshly newe, and lat Criseyde go!
It lith nat in my power, leeve brother;   *lies, dear*
And though I myght, I wolde nat do so.
460 But kanstow playen °raket, to and fro,
°Nettle in, dok out, now this, now that, Pandare?
°Now foule falle hire for thi wo that care!

"Thow farest ek by me, thow Pandarus,   *proceed*
As he that, whan a wight is wo bygon,
465 He cometh to hym a paas, and seith right thus,   *apace*
'Thynk nat on smert, and thow shalt fele non.'   *pain*
Thow moost me first °transmewen in a ston,   *transmutate, into*
And reve me my passiones alle,   *deprive me of*
Er thow so lightly do my wo to falle.   *cause, cease*

470 "The deth may wel out of my brest departe   *separate*
The lif, so longe may this sorwe myne;   *undermine (me)*
But fro my soule shal Criseydes darte   *javelin*
Out nevere mo; but down with °Proserpyne,
Whan I am ded, I wol go wone in pyne,   *dwell in misery*
475 And ther I wol eternaly compleyne
My wo, and how that twynned be we tweyne.   *put asunder*

"Thow hast here made an argument, for fyn,   *in conclusion*
How that it sholde a lasse peyne be   *less*
Criseyde to forgon, for she was myn,   *lose*

---

460 the game of rackets, a kind of tennis played off a wall
461 These are the first words of a charm for removing the sting of a nettle.
462 now bad luck to any lady that may care about your love-sickness
467 Cf. 4. 830.
473 queen of Hades, wife of Pluto

480 And lyved in ese and in felicite.   *(we) lived*
    Whi gabbestow, that seydest thus to me   *do you talk nonsense*
    That '°hym is wors that is fro wele ythrowe,   *from felicity cast away*
    Than he hadde erst noon of that wele yknowe?'   *(if) he, earlier*

    "But tel me now, syn that °the thynketh so lyght
485 To changen so in love ay to and fro,
    Whi hastow nat don bysyly thi myght   *solicitously*
    To chaungen hire that doth the al thi wo?   *causes*
    Why nyltow lete hire fro thyn herte go?
    Whi nyltow love an other lady swete,   *sweet*
490 That may thyn herte setten in quiete?

    "If thou hast had in love ay yet myschaunce,   *misfortune*
    And kanst it not out of thyn herte dryve,
    I, that levede in lust and in plesaunce   *lived*
    With hire, as muche as creature on lyve,
495 How sholde I that foryete, and that so blyve?   *forget, quickly*
    O, where hastow ben hid so longe in °muwe,   *mew*
    That kanst so wel and formaly arguwe?

    "Nay, God wot, nought worth is al thi red,   *knows, nothing, advice*
    For which, for what that evere may byfalle,   *wherefore*
500 Withouten wordes mo, I wol be ded.
    O deth, that endere art of sorwes alle,
    Com now, syn I so ofte after the calle;
    For °sely is that deth, soth for to seyne,   *felicitous*
    That, ofte ycleped, cometh and endeth peyne.   *invoked*

482-3 it is worse for him (Cf. 3. 1625-8.)
484 it seems to you so easy
496 Cf. 3. 602.
503 Cf. 2. 683 and 1. 35 and n.

505 "Wel wot I, whil my lyf was in quyete,   *know*
    °Er thow me slowe, I wolde have yeven hire;
    But now thi comynge is to me so swete
    That in this world I nothing so desire.   *nothing (else) so (much)*
    O deth, syn with this sorwe I am a-fyre,   *on fire*
510 Thow other do me anoon in teris drenche,   *either, drown*
    Or with thi colde strok myn hete quenche.

    "Syn that thou sleest so fele in sondry wyse   *many*
    Ayens hire wil, unpreyed, day and nyght,   *against, unasked for*
    Do me at my requeste this servise:
515 Delyvere now the world, so dostow right,
    Of me, that am the wofulleste wyght   *creature*
    That evere was; for tyme is that I sterve,   *die*
    Syn in this world of right nought may I serve."   *for nothing*

    This Troylus in teris gan distille,   *tears*
520 As licour out of a lambic ful faste;   *alembic (retort for distilling)*
    And Pandarus gan holde his tunge stille,
    And to the ground his eyen doun he caste.
    But natheles, thus thought he at the laste:
    "What! parde, rather than my felawe deye,   *indeed*
525 Yet shal I somwhat more unto hym seye."

    And seyde: "Frend, syn thow hast swych distresse,
    And syn thee list myn arguments to blame,   *it pleases you*
    Why nylt thiselven helpen don redresse,   *will you not*
    And with thy manhod letten al this grame?   *stop all this grief*
530 Go ravisshe hire ne kanstow not? for shame!   *carry her off by force*
    And other lat hire out of towne fare,   *either*
    Or hold hire stille, and leve thi nyce fare.   *quit, foolish behavior*

    °"Artow in Troie, and hast non hardyment   *courage*
    To take a womman which that loveth the,

---

506 before you had slain me, I would have given ransom (not to have been slain)
533-6 Recall, with P's question here, the case of Paris and Helen.

535 And wolde hireselven ben of thyn assent?
Now is nat this a nyce vanitee?
Ris up anon, and lat this wepyng be,
And kith thow art a man; for in this houre   *show*
I wol ben ded, or she shal bleven oure."   *remain ours*

540 To this answerde hym Troilus ful softe,
And seyde, "Parde, leve brother deere,   *indeed, beloved*
Al this have I myself yet thought ful ofte,
And more thyng than thow devysest here.   *consider*
But whi this thyng is laft, thow shalt wel here;   *ignored, hear*
545 And whan thow me hast yeve an audience,   *given*
Therafter maystow telle al thi sentence.

"First, syn thow woost this town hath al this werre   *since, war*
°For ravysshyng of wommen so by myght,   *because of*
It sholde nought be suffred me to erre,
550 As it stant now, ne don so gret unright.
I sholde han also blame of every wight,
My fadres graunt if that I so withstoode,   *decision to grant her*
Syn she is chaunged for the townes goode.   *exchanged*

"I have ek thought, so it were hire assent,   *provided she agreed*
555 To axe hire at my fader, of his grace;   *ask for her from*
Than thynke I, this were hire accusement,   *betrayal of her*
Syn wel I woot I may hire nought purchace.
For syn my fader, in so heigh a place
As parlement, hath hire eschaunge enseled,   *sealed*
560 He nyl for me his °lettre be repeled.   *repealed*

"Yet drede I moost hire herte to perturbe
With violence, if I do swich a game;   *strategy*

---

548 Hesione, Priam's sister, was carried off by Telamon, and when the Greeks refused to give her up, Paris in retaliation took Helen.
560 the letter (of his law)

For if I wolde it openly desturbe,   *interfere with the arrangement*
It mooste be disclaundre to hire name.   *a reproach*
565 And me were levere ded than hire diffame,   *I would prefer to be*
°As nolde God but if I sholde have
Hire honour levere than my lif to save!

"Thus am I lost, for aught that I kan see.
For certeyn is, syn that I am hire knyght,
570 I moste hire honour levere han than me   *must, dearer*
In every cas, as lovere ought of right.
Thus am I with desir and reson twight: *pulled (in two directions)*
Desir for to destourben hire me redeth,   *counsels*
And reson nyl nat, so myn herte dredeth."   *is apprehensive*

575 Thus wepyng that he koude nevere cesse,   *(such) that*
He seyde, "Allas! how shal I, wrecche, fare?   *wretch (that I am)*
For wel fele I alwey my love encresse,   *feel*
And hope is lasse and lasse alwey, Pandare.
Encressen ek the causes of my care.
580 So weilaway, whi nyl myn herte breste?   *burst*
For, as in love, ther is but litel reste."

Pandare answerde, "Frend, thow maist, for me,
Don as the list; but hadde ich it so hoote,   *as pleases you, hot*
And thyn estat, she sholde go with me,   *and (had)*
585 Though al this town °cride on this thyng by note.   *in unison*
I nolde sette at al that noys a grote!   *care for, fourpenny piece*
For whan men han wel cryd, than wol they rowne; *quieten to a whisper*
Ek wonder last but nyne nyght nevere in towne.

"Devyne not in resoun ay so depe   *examine*
590 Ne corteisly, but help thiselve anon.   *with respect for others*
Bet is that othere than thiselven wepe,

566-7 God forbid that I should not hold her honor dearer than saving my life
585 cried out against

200

And namely syn ye two ben al on.   *especially, one*
Ris up, for by myn hed, she shal not goon!   *bead*
And rather be in blame a lite ifounde   *little*
595 Than sterve here as a gnat, withouten wounde.   *die*

"It is no shame unto yow ne no vice,
Hire to withholden that ye love moost.
Peraunter, she myghte holde the for nyce,   *perhaps, a fool*
To late hire go thus to the Grekis oost.   *let, host*
600 Thenk ek Fortune, as wel thiselven woost,   *know*
Helpeth hardy man to his enprise,   *enterprise*
And weyveth wrecches for hire cowardise.   *forsakes*

"And though thy lady wolde a lite hire greve,   *grieve*
Thow shalt thiself thi pees hereafter make,   *peace*
605 But as for me, certeyn, I kan nat leve   *believe*
That she wolde it as now for yvel take.
Whi sholde thanne of ferd thyn herte quake?   *fear*
Thenk ek how Paris hath, that is thi brother,
A love; and whi shaltow nat have another?

610 "And Troilus, o thyng I dar the swere,   *dare swear to you*
That if Criseyde, which that is thi lief,   *beloved*
Now loveth the as wel as thow dost here,   *her*
God help me so, she nyl nat take a-grief,
Theigh thow do boote anon in this meschief.   *though, find remedy*
615 And if she wilneth fro the for to passe,   *wishes*
Thanne is she fals; so love hire wel the lasse.

"Forthi tak herte, and thynk right as a knyght,   *hence*
Thorugh love is broken alday every lawe.   *continually*
Kith now somwhat thi corage and thi myght;   *show*
620 Have mercy on thiself, for any awe.   *regardless of fear*
Lat nat this wrecched wo thyn herte gnawe,

201

But manly °sette the world on six and sevene;
And if thow deye a martyr, go to hevene!

"I wol myself ben with the at this dede,
625 Theigh ich and al my kyn, upon a stownde,   *though, in one hour*
Shulle in a strete as dogges liggen dede,   *shall, lie*
Thorugh-girt with many a wide and blody wownde;
In every cas I wol a frend be founde.
And if the liste here sterven as a wrecche,   *it pleases you, to die*
630 Adieu, the devel spede hym that it recche!"   *prosper, cares about it*

This Troilus gan with tho wordes quyken,   *come around*
And seyde, "Frend, graunt mercy, ich assente.
°But certeynly thow maist nat so me priken,   *goad on*
Ne peyne non ne may me so tormente,
635 That, for no cas, it is nat myn entente,
At shorte wordes, though I deyen sholde,   *die*
To ravysshe hire, but if hireself it wolde."   *carry off, unless*

"Whi, so mene I," quod Pandarus, "al this day.   *all this while*
But telle me thanne, hastow hire wil assayed,   *tried (to discover)*
640 That sorwest thus?" And he answerde hym, "Nay."
"Wherof artow," quod Pandare, "thanne amayed,   *dismayed*
That nost nat that she wol ben °yvele appayed,   *don't know*
To ravysshe hire, syn thow hast nought ben there,   *to (be) carried off*
But if that Jove told it in thyn ere?   *unless*

645 "Forthi ris up, °as nought ne were, anon,   *therefore*
And wassh thi face, and to the kyng thow wende,   *go*
Or he may wondren whider thow art goon.

---

622 stake the world on a throw of the dice
633-7 The sense is: there's nothing you or anyone can do to make me "ravysshe hire" if she doesn't want me to do it.
642 ill pleased
645 as if nothing were wrong

Thow most with wisdom hym and othere blende, *prudently, blind*
Or, upon cas, he may after the sende, *perchance*
650 Er thow be war; and shortly, brother deere, *aware (of it)*
Be glad, and lat me werke in this matere.

"For I shal shape it so, that sikerly *certainly*
Thow shalt this nyght som tyme, in som manere,
Come speken with thi lady pryvely *in private*
655 And by hire wordes ek, and by hire cheere, *demeanor*
Thow shalt ful sone aperceyve and wel here
Al hire entente, and of this cas the beste. *regarding*
And fare now wel, for in this point I reste."

The swifte Fame, which that false thynges
660 Egal reporteth lik the thynges trewe, *equally*
Was thorughout Troie yfled with preste wynges *swift*
Fro man to man, and made this tale al newe,
How Calkas doughter, with hire brighte hewe,
At parlement, withouten wordes more,
665 Ygraunted was in chaunge of Antenore.

The whiche tale anon-right as Criseyde *as soon as*
Hadde herd, she, which that of hire fader roughte, *cared*
As in this cas, right nought, ne whan he deyde,
Ful bisily to Jupiter bisoughte *prayed*
670 Yeve hem meschaunce °that this tretis broughte. *(to) give, bad luck*
But shortly, lest thise tales sothe were, *true*
She dorst at no wight asken it, for fere. *dared, fear*

As she that hadde hire herte and al hire mynde
On Troilus iset so wonder faste,
675 That al this world ne myghte hire love unbynde,
Ne Troilus out of hire herte caste,
She wol ben his, while that hire lif may laste.

---

670 that arranged this treaty

And thus she brenneth both in love and drede, *burns*
So that she nyste what was best to reede. *knew not, plan*

680 But as men seen in towne, and al aboute,
That wommen usen frendes to visite,
So to Criseyde of wommen com a route, *crowd*
For pitous joie, and wenden hire delite; *thought they'd please her*
And with hire tales, °deere ynough a myte,
685 Thise wommen, which that in the cite dwelle,
They sette hem down, and seyde as I shall telle.

Quod first that oon, "I am glad, trewely,
Bycause of yow, that shal youre fader see."
Another seyde, "Ywis, so nam nat I; *I'm not*
690 For al to litel hath she with us be."
Quod tho the thridde, "I hope, ywis, that she *third*
Shal bryngen us the pees on every syde, *peace*
That, whan she goth, almyghty God hire gide!" *guide*

Tho wordes and tho wommanysshe thynges, *those*
695 She herde hem right as though she thennes were; *were somewhere else*
For, God it woot, hire herte on othir thyng is. *knows*
Although the body sat among hem there,
Hire advertence is alwey elleswhere; *attention*
For Troilus ful faste hire soule soughte; *concertedly*
700 Withouten word, on hym alwey she thoughte.

Thise wommen, that thus wenden hire to plese, *expected*
Aboute naught gonne alle hire tales spende. *for nothing*
Swich vanyte ne kan don hire non ese,
As she that al this mene while brende *burned*
705 Of other passioun than that they wende, *suspected*
So that she felte almost hire herte dye
For wo and wery of that compaignie. *(she felt) weary*

---

684 dear enough at a mite—i.e., not worth much at all

For which no lenger myghte she restreyne
Hir teeris, so they gonnen up to welle,
710 That yaven signes of the bittre peyne   *gave*
In which hir spirit was, and moste dwelle;   *must*
Remembryng hir, fro heven into which helle   *what*
She fallen was, syn she forgoth the syghte   *is losing*
Of Troilus, and sorwfully she sighte.   *sighed*

715 And thilke fooles sittynge hire aboute   *these same*
Wenden that she wepte and siked sore   *thought, sighed*
Bycause that she sholde out of that route   *company*
Departe, and nevere pleye with hem more.   *associate*
And they that hadde yknowen hire of yore   *for some time*
720 Seigh hire so wepe, and thoughte it kyndenesse,   *saw*
And ech of hem wepte eke for hire destresse.

And bisyly they gonnen hire comforten
Of thyng, God woot, on which she litel thoughte;   *knows*
And with hire tales wenden hire disporten,   *thought to distract her*
725 And to be glad they often hire bysoughte.
But swich an ese therwith they hire wroughte,   *ease, did*
Right as a man is esed for to feele,
For ache of hed, to clawen hym on his heele!   *head, scratch*

But after al this nyce vanyte   *idle talk*
730 They toke hire leve, and hom they wenten alle.
Criseyde, ful of sorweful pite,
Into hire chambre up went out of the halle,
And on hire bed she gan for ded to falle,
In purpos nevere thennes for to rise;
735 And thus she wroughte, as I shal yow devyse.   *behaved*

Hire ownded heer, that sonnyssh was of hewe,   *wavy, hair*
She rente, and ek hire fyngeres longe and smale   *tore*
She wrong ful ofte, and bad God on hire rewe,   *prayed, have pity*
And with the deth to doon boote on hire bale.   *remedy, suffering*

740 Hire hewe, whilom bright, that tho was pale,   *hitherto, then*
    Bar witnesse of hire wo and hire constreynte;   *distress*
    And thus she spak, sobbyng in hire compleynte:

    "Allas!" quod she, "out of this regioun
    I, woful wrecche and infortuned wight,
745 °And born in corsed constellacioun,
    Moot goon, and thus departen fro my knyght.   *must*
    Wo worth, allas! that ilke dayes light   *woe unto, same*
    On which I saugh hym first with eyen tweyne,   *two*
    That causeth me, and ich hym, al this peyne!"

750 Therwith the teris from hire eyen two
    Down fille, as shour in Aperill ful swithe;   *swiftly*
    Hire white brest she bet, and for the wo   *beat*
    After the deth she cryed a thousand sithe,   *times*
    Syn he that wont hire wo was for to lithe,   *accustomed, ease*
755 She moot forgon; for which disaventure   *must leave, misfortune*
    She held hireself a forlost creature.

    She seyde, "How shal he don, and ich also?
    How sholde I lyve, if that I from hym twynne?   *separate*
    O deere herte eke, that I love so,   *also*
760 Who shal that sorwe slen that ye ben inne?   *slay*
    O Calkas, fader, thyn be al this synne!
    O moder myn, that cleped were Argyve,   *called*
    Wo worth that day that thow °me bere on lyve!   *woe be to*

    "To what fyn sholde I lyve and sorwen thus?   *purpose*
765 How sholde a fissh withouten water dure?   *endure*
    What is Criseyde worth, from Troilus?
    How sholde a plaunte or lyves creature   *living*
    Lyve withouten his kynde noriture?   *natural nourishment*

---

745 and born under a constellation in which the planets were unfavorably disposed
763 brought me into the world

For which ful ofte a by-word here I seye,   *proverb*
770 That 'rooteles moot grene soone deye.'   *rootless must green*

"I shal doon thus, syn neither swerd ne darte   *spear*
Dar I noon handle, for the crueltee,
That ilke day that I from you departe,
If sorwe of that nyl nat my bane be,   *death*
775 Thanne shal no mete or drynke come in me
Til I my soule out of my breste unshethe;   *unsheath*
And thus myselven wol I don to dethe.

"And, Troilus, my clothes everychon
Shul blake ben in tokenyng, herte swete,   *black*
780 That I am as out of this world agon,   *gone (like a nun)*
That wont was yow to setten in quiete;
And of myn ordre, ay til deth me mete,   *(religious) order*
The observance evere, in youre absence,   *(ritual) observance*
Shal sorwe ben, compleynt, and abstinence.

785 "Myn herte and ek the woful goost therinne
Byquethe I, with youre spirit to compleyne
Eternaly, for they shal nevere twynne.   *part*
For though in erthe ytwynned be we tweyne,   *separated, two*
Yet in the feld of pite, out of peyne,   *Elysian field (in Hades)*
790 That highte Elisos, shal we ben yfeere,   *together*
As Orpheus with Erudice, his fere.   *mate*

"Thus, herte myn, for Antenor, allas!   *sweetheart*
I soone shal be chaunged, as I wene.   *exchanged, expect*
But how shul ye don in this sorwful cas;
795 How shal youre tendre herte this sustene?
But, herte myn, foryete this sorwe and tene,   *forget, grief*
And me also; for, sothly for to seye,   *truly*
So ye wel fare, I recche naught to deye."   *I care not if I die*

How myghte it evere yred ben or ysonge,   *read*
800 The pleynte that she made in hire destresse?   *complaint*

207

I not; but as for me, my litel tonge, *do not know*
If I discryven wolde hire hevynesse,
It sholde make hire sorwe seme lesse
Than that it was, and childisshly deface
805 Hire heigh compleynte, and therfore ich it pace. *pass over*

Pandare, which that sent from Troilus
Was to Criseyde—as ye han herd devyse *related*
That for the beste it was acorded thus,
And he ful glad to doon hym that servyse—
810 Unto Criseyde, in a ful secree wise, *secret*
Ther as she lay in torment and in rage,
Com hire to telle al hoolly his message,

And fond that she hireselven gan to trete *had begun to behave*
Ful pitously; for with hire salte teris
815 Hire brest, hire face, ybathed was ful wete.
The myghty tresses of hire sonnysshe heeris, *heavy, hair*
Unbroiden, hangen al aboute hire eeris; *dissheveled, ears*
Which yaf hym verray signal of martire *gave, martyrdom*
Of deth, which that hire herte gan desire.

820 Whan she hym saugh, she gan for sorwe anon *saw*
Hire tery face atwixe hire armes hide; *tear-stained, between*
For which this Pandare is so wo-bygon
That in the hous he myghte unnethe abyde, *hardly*
As he that pite felt on every syde.
825 For if Criseyde hadde erst compleyned soore, *earlier*
Tho gan she pleyne a thousand tymes more.

And in hire aspre pleynte thus she seyde: *bitter*
"Pandare first of joies mo than two
Was cause causyng unto me, Criseyde, *the first cause*
830 That now °transmewed ben in cruel wo. *transformed*

---

830 Cf. 4. 467.

°Wher shal I seye to yow welcom or no,
That alderfirst me broughte unto servyse   *first of all*
Of love, allas! that endeth in swich wise?

"Endeth thanne love in wo? Ye, or men lieth!
835 And alle worldly °blisse, as thynketh me.
°The ende of blisse ay sorwe it occupieth;
And whoso troweth nat that it so be,   *believes*
Lat hym upon me, woful wrecche, ysee,   *look*
That myself hate, and ay my burthe acorse,   *birth, curse*
840 Felyng alwey, fro wikke I go to worse.   *wicked*

"Whoso me seeth, he seeth sorwe al °atonys,
Peyne, torment, pleynte, wo, distresse!
Out of my woful body harm ther noon is,   *apart from*
As angwissh, langour, cruel bitternesse,
845 Anoy, smert, drede, fury, and ek siknesse.   *pain*
I trowe, ywys, from hevene teeris reyne   *believe, rain*
For pite of myn aspre and cruel peyne."   *bitter*

"And thow, my suster, ful of discomfort,"
Quod Pandarus, "what thynkestow to do?
850 Whi ne hastow to thyselven som resport?   *regard*
Whi wiltow thus thiself, allas, fordo?   *harm*
Leef al this werk, and tak now heede to   *leave, behavior*
That I shal seyn; and herkne of good entente   *listen to*
This, which by me thi Troilus the sente."

855 Tornede hire tho Criseyde, a wo makynge   *turned*
So gret that it a deth was for to see.

---

831 whether I shall say to you welcome or not (I don't know)
835 "Blisse" is a subject of "endeth" also.
836 sorrow always takes possession of the end of bliss
841 Construe "atonys" with not only "sorwe" but also with the entire string of nouns
in 842.

209

"Allas!" quod she, "what wordes may ye brynge?
What wol my deere herte seyn to me,
Which that I drede nevere mo to see? *whom*
860 Wol he han pleynte or teris, er I wende? *complaint, tears, go*
I have ynough, if he therafter sende!" *if he sends for any*

°She was right swich to seen in hire visage
As is that wight that men on °beere bynde; *bier*
Hire face, lik of Paradys the ymage,
865 Was al ychaunged in another kynde.
The pleye, the laughter, men was wont to fynde *one was accustomed*
In hire, and ek hire joies everichone,
Ben fled, and thus lith now Criseyde allone. *are*

Aboute hire eyen two a purpre ryng *purple*
870 Bytrent, in sothfast tokenyng of hire peyne, *circles, true*
That to biholde it was a dedly thyng;
For which Pandare myghte nat restreyne
The teeris from his eighen for to reyne. *eyes*
But natheles, as he best myghte, he seyde
875 From Troilus thise wordes to Criseyde:

"Lo, nece, I trowe wel ye han herd al how *believe*
The kyng with othere lordes, for the beste,
Hath mad eschaunge of Antenor and yow,
That cause is of this sorwe and this unreste.
880 But how this cas dooth Troilus moleste,
That may non erthely mannes tonge seye;
For verray wo his wit is al aweye. *lost*

"For which we han so sorwed, he and I,
°That into litel bothe it hadde us slawe;

862-3 i.e., she looked like one of the dead
863 Cf. 2. 1638.
884 that it had almost slain us both

885 But thorugh my conseyl this day, finaly,
He somwhat is fro wepynge now withdrawe,
And semeth me that he desireth fawe   *willingly*
With yow to ben al nyght, for to devyse
Remedie in this, if ther were any wyse.   *way (to do it)*

890 "This, short and pleyn, th'effect of my message,
As ferforth as my wit kan comprehende;   *far*
For ye, that ben of torment in swich rage,
May to no long prologe as now entende.   *pay attention*
And hereupon ye may answere hym sende;
895 And, for the love of God, my nece deere,
So lef this wo er Troilus be here!"   *leave*

"Gret is my wo," quod she, and sighte soore,   *great, sighed*
As she that feleth dedly sharp distresse;
"But yit to me his sorwe is muchel more,
900 That love hym bet than he hymself, I gesse.   *better*
Allas! for me hath he swich hevynesse?
Kan he for me so pitously compleyne?
Iwis, this sorwe doubleth al my peyne.   *certainly*

"Grevous to me, God woot, is for to twynne,"   *separate*
905 Quod she, "but yet it harder is to me
To sen that sorwe which that he is inne;   *see*
For wel woot I it wol my bane be,   *know, death*
And deye I wol in certeyn," tho quod she;
"But bid hym come, er deth, that thus me threteth,   *threatens*
910 Dryve out that goost which in myn herte beteth."   *spirit, beats*

Thise wordes seyd, she on hire armes two
Fil gruf, and gan to wepen pitously.   *fell face down*
Quod Pandarus, "Allas! whi do ye so,
Syn wel ye woot the tyme is faste by,   *since, know, close*
915 That he shal come? Aris up hastily,

211

That he yow nat bywopen thus ne fynde,   *disfigured from crying*
But ye wole have hym wood out of his mynde.   *unless, mad*

"For wiste he that ye ferde in this manere,   *if he knew, behaved*
He wolde hymselven sle; and if I wende   *slay, had expected*
920 To han this fare, he sholde nat come here   *behavior*
For al the good that Priam may dispende.   *wealth, spend*
For to what fyn he wolde anon pretende,   *end, aim*
That knowe ich wel; and forthi yet I seye,   *therefore*
So lef this sorwe, or platly he wol deye.   *leave, plainly*

925 "And shapeth yow his sorwe for t'abregge,   *abbreviate*
And nought encresse, leeve nece swete!   *dear, sweet*
°Beth rather to hym cause of flat than egge,
And with som wisdom ye his sorwe bete.   *assuage*
What helpeth it to wepen ful a strete,   *weep a streetful*
930 °Or though ye bothe in salte teeris dreynte?   *drowned*
°Bet is a tyme of cure ay than of pleynte.

"I mene thus: whan ich hym hider brynge,   *hither*
Syn ye be wise, and bothe of oon assent,   *prudent*
°So shapeth how destourbe youre goynge,
935 Or come ayeyn, soon after ye be went.   *gone*
Women ben wise in short avysement;   *brief deliberations*
And lat sen how youre wit shal now availle,   *prove helpful*
And what that I may helpe, it shal nat faille."   *in any way*

---

927 In the conferring of knighthood the candidate was touched with the flat of a sword; hence the beneficial effect caused by the flat as opposed to the edge of a blade. S. Barney (*ad loc.*) suggests a medical antithesis, on the other hand—i.e., healing rather than wounding.
930 "Though ye, etc." also depends upon "what helpeth it, etc."
931 ever better is time spent on a remedy than on complaining
934-5 so plan how to frustrate your going or how to arrange your return

"Go," quod Criseyde, "and uncle, trewely,
940 I shal don al my myght me to restreyne
From wepyng in his sighte, and bisily,   *solicitously*
Hym for to glade I shal don al my peyne,   *effort*
°And in myn herte seken every veyne.
If to this sore ther may be fonden salve,
945 It shal nat lakke, certeyn, on my halve."   *part*

Goth Pandarus, and Troilus he soughte,
Til in a temple he fond hym al allone,
As he that of his lif no lenger roughte;   *cared*
But to the pitouse goddes everichone   *piteous, everyone*
950 Ful tendrely he preyed, and made his mone,   *moan*
To doon hym sone out of this world to pace;   *pass*
For wel he thoughte ther was non other grace.

And shortly, al the sothe for to seye,   *the whole truth*
He was so fallen in despeir that day,
955 That outrely he shop hym for to deye.   *utterly, prepared himself*
For right thus was his argument alway:
He seyde, he nas but lorn, so weylaway!   *lost, alas*
°"For al that comth, comth by necessitee:
Thus to ben lorn, it is my destinee.

960 "For certeynly, this wot I wel," he seyde,   *know*
"That forsight of divine purveyaunce   *providence*
Hath seyn alwey me to forgon Criseyde,   *lose*
Syn God seeth every thyng, out of doutaunce,   *doubt*
And hem disponyth, thorugh his ordinaunce,   *disposes them*
965 In hire merites sothly for to be,   *according to their deserts*
As they shul comen by predestyne.

---

943 and in my heart I shall search out every vein to find the cause of an illness and prescribe a remedy

958ff. T's reasoning about predestination and free will is not in Boccaccio. The passage is based on Boethius, *CP 5*, prose 2 and esp. 3.

213

"But natheles, allas! whom shal I leeve?   *believe*
For ther ben grete clerkes many oon,   *a one*
That destyne thorugh argumentes preve;   *prove*
970   And som men seyn that °nedely ther is noon,
But that fre chois is yeven us everychon.   *given*
O, welaway! so sleighe arn clerkes olde,   *cunning*
That I not whos opynyoun I may holde.   *do not know*

"For som men seyn, if God seth al biforn,
975   Ne God may nat deceyved ben, parde,   *certainly*
Than moot it fallen, theigh men hadde it °sworn,   *must*
That purveiance hath seyn before to be.   *(namely) what, providence*
Wherfore I sey, that from eterne if he   *eternity*
Hath wist byforn oure thought ek as oure dede,   *known*
980   We han no fre chois, as thise clerkes rede.   *claim*

"For other thought, nor other dede also,
Myghte nevere ben, but swich as purveyaunce,   *providence*
°Which may nat ben deceyved nevere mo,
Hath feled byforn, withouten ignoraunce.   *intuited*
985   For yf ther myghte ben a variaunce   *alternative*
To writhen out fro Goddis purveyinge,   *squirm out from (under)*
Ther nere no prescience of thyng comynge.   *would be no foreknowledge*

"But it were rather an opynyoun
Uncerteyn, and no stedfast forseynge.   *stable foresight*
990   And certes, that were an abusioun,   *absurdity*
That God sholde han no parfit cler wytynge   *perfect, knowing*
More than we men that han doutous wenynge.   *doubtful conjecture*
But swich an errour upon God to gesse   *to imagine in God*
Were fals and foul, and wikked corsednesse.   *cursedness*

---

970 there can't be any such thing
976 sworn (to the contrary)
983 which may never be deceived at all

995 "Ek this is an opynyoun of some
   °That han hire top ful heighe and smothe yshore: *scalps, shorn*
   They seyn right thus, that thyng is nat to come
   For that the prescience hath seyn byfore
   That it shal come; but they seyn that therfore   *because*
1000 That it shal come, therfore the purveyaunce
   Woot it byforn, withouten ignoraunce;   *knows*

   °"And in this manere this necessite
   Retorneth in his part contrarie agayn.
   For nedfully byhoveth it nat to bee
1005 That thilke thynges fallen in certayn
   That ben purveyed; but nedly, as they sayn,
   Byhoveth it that thynges whiche that falle,
   That they in certayn ben purveyed alle.

   "I mene as though I laboured me in this,   *worked diligently*
1010 To enqueren which thyng cause of which thyng be: *inquire*
   As wheither that the prescience of God is
   The certeyn cause of the necessite
   Of thynges that to comen ben, parde;   *are to come*
   Or if necessite of thyng comynge
1015 Be cause certeyn of the purveyinge.   *providence*

   "But now °n'enforce I me nat in shewynge   *demonstration*
   How the ordre of causes stant; but wel woot I   *stands, know*
   That it byhoveth that the byfallynge   *is necessary, happening*
   Of thynges wiste byforen certeynly   *foreknown*
1020 Be necessarie, al seme it nat therby   *must be, although seems*

---

996 i.e., clerks or scholars

1002–8 And in this argument this necessity doubles back to reside in its contrary:
for, in this argument, it is not necessary that those things happen certainly that are
foreseen; rather, as they say, those things that do happen must necessarily be foreseen
all of them certainly.

1016 I do not demand of myself

215

That prescience put fallynge necessaire   *affixes necessary happening*
To thyng to come, al falle it foule or faire.   *although, happens*

"For if ther sitte a man yond on a see,   *yonder, seat*
Than by necessite bihoveth it   *must it be*
1025 That, certes, thyn opynyoun sooth be,   *truth*
That wenest or conjectest that he sit.   *assumes, conjectures*
And further over now ayeynward yit,   *furthermore, on the other hand*
Lo, right so is it of the part contrarie,   *it is the same concerning*
As thus,—nowe herkne, for I wol nat tarie: *delay*

1030 "I sey, that if the opynyoun of the   *your opinion*
Be soth, for that he sitte, than sey I this,
That he mot siten by necessite;   *must*
And thus necessite in eyther is.
For in hym nede of sittynge is, ywys,
1035 And in the nede of soth; and thus, forsothe,   *in you*
There mot necessite ben in yow bothe.

"But thow mayst seyn, the man °sit nat therfore,
That thyn opynyoun of his sittynge soth is:
But rather, for the man sit ther byfore,   *because*
1040 Therfore is thyn opynyoun soth, ywis.   *true*
And I seye, though the cause of soth of this   *the truth*
Comth of his sittyng, yet necessite
Is entrechaunged both in hym and the.   *reciprocal*

"Thus in this same wise, out of doutaunce,   *doubt*
1045 I may wel maken, as it semeth me,
My resonyng of Goddes purveyaunce   *providence*
And of the thynges that to comen be;   *are to come*
By which resoun men may wel yse
That thilke thynges that in erthe falle,   *happen*
1050 That by necessite they comen alle.

1037 sits not for the reason

216

°"For although that, for thyng shal come, ywys,   *because*
Therfore is it purveyed, certeynly,   *foreseen*
Nat that it comth for it purveyed is;   *it comes because*
Yet natheles, bihoveth it nedfully,   *must it be necessarily*
1055 That thing to come be purveyed, trewely;
Or elles, thynges that purveyed be,
That they bitiden by necessite.   *happen*

"And this suffiseth right ynough, certeyn,
For to destruye oure fre chois °every del.   *destroy, free will*
1060 °But now is this abusioun, to seyn   *an absurdity*
That fallyng of the thynges temporel   *happening, temporal*
Is cause of Goddes prescience eternel.   *foreknowledge*
Now trewely, that is a fals sentence,
That thyng to come sholde cause his prescience.   *future events*

1065 "What myght I wene, and I hadde swich a thought,   *suppose, if*
But that God purveyeth thyng that is to come   *foresees*
For that it is to come, and ellis nought?   *because, otherwise*
So myghte I wene that thynges alle and some,
That whilom °ben byfalle and overcome,   *in the past*
1070 Ben cause of thilke sovereyne purveyaunce   *providence*
That forwoot al withouten ignoraunce.   *foreknows*

1051-7 For even though it is the case that, because a thing shall come and hence is foreseen, it does not come because it is foreseen, even so, it must necessarily be that a thing to come be foreseen truly (by God [supplied from Ch's translation of Boethius's *CP*]), or else, it must be that things that are foreseen (by God) happen by necessity.
1059 completely
1060 T now changes the direction of his argument, isolating the logical flaw in what he has been saying—namely that, in that argument, mortal events would determine divine knowing.
1069 have happened and transpired

"And over al this, yet sey I more herto, *in addition to this*
That right as whan I wot ther is a thyng, *know*
Iwys, that thyng moot nedfully be so; *must necessarily*
1075 Ek right so, whan I woot a thyng comyng, *to come*
So mot it come; and thus the bifallyng *must, happening*
Of thynges that ben wist bifore the tyde, *known, event*
They mowe nat ben eschued on no syde." *may, escaped*

Thanne seyde he thus: "Almyghty Jove in trone, *enthroned*
1080 That woost of al this thyng the sothfastnesse, *know, truth*
Rewe on my sorwe, and do me deyen sone, *take pity, die*
Or bryng Criseyde and me fro this destresse!"
And whil he was in al this hevynesse,
Disputyng with hymself in this matere,
1085 Com Pandare in, and seyde as ye may here. *bear*

"O myghty God," quod Pandarus, "in trone, *enthroned*
I! who say evere a wis man faren so? *saw, behave*
Whi, Troilus, what thinkestow to doone?
Hastow swich lust to ben thyn owen fo? *pleasure*
1090 What, parde, yet is nat Criseyde ago! *gone*
Whi list the so thiself fordoon for drede, *destroy*
That in thyn hed thyne eyen semen dede? *eyes appear*

"Hastow nat lyved many a yer byforn *year herebefore*
Withouten hire, and ferd ful wel at ese? *fared*
1095 Artow for hire and for noon other born?
Hath Kynde the wrought al only hire to plese? *Nature*
Lat be, and thynk right thus in thi disese: *misery*
That, in the dees right as ther fallen chaunces, *dice, happen*
Right so in love ther come and gon plesaunces.

1100 "And yet this is my wonder most of alle,
Whi thow thus sorwest, syn thow nost nat yit, *since, know not*
Touchyng hire goyng, how that it shal falle, *turn out*
Ne yif she kan hireself destourben it. *if, frustrate*

218

Thow hast nat yet assayed al hire wit.   *made trial of*
1105 °A man may al bytyme his nekke beede
Whan it shal of, and sorwen at the nede.

"Forthi tak hede of that I shal the seye: *hence*
I have with hire yspoke, and longe ybe,   *long have been (with her)*
So as acorded was bitwixe us tweye;   *between*
1110 And evere mo me thynketh thus, that she   *more*
Hath somwhat in hire hertes privete,   *heart's private thoughts*
Wherwith she kan, if I shal right arede,   *rightly guess*
Destourbe al this of which thow art in drede.   *prevent, dread*

"For which my counseil is, whan it is nyght,   *counsel*
1115 Thow to hire go, and make of this an ende;
And blisful °Juno, thorugh hire grete myght,
Shal, as I hope, hire grace unto us sende.
Myn herte seyth, 'Certeyn, she shal nat wende.'   *certainly, go*
And forthi put thyn herte a while in reste,
1120 And hold thi purpos, for it is the beste."

This Troilus answerd, and sighte soore: *sighed sorely*
'Thow seist right wel, and I wol don right so."   *say*
And what hym liste, he seyde unto it more.   *pleased, apropos of*
And whan that it was tyme for to go,
1125 Ful pryvely hymself, withouten mo,   *others*
Unto hire com, as he was wont to doone;   *accustomed*
And how they wroughte, I shal yow tellen soone.   *behaved*

Soth is, that whan they gonne °first to mete,   *truth*
So gan the peyne hire hertes for to twiste,   *pain*
1130 That neyther of hem other myghte grete,   *greet*

1105 a man may at the necessary time offer his neck—that is, when he must lose
his head—and he may sorrow when there is need
1116 Juno, wife of Jupiter and, traditionally, enemy of Aeneas and the Trojans
1128 to see each other

But hem in armes toke, and after kiste.   *each other, kissed*
The lasse woful of hem bothe nyste   *(even) the less woeful, knew not*
Wher that he was, ne myghte o word out brynge,   *express*
As I seyde erst, for wo and for sobbynge.   *before, because of*

1135 Tho woful teeris that they leten falle   *those, tears, let*
As bittre weren, out of teris kynde,   *beyond the nature of tears*
°For peyne, as is °ligne aloes or galle.
So bittre teeris weep nought, as I fynde,   *wept*
The woful °Mirra thorugh the bark and rynde,
1140 That in this world ther nys so hard an herte,   *(such) that, is not*
That nolde han rewed on hire peynes smerte.   *would not have pitied*

But whan hire wofulle weri goostes tweyne   *their, weary, spirits*
°Retourned ben ther as hem oughte to dwelle,
And that somwhat to wayken gan the peyne   *when, weaken*
1145 °By lengthe of pleynte, and ebben gan the welle   *recede*
Of hire teeris, and the herte unswelle,   *tears*
With broken vois, °al hoors forshright, Criseyde   *voice*
To Troilus thise ilke wordes seyde: *same*

"O Jove, I deye, and mercy I beseche!   *die*
1150 Help, Troilus!" and therwithal hire face
Upon his brest she leyde, and loste speche;   *laid*
Hire woful spirit from his propre place,   *her, its*
°Right with the word, alwey o poynt to pace.

1137 construe "for peyne" ("because of pain") with "woful teeris"
1137 lign-aloes, an aromatic wood
1139 Myrrha, changed into a myrrh tree for deceiving her father into committing incest with her, wept tears of myrrh—see Ovid, *Metam.* 10. 298–518.
1143 had returned to where they should dwell (i.e., when T & C had their wits about them again)
1145 because of the length of his complaint
1147 completely hoarse from shrieking
1153 with the very utterance of the word was always on the point of passing

And thus she lith with hewes pale and grene,   *lies, complexion*
1155 That whilom fressh and fairest was to sene.   *once*

This Troilus, that on hire gan biholde,
Clepyng hire name,—and she lay as for ded,   *calling, dead*
Withoute answere, and felte hir lymes colde,   *limbs*
Hire eyen throwen upward to hire hed,—   *rolled upward in*
1160 This sorwful man kan now noon other red,   *knows, counsel*
But ofte tyme hire colde mowth he kiste.   *mouth, kissed*
°Wher hym was wo, God and hymself it wiste!   *knew*

He rist hym up, and °long streght he hire leyde;   *he rose up*
For signe of lif, for aught he kan or may,   *anything, can (do)*
1165 Kan he non fynde in nothyng on Criseyde,   *anywhere*
For which his song ful ofte is "weylaway!"
But whan he saugh that specheles she lay,   *saw*
With sorweful vois, and herte °of blisse al bare,
He seyde how she was fro this world yfare.   *departed*

1170 So after that he longe hadde hire compleyned,   *complained over*
His hondes wrong, and seyd that was to seye,   *(had) his, what*
And with his teeris salt hire brest byreyned,   *rained upon*
He gan tho teeris wypen of ful dreye,   *wipe, dry*
And pitously gan for the soule preye,   *pray*
1175 And seyde, "O Lord, that set art in thi trone,   *throne*
Rewe ek on me, for I shal folwe hire sone!"   *have pity*

She cold was, and withouten sentement,   *sensation*
For aught he woot, for breth ne felte he non;   *knew*
And this was hym a pregnant argument   *to him*
1180 That she was forth out of this world agon.   *gone*
And whan he say ther was non other woon   *saw, alternative*

1162 whether it was woeful to him
1163 and he laid her down stretched out at length
1168 wholly barren of bliss

He gan hire lymes dresse in swich manere   *arrange*
As men don hem that shal ben layd on beere.   *bier (for burial)*

And after this, with sterne and cruel herte,   *heart*
1185 His swerd anon out of his shethe he twighte,   *sword, pulled*
Hymself to slen, how sore that hym smerte,   *slay, however, pained*
So that his soule hire soule folwen myghte   *might follow*
Ther as the doom of °Mynos wolde it dighte;   *judgment, ordain*
Syn Love and cruel Fortune it ne wolde,   *since, would not have it*
1190 That in this world he lenger lyven sholde.   *longer*

Than seyde he thus, fulfild of heigh desdayn: *full of high*
"O cruel Jove, and thow, Fortune adverse,
This al and som, that falsly have ye slayn   *this is the whole of it*
Criseyde, and syn ye may do me no werse,
1195 Fy on youre myght and werkes so dyverse!   *a curse on*
Thus cowardly ye shul me nevere wynne;   *conquer*
Ther shal no deth me fro my lady twynne.   *separate*

"For I this world, syn ye have slayn hire thus,
Wol lete, and folwe hire spirit low or hye.   *abandon, follow*
1200 Shal nevere lovere seyn that Troilus   *say*
Dar nat, for fere, with his lady dye;   *dared*
For, certeyn, I wol beere hire compaignie.   *bear*
But syn ye wol nat suffre us lyven here,
Yet suffreth that oure soules ben yfere.   *together*

1205 "And thow, cite, which that I leve in wo,   *city, leave*
And thow, Priam, and bretheren al yfeere,   *together*
And thow, my moder, farwel! for I go;
And °Atropos, make redy thow my beere.   *bier*

1188 Mynos was a king of Crete who after his death became one of the judges of the shades in the lower world.

1208 the one of the three fates who cuts the thread of life (See 5. 1–3 and n.; also 3. 1546.)

And thow, Criseyde, o swete herte deere,
1210 Receyve now my spirit!" wolde he seye,
With swerd at herte, al redy for to deye.   *heart*

But, as God wolde, °of swough therwith sh'abreyde,   *she awoke*
And gan to sike, and "Troilus" she cride;   *sigh*
And he answerde, "Lady myn, Criseyde,
1215 Lyve ye yet?" and leet his swerd down glide.   *let*
"Ye, herte myn, that thonked be Cipride!"   *thanked, Cipride (Venus)*
Quod she, and therwithal she soore syghte,   *sighed*
And he bigan to glade hire as he myghte;   *cheer*

Took hire in armes two, and kiste hire ofte,   *kissed*
1220 And hire to glade he did al his entente;   *cheer*
For which hire goost, that flikered ay on lofte,   *ever aloft*
Into hire woful herte ayeyn it wente.   *heart again*
But at the laste, as that hire eye glente   *glanced*
Asyde, anon she gan his swerd espie,   *see*
1225 As it lay bare, and gan for fere crye,   *fear*

And asked hym, whi he it hadde out drawe.
And Troilus anon the cause hire tolde,
And how hymself therwith he wolde han slawe;   *slain*
For which Criseyde upon hym gan biholde,
1230 And gan hym in hire armes faste folde,
And seyde, "O mercy, God, lo, which a dede!   *what a deed*
Allas, how neigh we weren bothe dede!   *nearly, dead*

"Than if I nadde spoken, as grace was,   *then, had not*
Ye wolde han slayn yowreself anon?" quod she.
1235 "Yee, douteles"; and she answerde, "Allas!
For, by that ilke Lord that made me,   *same*
°I nolde a forlong wey on lyve have be,

1212 out of (her) swoon
1237 I would not even for a few minutes have remained alive

After youre deth, to han ben crowned queene   *(even) to have been*
Of al the lond the sonne on shyneth sheene.   *shines brightly on*

1240 "But with this selve swerd, which that here is,   *same*
Myselve I wolde han slayn," quod she tho.
"But hoo, for we han right ynough of this,   *have (had)*
And lat us rise, and streght to bedde go,   *straight*
And there lat us speken of oure wo.
1245 For, by the °morter which that I se brenne,   *burn*
Knowe I ful wel that day is nat far henne."   *from now*

Whan they were in hire bed, in armes folde,   *their, folded*
Naught was it lik tho nyghtes here-byforn.   *those*
For pitously ech other gan byholde,
1250 As they that hadden al hire blisse ylorn,   *lost*
Bywaylinge ay the day that they were born;
Til at the laste this sorwful wight, Criseyde,   *creature*
To Troilus thise ilke wordes seyde: *same*

"Lo, herte myn, wel woot ye this," quod she,   *know*
1255 "That if a wight alwey his wo compleyne,   *person, complain of*
And seketh nought how holpen for to be,   *helped*
It nys but folie and encrees of peyne;   *folly, increase*
And syn that here assembled be we tweyne   *two*
To fynde boote of wo that we ben inne,   *remedy*
1260 It were al tyme soone to bygynne.   *high time*

"I am a womman, as ful wel ye woot,   *know*
And as I am avysed sodeynly,   *have concluded suddenly*
So wol I telle yow, whil it is hoot.   *hot*
Me thynketh thus, that nouther ye nor I   *neither*
1265 Ought half this wo to maken, skilfully;   *reasonably speaking*

1245 A "morter" is a night light consisting either of a wax candle or a bowl of wax or oil with a wick. It was made to last a certain number of hours.

224

For ther is art ynough for to redresse   *means*
That yet is mys, and slen this hevynesse.   *what, amiss, slay*

"Soth is, the wo, the which that we ben inne,   *are*
For aught I woot, for nothyng ellis is   *know, else*
1270 But for the cause that we sholden twynne.   *separate*
Considered al, ther nys namore amys.   *all things considered*
But what is thanne a remede unto this,
But that we shape us soone for to meete?   *arrange*
This al and som, my deere herte sweete.   *the sum of it*

1275 "Now, that I shal wel bryngen it aboute,
To come ayeyn, soone after that I go,
Therof am I no manere thyng in doute.   *in no way*
For, dredeles, withinne a wowke or two,   *doubtless, week*
I shal ben here; and that it may be so
1280 By alle right, and in a wordes fewe,   *in all justice*
I shal yow wel an heep of weyes shewe.   *ways show*

"For which I wol nat make long sermoun,   *a long speech of it*
For tyme ylost may nought recovered be;
But I wol gon to my conclusioun,
1285 And to the beste, in aught that I kan see.   *for the best*
And, for the love of God, foryeve it me,   *forgive*
If I speke aught ayeyns youre hertes reste,   *against, contentment*
For trewely, I speke it for the beste;

"Makyng alwey a protestacioun,
1290 That now thise wordes, which that I shal seye,
Nis but to shewen yow my mocioun   *they are, intention*
To fynde unto oure help the beste weye;
And taketh it non other wise, I preye.   *way*
For in effect, what so ye me comaunde,
1295 That wol I don, for that is no demaunde.   *of that there is no question*

"Now herkneth this: ye han wel understonde,
My goyng graunted is by parlement

225

So ferforth that it may nat be withstonde   *far*
For al this world, as by my jugement.   *as I see it*
1300 And syn ther helpeth non avisement   *since, plan*
To letten it, lat it passe out of mynde,   *prevent*
And lat us shape a bettre wey to fynde.   *arrange*

"The soth is this: the twynnyng of us tweyne   *truth, separation*
Wol us disese and cruelich anoye;   *distress, annoy*
1305 But hym byhoveth somtyme han a peyne,   *it's necessary for, to have*
That serveth Love, if that he wol have joye.
And syn I shal no ferther out of Troie   *since*
Than I may ride ayeyn on half a morwe,   *again*
It oughte lesse causen us to sorwe;

1310 "So as I shal not so ben hid °in mewe,   *since, be hidden*
That day by day, myn owne herte deere,
Syn wel ye woot that it is now a trewe,   *since, know, truce*
Ye shal ful wel al myn estat yheere.   *hear*
And er that trewe is doon, I shal ben heere;
1315 And thanne have ye both Antenore ywonne
And me also. Beth glad now, if ye konne,   *can*

"And thenk right thus, 'Criseyde is now agon.   *think*
But what! she shal come hastiliche ayeyn!'   *again*
And whanne, allas? By God, lo, right anon,
1320 Er dayes ten, this dar I saufly seyn.   *before, dare, safely*
And than at erste shal we be so fayn,   *at last, glad*
So as we shal togidres evere dwelle,   *since, together*
That al this world ne myghte oure blisse telle.

"I se that ofte tyme, there as we ben now,   *where we are*
1325 That for the beste, oure counseyl for to hide,   *in order*
Ye speke nat with me, nor I with yow

1310 a molting cage

226

In fourtenyght, °ne se yow go ne ride. | *two week period*
May ye naught ten dayes thanne abide, | *wait*
For myn honour, in swich an aventure? | *situation (as the present one)*
1330 Iwys, ye mowen ellis lite endure! | *otherwise have little patience*

"Ye knowe ek how that al my kyn is heere, | *also*
But if that onliche it my fader be; | *unless, only*
And ek myn othere thynges alle yfeere, | *goods, together*
And nameliche, my deere herte, ye,
1335 Whom that I nolde leven for to se | *would not cease to see*
For al this world, as wyd as it hath space; | *wide*
°Or ellis se ich nevere Joves face! | *else may I see*

"Whi trowe ye my fader in this wise | *do you think, way*
Coveyteth so to se me, but for drede | *desires, dread*
1340 Lest in this town that folkes me despise
Because of hym, for his unhappy dede? | *deed*
What woot my fader what lif that I lede? | *knows, lead*
For if he wiste in Troie how wel I fare, | *knew*
°Us neded for my wendyng nought to care.

1345 "Ye sen that every day ek, more and more, | *see*
Men trete of pees; and it supposid is | *treat of peace*
That men the queene Eleyne shal restore,
And Grekis us restoren that is mys. | *what is lost*
So, though ther nere comfort non but this, | *there were no comfort*
1350 That men purposen pees on every syde,
Ye may the bettre at ese of herte abyde. | *rest at ease*

"For if that it be pees, myn herte deere, | *peace*
The nature of the pees moot nedes dryve | *must, compel*
That men moost entrecomunen yfeere, | *must communicate together*

1327 nor do I see
1337 i.e., may I never come to bliss in after life
1344 we would never have needed to care about my departing

227

1355 And to and fro ek ride and gon as blyve	*also, quickly*
Alday as thikke as been fleen from an hyve,	*continually, bees fly*
And every wight han liberte to bleve	*stay*
°Where as hym liste the bet, withouten leve.	

"And though so be that pees ther may be non,	*it so be*
1360 Yet hider, though ther °nevere pees ne were,	*hither, peace*
I moste come; for whider sholde I gon,	*must, where*
Or how, meschaunce, sholde I dwelle there	*confound it!*
Among tho men of armes evere in feere?	*those, fear*
For which, as wisly God my soule rede,	*surely, instruct*
1365 I kan nat sen wherof ye sholden drede.	*see, have dread*

"Have here another wey, if it so be	*way (plan)*
That al this thyng ne may yow nat suffise.	
My fader, as ye knowen wel, parde,	*certainly*
Is old, and elde is ful of coveytise;	*old age, covetousness*
1370 And I right now have founden al the gise,	*method*
Withouten net, wherwith I shal hym hente.	*without a net, catch*
And herkeneth now, if that ye wol assente.	*will*

"Lo, Troilus, men seyn that hard it is	
The wolf ful, and °the wether hool to have;	*full (of food)*
1375 This is to seyn, that men ful ofte, iwys,	*indeed*
Mote spenden part the remenant for to save.	*must, rest*
For ay with gold men may the herte grave	*make an impression on*
Of hym that set is upon coveytise;	*is obsessed with*
And how I mene, I shal it yow devyse.	*mean, explain*

1380 "The moeble which that I have in this town	*personal property*
Unto my fader shal I take, and seye,	

1358 wherever it pleases him best (lit. "better") without (anyone's) permission
1360 never were peace
1374 sheep whole (healthy)

That right °for trust and for savacioun
It sent is from a frend of his or tweye,   *two*
The whiche frendes ferventliche hym preye   *pray*
1385 To senden after more, and that in hie,   *speedily*
Whil that this town stant thus in jupartie.   *stands, jeopardy*

"And that shal ben an huge quantite,—
Thus shal I seyn,—but lest it folk espide,   *discovered*
This may be sent by no wight but by me.   *person*
1390 I shal ek shewen hym, if pees bitide,   *peace, come to pass*
What frendes that ich have on every side   *friends*
Toward the court, °to don the wrathe pace   *in the direction of*
Of Priamus, and don hym stonde in grace.   *cause, him (i.e., Calkas)*

"So, what for o thyng and for oother, swete,   *one*
1395 I shal hym so enchaunten with my sawes,   *words*
That right in hevene °his sowle is, shal he meete.   *dream*
For al Appollo, or his clerkes lawes,
Or calkulyng, °availeth nought thre hawes;   *divination*
Desir of gold shal so his soule blende,   *blind*
1400 That, as me list, I shal wel make an ende.   *it pleases me*

"And yf he wolde aught by his °sort it preve,   *in any way*
If that I lye, in certayn I shal fonde   *lie, try*
Distourben hym, and °plukke hym by the sleve,   *to frustrate*
Makynge his sort, and beren hym on honde
1405 He hath not wel the goddes understonde;

1382 because of trust in him and for reasons of safe keeping
1392-3 to cause the wrath of Priam to pass
1396 he shall dream that his soul is
1398 i.e., is worth little or nothing at all
1401 divination prove it
1403-4 and pluck him by the sleeve (as he is) making his forecast and make him believe

229

For goddes speken in amphibologies,   *ambiguities*
And for oo sooth they tellen twenty lyes.   *one, truth*

"Eke drede fond first goddes, I suppose,—"   *fear invented*
Thus shal I seyn,—and that his coward herte   *say*
1410 Made hym amys the goddes text to glose,   *in error, interpret*
Whan he for fered out of Delphos sterte.   *fear, Delphi started*
And but I make hym soone to converte,   *unless, change his mind*
And don my red withinne a day or tweye,   *follow my advice*
I wol to yow oblige me to deye."   *pledge myself, die*

1415 And treweliche, as writen wel I fynde,   *truly*
That al this thyng was seyd of good entente;   *with good intentions*
And that hire herte trewe was and kynde
Towardes hym, and spak right as she mente,
And that she starf for wo neigh, whan she wente,   *died, nearly*
1420 And was in purpos evere to be trewe: *(she) was*
Thus writen they that of hire werkes knewe.   *deeds*

This Troilus, with herte and erys spradde,   *ears receptive*
Herde al this thyng devysen to and fro;   *explained*
And verrayliche hym semed that he hadde   *truthfully, it seemed to*
1425 The selve wit; but yet to late hire go   *like mind, let*
His herte mysforyaf hym evere mo.   *had misgivings ever more*
But fynaly, he gan his herte wreste   *turn*
To trusten hire, and took it for the beste.

°For which the grete furie of his penaunce   *great, suffering*
1430 Was queynt with hope, and therwith hem bitwene   *quenched*
Bigan for joie th'amorouse daunce.   *dance (love-making)*
And as the briddes, whanne the sonne is shene,   *birds, bright*
Deliten in hire song in leves grene,   *delight*
Right so the wordes that they spake yfeere   *together*
1435 Delited hem, and made hire hertes clere.   *unclouded*

1429 as a result of which

But natheles, the wendyng of Criseyde,   *nevertheless, leaving*
For al this world, may nat out of his mynde;   *part from*
For which ful ofte he pitously hire preyde   *piteously*
That of hire heste he myghte hire trewe fynde,   *promise*
1440 And seyde hire, "Certes, if ye be unkynde,
And but ye come at day set into Troye,   *unless, the appointed day*
Ne shal I nevere have hele, honour, ne joye.   *health*

°"For also soth as sonne uprist o-morwe—
And God, so wisly thow me, woful wrecche,
1445 To reste brynge out of this cruel sorwe—
I wol myselven sle if that ye drecche!
But of my deeth though litel be to recche,   *reckon*
Yet, er that ye me causen so to smerte,   *suffer*
Dwelle rather here, myn owen swete herte.

1450 "For trewely, myn owne lady deere,
°Tho sleghtes yet that I have herd yow stere   *propose*
Ful shaply ben to faylen alle yfeere.   *likely, fail, together*
For thus men seyth, 'that on thenketh the beere,   *one (thing), bear*
But al another thenketh his ledere.'   *leader*
1455 Youre syre is wys; and seyd is, out of drede   *it is said, doubtless*
'Men may the wise atrenne, and naught atrede.'   *outrun, outwit*

"It is ful hard to halten unespied   *limp undetected*
Byfore a crepel, for he kan the craft;   *cripple, knows, trick*
Youre fader is in sleght as °Argus eyed;   *cunning*
1460 For al be that his °moeble is hym biraft,   *is taken from him*
His olde sleighte is yet so with hym laft,   *left*

1443-6 for as truly as the sun rises on the morrow—and God, woeful wretch that
I am, as surely bring me to rest out of this cruel sorrow—I will slay myself if you delay
1451 those stratagems
1459 provided with as many eyes as Argus—i.e., a hundred
1460 personal property

Ye shal nat blende hym °for youre wommanhede,   *blind*
Ne feyne aright; and that is al my drede.   *pretend, dread*

"I not if pees shal evere mo bitide;   *do not know, peace, befall*
1465 But pees or no, for ernest ne for game,   *under any circumstances*
I woot, syn Calkas on the Grekis syde   *know*
Hath ones ben, and lost so foule his name,   *once, foully*
He dar nomore come here ayeyn for shame;   *again*
For which that wey, for aught I kan espie,   *way (i.e., plan), see*
1470 To trusten on, nys but a fantasie.   *is only*

"Ye shal ek sen, youre fader shal yow glose   *see, cajole*
To ben a wif, and as he kan wel preche,   *wife*
He shal som Greke so preyse and wel alose,   *commend*
That ravysshen he shal yow with his speche,   *he shall carry you away*
1475 Or do yow don by force as he shal teche;   *force you to do*
And Troilus, of whom ye nyl han routhe,   *you will have no pity*
Shal causeles so sterven in his trouthe!   *without cause, die*

"And over al this, youre fader shal despise   *in addition*
Us alle, and seyn this cite nys but lorn,   *city is but lost*
1480 And that th'assege nevere shal aryse,   *siege, be lifted*
For-whi the Grekis han it alle sworn,   *because, all this*
Til we be slayn, and down oure walles torn.
And thus he shal yow with his wordes fere,   *frighten*
°That ay drede I, that ye wol bleven there.   *dread, remain*

1485 "Ye shal ek seen so many a lusty knyght
Among the Grekis, ful of worthynesse,
And ech of hem with herte, wit, and myght
To plesen yow °don al his bisynesse,   *effort*

1462 even granted your woman's wiles
1484 Construe "that" with "thus. . . ."
1488 Construe "don, etc." with "seen" (1485): you shall also see many a lusty knight
do his best to please you.

That ye shul dullen of the rudenesse   *grow weary*
1490 Of us sely Troians, but if routhe   *simple, unless pity*
°Remorde yow, or vertu of youre trouthe.   *the quality of your loyalty*

"And this to me so grevous is to thynke,   *grievous is to consider*
That fro my brest it wol my soule rende;   *tear out*
°Ne dredeles, in me ther may nat synke   *deeply dwell*
1495 A good opynyoun, if that ye wende;   *comforting anticipation, depart*
For which youre fadres °sleghte wol us shende.   *because of*
And if ye gon, as I have told yow yore,   *before*
So thenk I n'am but ded, withoute more.   *I consider myself but dead*

"For which, with humble, trewe, and pitous herte,   *sorrowful*
1500 A thousand tymes mercy I yow preye;
So rueth on myn aspre peynes smerte,   *have pity, bitter, sharp*
And doth somwhat as that I shal yow seye,   *proceed, along the lines*
And lat us stele awey bitwixe us tweye;   *steal, two*
And thynk that folie is, whan man may chese,   *foolishness, choose*
1505 °For accident his substaunce ay to lese.

"I mene thus: that syn we mowe er day   *mean, since, may*
Wel stele awey, and ben togidere so,   *steal, together*
°What wit were it to putten in assay,
In cas ye sholden to youre fader go,

1491 cause you remorse
1494 nor without a doubt
1496 stratagem will tear us apart
1505 Expand thus: "if he loses his essential felicity for inessential things." Ch draws on philosophical terminology: "accident" is this or that particular variable (e.g., color or size) contingent on "substaunce" which is understood to transcend that variable— see, further, *CT* VI C 538–9; commentators also usually observe the pun in "accident" which suggests the sense of "uncertain (and probably catastrophic) event" in addition to the philosophical sense.
1508 what sense would it make to put to experiment whether, in case you should go to your father, you might come back or not

1510 If that ye myghten come ayeyn or no?
Thus mene I, that it were a gret folie   *folly*
To putte that sikernesse in jupertie.   *certainty in jeopardy*

°"And vulgarly to speken of substaunce
Of tresour, may we bothe with us lede   *carry*
1515 Inough to lyve in honour and plesaunce,
Til into tyme that we shal ben dede;   *until, dead*
And thus we may eschuen al this drede.   *avoid, uncertainty*
For everich other wey ye kan recorde,   *call to mind*
Myn herte, ywys, may therwith naught acorde.

1520 "And hardily, ne dredeth no poverte,   *indeed, dread*
For I have kyn and frendes elleswhere
That, though we comen in oure bare sherte,   *shirt*
Us sholde neyther lakken gold ne gere,   *lack, gold*
But ben honured while we dwelten there.   *we shall be honored*
1525 And °go we anon; for, as in myn entente,   *understanding*
This is the beste, if that ye wole assente."

Criseyde, with a sik, right in this wise,   *sigh*
Answerde, "Ywys, my deere herte trewe,   *indeed*
We may wel stele awey, as ye devyse,   *steal, suggest*
1530 And fynden swich unthrifty weyes newe;   *unprofitable ways*
But afterward, °ful soore it wol us rewe.
°And helpe me God so at my moost nede,
As causeles ye suffren al this drede!

1513 "Vulgarly" means "in the ordinary sense." T here contrasts his use of "substaunce" in the sense of "amount" (of treasure, wealth) with his earlier use of it in a philosophical sense (1505).

1525 let us go immediately

1531 full sorely it will make us regret (our action)

1532-3 and so help me God in my hour of greatest need, you suffer all this dread for no reason

"For thilke day that I for cherisynge   *on that day, cherishing*
1535 Or drede of fader, or for other wight,   *creature*
Or for estat, delit, or for weddynge,   *my economic condition*
Be fals to yow, my Troilus, my knyght,
Saturnes doughter, °Juno, thorugh hire myght,
As wood as °Athamante do me dwelle   *mad*
1540 Eternalich in °Stix, the put of helle!   *pit*

"And this on every god celestial
I swere it yow, and ek on ech goddesse,   *swear*
On every nymphe and deite infernal,
On satiry and fawny °more and lesse,   *satyrs, fawns*
1545 That halve goddes ben of °wildernesse;   *demigods*
And °Attropos my thred of lif tobreste,   *break in two*
If I be fals! now trowe me if yow leste!   *believe, it please*

"And thow, °Symois, that as an arwe clere   *arrow*
Thorugh Troie rennest ay downward to the se,   *run, sea*
1550 Ber witnesse of this word that seyd is here,
That thilke day that ich untrewe be
To Troilus, myn owene herte fre,   *noble beloved*
That thow retourne bakward to thi welle,   *source*
And I with body and soule synke in helle!

1555 "But that ye speke, awey thus for to go   *propose*
And leten alle youre frendes, God forbede,   *forsake*

1538 Juno, daughter of Saturn, wife of Jupiter, goddess of the moneyers in ancient Rome

1539 Athamas was driven mad at Juno's command—see *Inf.* 30. 1–12.

1540 Stix is one of the rivers of Hell, commonly equated with hell-pit in the Middle Ages.

1544 greater and lesser

1545 Satyrs and fauns haunted the woods and glades.

1546 See 3. 1208 and n.

1548 Symois: a river in Troy

For any womman, that ye sholden so!
And namely syn Troie hath now swich nede   *since*
Of help. And ek of o thyng taketh hede: *one*
1560 If this were wist, my lif lay in balaunce,   *known, would lie*
And youre honour; God shilde us fro meschaunce!   *shield, misfortune*

"And if so be that pees heereafter take,   *peace, take place*
As alday happeth after anger °game,   *continually happens*
Whi, Lord, the sorwe and wo ye wolden make,
1565 That ye ne dorste come ayeyn for shame!   *would not dare*
And er that ye juparten so youre name,   *put in jeopardy*
Beth naught to hastif in this hoote fare;   *hasty, rash action*
For hastif man ne wanteth nevere care.   *never lacks for anxiety*

"What trowe ye the peple ek al aboute   *think, also*
1570 Wolde of it seye? It is ful light t'arede.   *say, easy to predict*
They wolden seye, and swere it, out of doute,
That love ne drof yow naught to don this dede,   *drove*
But lust voluptuous and coward drede.   *fear*
Thus were al lost, ywys, myn herte deere,   *indeed*
1575 Youre honour, which that now shyneth so clere.

"And also thynketh on myn honeste,   *good repute*
That floureth yet, °how foule I sholde it shende,   *flourishes*
And with what filthe it spotted sholde be,
If in this forme I sholde with yow wende.   *manner, go*
1580 Ne though I lyved unto the werldes ende,
My name sholde I nevere ayeynward wynne.   *good name, get back*
Thus were I lost, and that were routhe and synne.   *pity, sin*

"And forthi sle with resoun al this hete!   *therefore, slay, heat*
°Men seyn, 'the suffrant overcomith,' parde;

1563 "recreation" in the sense of reconcilement and good will
1577 how badly I should ruin it
1584 Men say, 'he who suffers conquers,' certainly

236

1585 °Ek 'whoso wol han lief, he lief moot lete.'
       Thus maketh vertu of necessite
       By pacience, and thynk that lord is he
       Of Fortune ay, that naught wole of hire recche;   *ever, will, care*
       And she °ne daunteth no wight but a wrecche.   *wretch*

1590 "And trusteth this, that certes, herte swete,   *certainly, sweetheart*
       °Er Phebus suster, Lucina the sheene,
       The Leoun passe out of this Ariete,
       I wol ben here, withouten any wene.   *doubt*
       I mene, as helpe me Juno, hevenes quene,   *mean*
1595 The tenthe day, but if that deth m'assaile,   *unless, attack*
       I wol yow sen, withouten any faille."   *see, fail*

       "And now, so this be soth," quod Troilus,   *true*
       "I shal wel suffre unto the tenthe day.   *endure*
       Syn that I se that nede it mot be thus.   *see, needs, must*
1600 But, for the love of God, if it be may,
       So late us stelen privelich away;   *let us steal secretly*
       For °evere in oon, as for to lyve in reste,   *as for living*
       Myn herte seyth that it wol be the beste."   *says*

       "O mercy, God, what lif is this?" quod she.   *life*
1605 "Allas, ye sle me thus for verray tene!   *slay, sorrow*
       I se wel now that ye mystrusten me,   *see*
       For by youre wordes it is wel yseene.
       Now, for the love of Cinthia the sheene,   *Cinthia (the moon), bright*

1585 And 'whoever will fain have something must give up something he fain would
have'
   1589 and she frightens no one
   1591-2 Expand thus: before the sun's sister, Lucina the bright (the moon), having
left the sign Aries, passes Leo (Taurus, Gemini, and Cancer, too, lying in between).
This would take a little more than nine days—hence "tenthe day" (1595).
   1602 invariably

237

Mistrust me nought thus causeles, for routhe,   *pity's sake*
1610 Syn to be trewe I have yow plight my trouthe.   *pledged, loyalty*

"And thynketh wel, that somtyme it is wit   *wisdom*
To spende a tyme, a tyme for to wynne.   *gain*
Ne, parde, lorn am I naught fro yow yit,   *indeed, lost, yet*
Though that we ben a day or two atwynne.   *apart*
1615 Drif out the fantasies yow withinne,   *drive, within you*
And trusteth me, and leveth ek youre sorwe,   *abandon, sorrow*
°Or here my trouthe, I wol naught lyve tyl morwe.

"For if ye wiste how soore it doth me smerte,   *sorely, pain*
Ye wolde cesse of this; for, God, thow wost,   *stop this, you know*
1620 The pure spirit wepeth in myn herte   *(my) very soul, weeps*
To se yow wepen that I love most,
And that I mot gon to the Grekis oost.   *and because, must, host*
Ye, nere it that I wiste remedie   *were it not, knew a remedy for*
To come ayeyn, right here I wolde dye!   *returning, die*

1625 "But certes, I am naught so °nyce a wight   *certainly*
That I ne kan ymaginen a wey
To come ayeyn that day that I have hight.   *return, promised*
For who may holde a thing that wol awey?   *(flee) away*
My fader naught, for al his queynte pley!   *cunning devices*
1630 °And by my thrift, my wendyng out of Troie   *leaving*
Another day shal torne us alle to joie.   *turn*

"Forthi with al myn herte I yow biseke,   *therefore, beseech*
°If that yow list don ought for my preyere,
And for that love which that I love yow eke,   *love with which, also*
1635 That er that I departe fro yow here,   *before*

1617 or have here my oath, I will not live until morning
1625 foolish a person
1630 C swears a mild oath by her prosperity.
1633 if it pleases you to do anything at my prayer

°That of so good a confort and a cheere
I may yow sen, that ye may brynge at reste   *to rest*
Myn herte, which that is o poynt to breste.   *on the verge of bursting*

"And over al this I prey yow," quod she tho,   *in addition to*
1640 "Myn owene hertes °sothfast suffisaunce,
Syn I am thyn al hol, withouten mo,   *since, wholly, other lovers*
That whil that I am absent, no plesaunce
Of oother do me fro youre remembraunce.   *remove me from*
For I am evere agast, forwhy men rede   *fearful, wherefore men say*
1645 That love is thyng ay ful o bisy drede.   *ever, anxiety*

"For in this world ther lyveth lady non,
If that ye were untrewe (as God defende!),   *prevent*
That so bitraised were or wo-bigon   *would be so betrayed*
As I, that alle trouthe in yow entende.   *apprehend*
1650 And douteles, if that ich other wende,   *suspected otherwise*
I ner but ded, and °er ye cause fynde,   *would be*
For Goddes love, so beth me naught unkynde!"   *be not cruel to me*

To this answerde Troilus and seyde,
°"Now God, to whom ther nys no cause ywrye,   *hidden*
1655 Me glade, as wys I nevere unto Criseyde,   *gladden, as indeed*
Syn thilke day I saugh hire first with yë,   *that very, saw, eyes*
Was fals, ne nevere shal til that I dye.
At shorte wordes, wel ye may me leve: *in short, believe*
I kan no more, it shal be founde at preve."   *by proof*

1660 "Grant mercy, goode myn, iwys!" quod she,   *my treasure, indeed*
"And blisful Venus lat me nevere sterve   *die*

1636-7 I may see you of such good comfort and good cheer that you may, etc.
1640 truthful source of satisfaction
1651 until you have reason to be
1654-7 The basic syntax is: as I hope God may favor me, I was never false.

°Er I may stonde of plesaunce in degree
To quyte hym wel, that so wel kan deserve.
And while that God my wit wol me conserve,   *mind, for me*
1665 I shal so don, so trewe I have yow founde,   *behave*
That ay honour to me-ward shal rebounde.   *toward me*

"For trusteth wel, that youre estat roial,   *royal condition*
Ne veyn delit, nor only worthinesse   *empty delight, unique*
Of yow in werre or torney marcial,   *war, martial tournament*
1670 Ne pompe, array, nobleye, or ek richesse   *nobility*
Ne made me to rewe on youre destresse;   *have pity*
But moral vertu, grounded upon trouthe,
That was the cause I first hadde on yow routhe!   *pity*

"Eke gentil herte and manhod that ye hadde,
1675 And that ye hadde, as me thoughte, in despit   *disdain*
Every thyng that souned into badde,   *tended toward evil*
As rudenesse and poeplissh appetit,   *(such) as, vulgar*
And that youre °resoun bridlede youre delit;
This made, aboven every creature,   *caused (it)*
1680 That I was youre, and shal while I may dure.   *shall (be), live*

"And this may lengthe of yeres naught fordo,   *destroy*
Ne remuable Fortune deface.   *changeable*
But Juppiter, that of his myght may do   *cause*
The sorwful to be glad, so yeve us grace,   *sorrowful, give*
1685 Or nyghtes ten, to meten in this place,   *before, meet*
So that it may youre herte and myn suffise!   *be enough for*
And fareth now wel, for tyme is that ye rise."

And after that they longe ypleyned hadde,   *complained*
And ofte ykist, and °streite in armes folde,   *kissed*

1662–3 before I may be in such a condition of happiness as to recompense him well who so well deserves
1678 reason bridled (or reined in) your delight in gratifying your desires
1689 tightly clasped (each other) in their arms

1690 The day gan rise, and Troilus hym cladde,   *clothed*
      And rewfullich his lady gan byholde,   *ruefully*
      As he that felte dethes cares colde,   *death's*
      And to hire grace he gan hym recomaunde.   *to commend himself*
      °Wher him was wo, this holde I no demaunde.

1695 For mannes hed ymagynen ne kan,   *head cannot imagine*
      N'entendement consider, ne tonge telle   *understanding*
      The cruel peynes of this sorwful man,
      That passen every torment down in helle.   *surpass*
      For whan he saugh that she ne myghte dwelle,   *saw*
1700 Which that his soule out of his herte rente,   *tore*
      Withouten more, out of the chaumbre he wente.

1694 whether he felt woeful is hardly a question, I think

241

BOOK FIVE

°Aprochen gan the fatal destyne   *approach*
That Joves hath in disposicioun,   *in his disposition*
And to yow, angry Parcas, sustren thre,   *and (that he, Jove)*
Committeth, to don execucioun;   *perform (for him)*
5 For which Criseyde moste out of the town,   *must*
And Troilus shal dwellen forth in pyne   *sorrow*
Til °Lachesis his thred no lenger twyne.   *spin*

°The golde-tressed Phebus heighe on-lofte   *high*
Thries hadde alle with his bemes clene   *thrice*
10 The snowes molte, and Zepherus as ofte   *melted*
Ibrought ayeyn the tendre leves grene,
Syn that the sone of Ecuba the queene   *son (i.e., Troilus)*
Bigan to love hire first for whom his sorwe
Was al, that she departe sholde a-morwe.

15 Ful redy was at prime °Diomede,   *prime (9 a.m.)*
Criseyde unto the Grekis oost to lede,   *host, lead*
For sorwe of which she felt hire herte blede,   *bleed*

1-3 Jove is represented as leagued with the Parcas (accusative form) or Fates, to whom he commits the carrying out ("to don execucioun") of destiny. The three Fates are the sisters, Clotho (who spins the thread of life), Lachesis (who determines its length), and Atropos (who cuts it off). Atropos is also mentioned at 4. 1208 and 1546.

7 The distinct functions of the three Fates were not always carefully observed.

8-11 The melting of winter's snow and the return of spring, symbolized by Zephyrus, the West Wind, three times give us the duration of the action. T first observed C at the Palladium, in April—see 1. 156.

15 Diomede was the Greek warrior next in bravery to Achilles.

242

°As she that nyste what was best to rede.
And trewely, as men in bokes rede,   *read*
20 Men wiste nevere womman han the care,   *knew, to have*
Ne was so loth out of a town to fare.   *reluctant, go*

This Troilus, withouten reed or loore,   *counsel or advice*
As man that hath his joies ek forlore,   *utterly lost*
Was waytyng on his lady evere more   *waiting for*
25 As she that was the sothfast °crop and more
Of al his lust or joies here-bifore.   *pleasure*
But Troilus, now far-wel al thi joie,   *good-bye to*
For shaltow nevere sen hire eft in Troie!   *see, again*

Soth is that while he bood in this manere,   *true it is, abode*
30 He gan his wo ful manly for to hide,
That wel unnethe it sene was in his chere;   *hardly, seen, face*
But at the yate ther she sholde out ride,   *gate*
With certeyn folk he hoved hire t'abide,   *remained, to wait for her*
So wo-bigon, al wolde he naught hym pleyne,   *although, complain*
35 That on his hors unnethe he sat for peyne.   *hardly, grief*

For ire he quook, °so gan his herte gnawe,   *rage, quaked*
Whan Diomede on horse gan hym dresse,   *began to mount his horse*
And seyde to hymself this ilke sawe: *very saying*
"Allas!" quod he, "thus foul a wrecchednesse,
40 Whi suffre ich it? Whi nyl ich it redresse?   *will I not set it right*
Were it nat bet atones for to dye   *better, at once*
Than evere more in langour thus to drye?   *distress, suffer*

---

18 as she that did not know what plan would be best to follow (The rhyme
"rede"/"rede" is *rime riche* or identical rhyme, a license Ch uses on occasion elsewhere.)
25 "crop" in the sense of the top of a tree; "more," the root (We would say "the be-
ginning and the end.")
36 so his heart began to gnaw itself within

"Whi nyl I make atones riche and pore   *will I not, at once*
To have inough to doone, er that she go?
45 Why nyl I brynge al Troie upon a roore?   *uproar*
Whi nyl I slen this Diomede also?   *slay*
Why nyl I rather with a man or two
Stele hire away? Whi wol I this endure?   *steal, will*
Whi nyl I helpen to myn owen cure?"   *remedy*

50 But why he nolde don so fel a dede,   *would not, wicked a deed*
That shal I seyn, and °whi hym liste it spare:
He hadde in herte alweyes a manere drede   *dread*
Lest that Criseyde, °in rumour of this fare,
Sholde han ben slayn; lo, this was al his care.
55 And ellis, certayn, as I seyde yore,   *otherwise, earlier*
He hadde it don, withouten wordes more.

Criseyde, whan she redy was to ride,
Ful sorwfully she sighte, and seyde "allas!"   *sighed*
But forth she moot, °for aught that may bitide,   *must*
60 And forth she rit sorwfully a pas.   *rides, step*
Ther is non other remedie in this cas.   *case*
What wonder is, though that hire sore smerte,   *it pained her sorely*
Whan she forgoth hire owen swete herte?   *is losing*

This Troilus, in wise of curteysie,   *in a courteous manner*
65 With hauke on honde, and with an huge route   *hawk, crowd*
Of knyghtes, rood and did hire companye,   *rode, kept*
Passyng al the valeye fer withoute;   *valley far*
And ferther wolde han riden, out of doute,
Ful fayn, and wo was hym to gon so sone;   *gladly, soon*
70 But torne he moste, and it was ek to done.   *must, it had to be done*

---

51 why it suited him to refrain from it
53 upon report of this conduct
59 whatever may happen

And right with that was Antenor ycome
Out of the Grekis oost, and every wight   *host, person*
Was of it glad, and seyde he was welcome.
And Troilus, al nere his herte light,   *although, was not*
75 He peyned hym with al his fulle myght   *strove*
Hym to withholde of wepyng atte leeste,   *to refrain from, least*
And Antenor he kiste, and made feste.   *kissed, showed (him) honor*

And therwithal he moste his leve take,   *must*
And caste his eye upon hire pitously,   *wretchedly*
80 And neer he rood, his cause for to make,   *nearer, to plead his case*
To take hire by the honde al sobrely.   *gravely*
And Lord! so she gan wepen tendrely!
And he ful softe and sleighly gan hire seye,   *softly and secretively*
°"Now holde youre day, and do me nat to deye."

85 With that his courser torned he aboute
With face pale, and unto Diomede
No word he spak, ne non of al his route;   *group*
Of which the sone of Tideus took hede,   *son (i.e., Diomede), heed*
°As he that koude more than the crede
90 In swich a craft, and by the reyne hire hente;   *reins, took*
And Troilus to Troie homward he wente.

This Diomede, that ledde hire by the bridel,
Whan that he saugh the folke of Troie aweye,   *saw, away*
Thoughte, "Al my labour shal nat ben on ydel,   *in vain*
95 °If that I may, for somwhat shal I seye.
For at the werste it may yet shorte oure weye.   *worst, shorten*
I have herd seyd ek tymes twyes twelve,   *said also times twice*
'He is a fool that wole foryete hymselve."   *forget*

---

84 now keep your promise to return the tenth day, and do not cause me to die
89-90 as one who had more than elementary knowledge of such a business
95 if I may have anything to do with it, for I shall strike up a conversation

But natheles, this thoughte he wel ynough,
100 That "certeynlich I am aboute nought,   *accomplishing nothing*
If that I speke of love, or make it tough;   *am too forward*
For douteles, if she have in hire thought
Hym that I gesse, he may nat ben ybrought   *guess*
So soon awey; but I shal fynde a meene,   *out of her mind, means*
105 That she naught wite as yet shal what I mene."   *know, mean*

This Diomede, as he that koude his good,   *knew what he was about*
°Whan this was don, gan fallen forth in speche
Of this and that, and axed whi she stood
In swich disese, and gan hire ek biseche,   *distress, also beseech*
110 That if that he encresse myghte or eche   *improve by adding to*
With any thyng hire ese, that she sholde   *comfort*
Comaunde it hym, and seyde he don it wolde.   *(he) said he would do it*

For treweliche he swor hire, as a knyght,   *swore to*
°That ther nas thyng with which he myghte hire plese,
115 That he nolde don his peyne and al his myght
To don it, for to done hire herte an ese;
And preyede hire, she wolde hire sorwe apese,   *quiet*
And seyde, "Iwis, we Grekis kan have joie   *certainly*
To honouren yow, as wel as folk of Troie."

120 °He seyde ek thus, "I woot yow thynketh straunge,—
Ne wonder is, for it is to yow newe,—
Th'aquayntaunce of thise Troians to chaunge
For folk of Grece, that ye nevere knewe.

---

107 The reference may be either to Diomede's taking C's bridle and setting out or to the decision as to his course of conduct.

114-16 that there was nothing with which he might please her that he would not do his utmost to perform in order to do her heart ease

120-1 He also spoke thus: I know it seems strange to you—and no wonder, since it's new to you—to change acquaintance

°But wolde nevere God but if as trewe
125 A Greke ye sholde among us alle fynde
As any Troian is, and ek as kynde.

°"And by the cause I swor yow right, lo, now,   *because, swore*
To ben youre frend, °and helply, to my myght,
And for that more aquayntaunce ek of yow   *because*
130 Have ich had than another straunger wight,   *person*
So fro this forth, I pray yow, day and nyght,
Comaundeth me, how soore that me smerte,   *however sorely it taxes me*
To don al that may like unto youre herte;   *be pleasing*

"And that ye me wolde as youre brother trete;   *treat*
135 And taketh naught my frendshipe in despit;   *hold, despicable*
And though youre sorwes be for thynges grete,
Not I nat whi, but °out of more respit,   *I know not why*
Myn herte hath for t'amende it gret delit.
And if I may youre harmes nat redresse,   *set right*
140 I am right sory for youre hevynesse.   *melancholy*

"For though ye Troians with us Grekes wrothe   *angry*
Han many a day ben, alwey yet, parde,   *have, indeed*
O god of Love in soth we serven bothe.   *one, truth*
And, for the love of God, my lady fre,
145 Whomso ye hate, as beth nat wroth with me;   *whomever*
For trewely, ther kan no wyght yow serve,   *person*
That half so loth youre wratthe wold disserve.   *reluctantly, deserve*

124-6 But God forbid that you should not find as true a Greek among us all as any Trojan is and also as kind

127ff. The gross syntax of the stanza is: "because . . . because . . . then command me."

128 to be helpful to the best of my ability

137-8 without further delay my heart has great delight in bettering your condition (of sorrow)

"And nere it that we ben so neigh the tente *were it not, near*
Of Calcas, which that sen us bothe may, *see*
150 I wolde of this yow telle al myn entente;
But this enseled til anothir day. *is to be sealed up*
Yeve me youre hond; I am, and shal ben ay, *give, ever*
God helpe me so, while that my lyf may dure, *last*
Youre owene aboven every creature. *your own (man)*

155 "Thus seyde I nevere er now to womman born; *before*
°For, God myn herte as wisly glade so,
I loved never womman here-biforn
As paramours, ne nevere shal no mo. *in the manner of a lover, more*
And, for the love of God, beth nat my fo, *foe*
160 Al kan I naught to yow, my lady deere, *although*
Compleyne aright, for I am yet to leere. *I have yet to learn*

"And wondreth nought, myn owen lady bright, *wonder*
Though that I speke of love to yow thus blyve; *quickly*
For I have herd er this of many a wight, *person*
165 Hath loved thyng he nevere saigh his lyve. *saw before in his life*
Ek I am nat of power for to stryve *able*
Ayeyns the god of Love, but hym obeye *against*
I wole alwey; and mercy I yow preye. *will*

"Ther ben so worthi knyghtes in this place, *such*
170 And ye so fayr, that everich of hem alle *fair, everyone*
Wol peynen hym to stonden in youre grace. *strive, win your favor*
°But myghte me so faire a grace falle, *happen to*
That ye me for youre servant wolde calle,
So lowely ne so trewely yow serve *humbly*
175 Nil non of hem, as I shal, til I sterve." *will none, die*

---

156 as certainly as may God gladden my heart
172-5 but might so fair a grace happen to me that you would call me your servant,
so humbly or faithfully none of them will serve you as I shall until I die

Criseyde unto that purpos lite answerde,   *subject answered little*
As she that was with sorwe oppressed so   *like someone who*
That, in effect, she naught his tales herde
But her and ther, now here a word or two.   *here*
180 °Hire thoughte hire sorwful herte brast a-two;
For whan she gan hire fader fer espie,   *discern afar*
Wel neigh down of hire hors she gan to sye.   *nigh, from, sink*

But natheles she thonked Diomede   *thanked*
Of al his travaile and his goode cheere,   *effort*
185 °And that hym list his frendshipe hire to bede;
And she accepteth it in good manere,
And wol do fayn °that is hym lief and dere,   *gladly*
And trusten hym she wolde, and wel she myghte,
As seyde she; and from hire hors sh'alighte.   *she dismounted*

190 Hire fader hath hire in his armes nome,   *taken*
And twenty tyme he kiste his doughter sweete,   *kissed*
And seyde, "O deere doughter myn, welcome!"
She seyde ek, she was fayn with hym to mete,   *glad, meet*
And stood forth muwet, milde, and mansuete.   *mute, meek*
195 But here I leve hire with hire fader dwelle,   *let*
And forth I wol of Troilus yow telle.

To Troie is come this woful Troilus,
In sorwe aboven alle sorwes smerte,   *painful*
With feloun look and face dispitous.   *angry, cruel*
200 Tho sodeynly doun from his hors he sterte,   *jumped*
And thorugh his paleis, with a swollen herte,   *palace*
To chaumbre he wente; of nothyng took he hede,   *heed*
Ne non to hym dar speke a word for drede.   *dare, dread*

---

180 it seemed to her that her sorrowful heart would burst asunder
185 and (she thanked him) that it pleased him to offer her his friendship
187 whatever is pleasing and dear to him

And ther his sorwes that he spared hadde   *held back*
205 He yaf an issue large, and "deth!" he criede;   *gave free vent to*
And in his throwes frenetik and madde   *frantic*
He corseth Jove, Appollo, and ek Cupide,   *cursed*
He corseth °Ceres, °Bacus, and °Cipride,   *Venus*
His burthe, hymself, his fate, and ek nature,   *birth*
210 And, save his lady, every creature.   *except for*

To bedde he goth, and walweth ther and torneth   *wallows, turns*
In furie, as doth he °Ixion in helle;
°And in this wise he neigh til day sojorneth.
°But tho bigan his herte a lite unswelle   *then, little*
215 Thorugh teris, which that gonnen up to welle;   *to well up*
And pitously he cryde upon Criseyde,   *piteously*
And to hymself right thus he spak, and seyde:

"Wher is myn owene lady, lief and deere?   *beloved*
Wher is hire white brest? wher is it, where?
220 Wher ben hire armes and hire eyen cleere,   *eyes*
That yesternyght this tyme with me were?   *at this time*
Now may I wepe allone many a teere,   *weep*
And graspe aboute I may, but in this place,   *feel about (me)*
Save a pilowe, I fynde naught t'enbrace.   *except for, pillow*

225 "How shal I do? whan shal she come ayeyn?   *again*
I not, allas! whi lete ich hire to go.   *do not know, I let her go*
°As wolde God ich hadde as tho ben sleyn!
O herte myn, Criseyde, O swete fo!   *foe*

---

208 Ceres, goddess of the harvest; Bacus, god of wine; Cipride—i.e., Venus
212 Because Ixion tried to make love to Juno, Jupiter had him chained hand and foot to a revolving wheel.
213 and in this state he remains till nearly day
214-15 The sense is that the pressure in his heart relents as the upwelling tears are released.
227 "As" introduces an exclamation: Would God I had been slain then!

O lady myn, that I love and na mo!   *no others*
230 To whom for evermo myn herte I dowe,   *bequeath*
Se how I dey, ye nyl me nat rescowe!   *die, rescue*

"Who seth yow now, °my righte lode-sterre?   *sees*
Who sit right now or stant in youre presence?   *sits, stands*
Who kan conforten now youre hertes werre?   *comfort, struggle*
235 Now I am gon, whom yeve ye audience?   *do you give*
Who speketh for me right now in myn absence?   *speaks*
Allas, no wight; and that is al my care!   *one, worry*
For wel woot I, °as yvele as I ye fare.   *know*

"How sholde I thus ten dayes ful endure,
240 Whan I the firste nyght have al this tene?   *sorrow*
How shal she don ek, sorwful creature?
°For tendernesse, how shal she ek sustene   *sustain*
Swich wo for me? °O pitous, pale, and grene
Shal ben youre fresshe, wommanliche face
245 For langour, er ye torne unto this place."   *distress, return*

And whan he fil in any slomberynges,   *slumberings (i.e., asleep)*
Anon bygynne he sholde for to grone,   *immediately, groan*
And dremen of the dredefulleste thynges   *dream*
That myghte ben; as, mete he were allone   *as (for example) dream*
250 In place horrible, makyng ay his mone,   *moan*
Or meten that he was amonges alle
His enemys, and in hire hondes falle.   *hands fallen*

---

232 "my very own lodestar"—i.e., source of light by which I guide my life (The metaphor continues a pattern of T as sailor on the ocean of life and love consistent throughout the poem—see, e.g., 1. 416–18.)

238 you are faring as ill as I

242 given her gentle nature, etc.

243 The word "grene" is often coupled in ME with *wan* and has much the same meaning (i.e., "pale," "without natural color").

And therwithal his body sholde sterte,   *jerk*
And with the sterte al sodeynliche awake,   *would he suddenly awaken*
255 And swich a tremour fele aboute his herte,
That of the fere his body sholde quake;   *fear*
And therwithal he sholde a noyse make,
And seme as though he sholde falle depe   *seem, deep*
From heighe o-lofte; and thanne he wolde wepe,   *high in the air*

260 And rewen on hymself so pitously,   *pity*
That wonder was to here his fantasie.   *it was a wonder to hear*
Another tyme he sholde myghtyly
Conforte hymself, and sein it was folie,   *say, foolishness*
So causeles swich drede for to drye;   *without cause, suffer*
265 And eft bygynne his aspre sorwes newe,   *again, bitter*
That every man myght on his sorwes rewe.   *pity*

Who koude telle aright or ful discryve   *fully describe*
His wo, his pleynt, his langour, and his pyne?   *sorrow, suffering*
Naught alle the men that han or ben on lyve.   *have been or are alive*
270 Thow, redere, maist thiself ful wel devyne   *reader, guess*
That swich a wo my wit kan nat diffyne.   *define*
On ydel for to write it sholde I swynke,   *in vain, labor*
Whan that my wit is wery it to thynke.   *weary even to think of it*

On hevene yet the sterres weren seene,   *in, still visible*
275 Although ful pale ywoxen was the moone;   *grown*
°And whiten gan the orisonte shene
Al estward, as it wont is for to doone;   *accustomed to do*
And Phebus with his rosy carte soone   *Phebus (the sun), chariot*
Gan after that to dresse hym up to fare   *prepare, rise*
280 Whan Troilus hath sent after Pandare.

This Pandare, that of al the day biforn   *during*
Ne myghte han comen Troilus to se,   *was not able to come*

---

276 and the bright horizon began to grow white in all the east

Although he on his hed it hadde sworn, *by his (own) head*

For with the kyng Priam alday was he, *continually*

285 So that it lay nought in his libertee

Nowher to gon,—but on the morwe he wente

To Troilus, whan that he for hym sente.

For in his herte he koude wel devyne *guess*

That Troilus al nyght for sorwe wook; *was awake*

290 And that he wolde telle hym of his pyne, *sorrow*

This knew he wel ynough, °withoute book.

For which to chaumbre streght the wey he took, *straight, way*

And Troilus tho sobrelich he grette, *then, soberly, greeted*

And on the bed ful sone he gan hym sette.

295 "My Pandarus," quod Troilus, "the sorwe

Which that I drye, I may nat longe endure. *suffer*

I trowe I shal nat lyven til to-morwe. *believe*

°For which I wolde alweys, on aventure,

To the devysen of my sepulture

300 The forme; and of my moeble thow dispone,

Right as the semeth best is for to done.

"But of the fir and flaumbe funeral *fire and funeral flame*

In which my body brennen shal to glede, *shall burn to ashes*

°And of the feste and pleyes palestral

305 At my vigile, I prey the, tak good hede *wake*

That that be wel; and °offre Mars my steede, *well done*

---

291 he did not need a book to tell him this

298-301 considering which, on the chance (that I may be dead), I am deeply concerned to describe to you the form and arrangement of my sepulchre; also do you see to the disposal of my goods, just as it seems best to you to do

304 and of the feast and athletic contests (Epics, such as the *Iliad* and the *Aen.*, contain accounts of funeral games in honor of fallen heroes.)

306 and sacrifice to Mars my horse

My swerd, myn helm, and, leve brother deere,
My sheld to Pallas yef, that shyneth cleere.   *give*

°"The poudre in which myn herte ybrend shal torne,
310 That preye I the thow take and it conserve   *pray, save*
In a vessell that men clepeth an urne,   *call*
Of gold, and to my lady that I serve,
For love of whom thus pitouslich I sterve,   *piteously, die*
So yeve it hire, and do me this plesaunce,   *give, favor*
315 To preyen hire kepe it for a remembraunce.

"For wele I fele, by my maladie,   *well, illness*
And by my dremes now and yore ago,   *dreams, earlier*
Al certeynly that I mot nedes dye.   *must*
The owle ek, which that hette °Escaphilo,   *owl, is called*
320 Hath after me shright °al thise nyghtes two.   *shrieked*
And, °god Mercurye! of me now, woful wrecche,
The soule gyde, and, °whan the liste, it fecche!"   *guide*

Pandare answerde and seyde, "Troilus,
My deere frend, as I have told the yore,   *before*
325 That it is folye for to sorwen thus,   *it is folly to*
And causeles, °for which I kan namore.
°But whoso wil nought trowen reed ne loore,
I kan nat sen in hym no remedie,   *see, any remedy*
But lat hym worthen with his fantasie.   *dwell*

---

309 the ashes into which my burned heart will turn
319 The screeching of the owl has been considered a foreboding of death since clas-
sical times; in this instance, T cites Ascalaphus, who, because he tattled on Proserpina,
was changed into an owl.
320 the past two nights
321 Mercury is the *Psychopomp* or guide and conveyer of the soul after death.
322 when it pleases you fetch it
326 regarding which there's no more I can say or do
327 he who will not believe advice or instruction

330 "But, Troilus, I prey the, tel me now
     If that thow trowe, er this, that any wight   *believe, before, one*
     Hath loved paramours as wel as thow?   *as a lover*
     Ye, God woot! and fro many a worthi knyght   *knows*
     Hath his lady gon a fourtenyght,   *fortnight (two weeks)*
335 And he nat yet made halvendel the fare.   *half the fuss*
     What nede is the to maken al this care?   *need is it for you*

     "Syn day by day thow maist thiselven se   *since, see*
     That from his love, or ellis from his wif,
     A man mot twynnen of necessite,   *must be parted*
340 Ye, though he love hire as his owene lif;
     Yet nyl he with hymself thus maken strif.   *will be not, strife*
     For wel thou woost, my leve brother deere,   *know*
     That alwey frendes may nat ben yfeere.   *together*

     "How don this folk that seen hire loves wedded   *these people*
     °By frendes myght, as it bitit ful ofte,   *happens, often*
345 And sen hem in hire spouses bed ybedded?
     God woot, they take it °wisly, faire, and softe,   *knows*
     Forwhi good hope halt up hire herte o-lofte.
     And, for they kan a tyme of sorwe endure,   *since*
350 As tyme hem hurt, a tyme doth hem cure.

     "So sholdestow endure, and laten slide   *should you, let*
     The tyme, and fonde to ben glad and light.   *strive, lighthearted*
     Ten dayes nys so longe nought t'abide.   *is not, wait*
     And syn she the to comen hath bihyght,   *since, to you, promised*
355 She nyl hire heste breken for no wight.   *promise, break, one*
     For dred the nat that she nyl fynden weye   *do not doubt, will find*
     To come ayein; my lif that dorste I leye.   *on that dare I wager*

---

344 by the influence and might of friends
346-47 prudently, fairly, and with restraint because good hope holds up

"Thy swevenes ek and al swich fantasie   *dreams*
    Drif out, and °lat hem faren to meschaunce;   *drive*
360 For they procede of thi melencolie,   *come from*
    That doth the fele in slep al this penaunce.   *makes you, suffering*
    A straw for alle swevenes signifiaunce!   *dreams'*
    God helpe me so, I counte hem nought a bene!   *not worth a bean*
    Ther woot no man aright what dremes mene.   *knows, mean*

365 "For prestes of the temple tellen this,   *priests*
    That dremes ben the revelaciouns
    Of goddes, and as wel they telle, ywis,
    That they ben infernals illusiouns;   *illusions from hell*
    And leches seyn that of complexiouns   *physicians, bodily humors*
370 Proceden they, or fast, or glotonye.   *fasting, gluttony*
    Who woot in soth thus what thei signifie?   *knows in truth*

    "Ek oother seyn that thorugh impressiouns,   *others say*
    As if a wight hath faste a thyng in mynde,   *person*
    That therof cometh swiche avysiouns;   *dreams*
375 And other seyn, as they in bokes fynde,
    °That after tymes of the yer, by kynde,
    Men dreme, and that th'effect goth by the moone.
    But leve no drem, for it is °nought to doone.   *believe*

    °"Wel worthe of dremes ay thise olde wives,
380 And treweliche ek °augurye of thise fowles,
    For fere of which men wenen lese here lyves,   *think they will lose*
    °As revenes qualm, or shrichyng of thise owles.
    To trowen on it bothe fals and foul is.   *believe in*

---

359 and let them go to the devil
376 according to the seasons of the year, by natural revolution, etc.
378 it is not to be done
379 let old women believe in dreams
380 divination from these birds
382 such as ravens' croaking or shrieking of these owls

Allas, allas, so noble a creature   *alas (that)*
385 As is a man shal dreden swich ordure!   *dread, filth*

"For which with al myn herte I the biseche,   *beg you*
Unto thiself that al this thow foryyve;   *have mercy on yourself*
And ris now up withowten more speche,   *rise*
And lat us caste how forth may best be dryve   *plan, made to pass*
390 This tyme, and ek how fresshly we may lyve   *blithely*
Whan that she comth, the which shal be right soone.   *comes*
God helpe me so, the best is thus to doone.

"Ris, lat us speke of lusty lif in Troie   *rise*
That we han led, and forth the tyme dryve;   *make the time pass*
395 And ek of tyme comyng us rejoie,   *let us rejoice in time coming*
That bryngen shal oure blisse now so blyve;   *soon*
And langour of thise twyes dayes fyve   *suffering, twice*
We shal therwith so foryete or oppresse,   *forget or suppress*
That wel unneth it don shal us duresse.   *hardly, hardship*

400 "This town is ful of lordes al aboute,
And trewes lasten al this mene while.   *(days of) truce*
Go we pleye us in som lusty route   *amuse ourselves, company*
To Sarpedoun, nat hennes but a myle;   *hence*
And thus thow shalt the tyme wel bygile,   *beguile*
405 And dryve it forth unto that blisful morwe,
That thow hire se, that cause is of thi sorwe.   *when, see*

"Now ris, my deere brother Troilus,
For certes, it non honour is to the
To wepe, and in thi bedde to jouken thus.   *weep, lie at rest*
410 For trewelich, of o thyng trust to me,   *one*
If thow thus ligge a day, or two, or thre,   *lie*
The folk wol wene that thow, for cowardise,   *suspect*
°The feynest sik, and that thow darst nat rise!"   *dare*

---

413 pretend to be ill

This Troilus answerde, "O brother deere,
415 This knowen folk that han ysuffred peyne,
°That though he wepe and make sorwful cheere,
That feleth harm and smert in every veyne,
No wonder is; and though ich evere pleyne,   *forever complain*
Or alwey wepe, I am no thyng to blame,   *weep, in no way*
420 Syn I have lost the cause of al my game.   *joy*

"But syn of fyne force I mot arise,   *of sheer necessity, must*
I shal arise as soone as evere I may;
And God, to whom myn herte I sacrifice,
So sende us hastely the tenthe day!   *hastily*
425 For was ther nevere fowel so fayn of May   *bird, glad*
As I shal ben, whan that she comth in Troie,   *comes into*
That cause is of my torment and my joie.

"But whider is thi reed," quod Troilus,   *whither, counsel*
"That we may pleye us best in al this town?   *amuse ourselves*
430 "By God, my conseil is," quod Pandarus,
"To ride and pleye us with kyng Sarpedoun."
So longe of this they speken °up and down,
Til Troilus gan at the laste assente
To rise, and forth to Sarpedoun they wente.

435 This Sarpedoun, as he that honourable
Was evere his lyve, and ful of heigh largesse,   *in his lyve*
With al that myghte yserved ben on table,
That deynte was, al coste it gret richesse,   *though it cost a fortune*
He fedde hem day by day, that swich noblesse,   *splendor*
440 As seyden bothe the mooste and ek the leeste,   *greatest and the least*
Was nevere er that day wist at any feste.   *known, feast*

416-18 it is no wonder if someone who feels harm and pain everywhere in his body
should weep and appear miserable
432 up and down (i.e., back and forth)

Not in this world ther is non instrument
Delicious, thorugh wynd or touche of corde,
As fer as any wight hath evere ywent,   *far, person, gone*
445 That tonge telle or herte may recorde,   *remember*
That at that feste it °nas wel herd acorde;
Ne of ladys ek so fair a compaignie
°On daunce, er tho, was nevere iseye with ië.

But what availeth this to Troilus,
450 That for his sorwe nothyng of it roughte?   *cared nothing about it*
For evere in oon his herte pietous   *continually, piteous*
Ful bisyly Criseyde, his lady, soughte.   *anxiously*
On hire was evere al that his herte thoughte,
Now this, now that, so faste ymagenynge,   *imagining*
455 That glade, iwis, kan hym no festeyinge.   *make glad, festivity*

Thise ladies ek that at this feste ben,   *feast*
Syn that he saugh his lady was aweye,   *saw*
It was his sorwe upon hem for to sen,   *to look upon them*
Or for to here on instruments so pleye.   *hear*
460 For she, that of his herte berth the keye,   *since, bears, key*
Was absent, lo, this was his fantasie,
That no wight sholde maken melodie.   *person*

Nor ther nas houre in al the day or nyght,   *nor was there*
Whan he was there as no wight myghte hym heere,   *where no one, hear*
465 That he ne seyde, "O lufsom lady bryght,   *lovely*
How have ye faren syn that ye were here?   *fared*
°Welcome, ywis, myn owne lady deere!"
But weylaway, al this nas but a maze.   *was only a delusion*
°Fortune his howve entended bet to glaze!

---

446 was not heard played well in harmony
448 in the dance, before then, was never seen with eyes
469 Fortune intended rather by deceiving him to cheat him (To glaze one's hood
is to mock or delude a person.)

470 The lettres ek that she of olde tyme   *in earlier times*
     Hadde hym ysent, he wolde allone rede
     An hondred sithe atwixen noon and prime,   *times, between*
     Refiguryng hire shap, hire wommanhede,
     Withinne his herte, and every word or dede
475 That passed was; and thus he drof t'an ende   *had passed, drove*
     The ferthe day, and seyde he wolde wende.   *fourth, go*

     And seyde, "Leve brother Pandarus,
     Intendestow that we shal here bleve   *do you intend, remain*
     Til Sarpedoun wol forth congeyen us?   *invite us to leave*
480 Yet were it fairer that we toke our leve.   *took, leave*
     For Goddes love, lat us now soone at eve   *promptly*
     Oure leve take, and homward lat us torne;   *turn*
     For treweliche, I nyl nat thus sojourne."

     Pandare answerde, "Be we comen hider   *hither*
485 To fecchen fir, and rennen hom ayein?   *fetch, run*
     God help me so, I kan nat tellen whider   *where*
     We myghte gon, if I shal sothly seyn,   *truthfully speak*
     Ther any wight is of us more feyn   *where, person, glad*
     Than Sarpedoun; and if we hennes hye   *hasten hence*
490 Thus sodeynly, I holde it vilanye,   *bad manners*

     "Syn that we seyden that we wolde bleve   *said, remain*
     With hym a wowke; and now, thus sodeynly,   *week*
     The ferthe day to take of hym owre leve, *on the fourth day, leave*
     He wolde wondren on it trewely!
495 Lat us holde forth oure purpos fermely.   *stick to*
     And syn that ye bihighten hym to bide,   *promised*
     Holde forward now, and after lat us ride." *keep your promise*

     Thus Pandarus, with alle peyne and wo,   *effort*
     Made hym to dwelle; and at the wikes ende,   *week's*
500 Of Sarpedoun they toke hire leve tho,   *leave then*
     And on hire wey they spedden hem to wende.   *go*

260

Quod Troilus, "Now Lord me grace sende,
That I may fynden, at my hom-comynge
Criseyde comen!" and therwith gan he synge.   *returned*

505 "Ye, °haselwode!" thoughte this Pandare,
And to hymself ful softeliche he seyde,
"God woot, refreyden may this hote fare,   *cool off, hot eagerness*
Er Calkas sende Troilus Criseyde!"
But natheles, he japed thus, and pleyde,   *joked*
510 And swor, ywys, his herte hym wel bihighte,   *his heart promised him*
She wolde come as soone as evere she myghte.

Whan they unto the paleys were ycomen
Of Troilus, they doun of hors alighte,   *dismounted*
And to the chambre hire wey than han they nomen.   *way, taken*
515 And into tyme that it gan to nyghte,   *grow dark*
They spaken of Criseÿde the brighte;   *spoke*
And after this, whan that hem bothe leste,   *it pleased them both*
They spedde hem fro the soper unto reste.   *supper*

On morwe, as soone as day bygan to clere,   *to dawn*
520 This Troilus gan of his slep t'abrayde,   *awaken*
And to Pandare, his owen brother deere,
"For love of God," ful pitously he sayde,   *piteously*
"As go we sen the palais of Criseyde;   *let us go see, palace*
For syn we yet may have namore feste,   *no more pleasure*
525 So lat us sen hire paleys atte leeste."   *least*

And therwithal, his °meyne for to blende,
A cause he fond in towne for to go,   *invented a reason*
And to Criseydes hous they gonnen wende.   *go*

---

505 a form of exclamation whose sense is something like "what a waste of time!"
(See n. to 3. 890.)
526 to deceive the members of his household

But Lord! this °sely Troilus was wo!   *full of woe*
530 °Hym thoughte his sorwful herte braste a-two.
For, whan he saugh hire dores spered alle,   *saw, barred*
Wel neigh for sorwe adoun he gan to falle.   *nigh, down*

Therwith, whan he was war and gan biholde   *aware*
How shet was every wyndow of the place,   *shut*
535 As frost, hym thoughte, his herte gan to colde;   *grow cold*
For which with chaunged dedlich pale face,   *deathly*
Withouten word, he forthby gan to pace,   *to go away*
And, as God wolde, he gan so faste ride,
That no wight of his contenance espide.   *person, caught sight*

540 Than seide he thus: "O paleys desolat,
O hous of houses whilom best ihight,   *once, called*
O paleys empty and disconsolat,
O thow lanterne of which queynt is the light,   *extinguished*
O paleys, whilom day, that now art nyght,   *once*
545 Wel oughtestow to falle, and I to dye,
Syn she is went that wont was us to gye!   *gone, accustomed, guide*

"O paleis, whilom crowne of houses alle,   *once*
Enlumyned with sonne of alle blisse!   *illuminated*
O ryng, fro which the ruby is out falle,
550 O cause of wo, that cause hast ben of lisse!   *joy*
Yet, syn I may not bet, fayn wolde I kisse   *(do) better, gladly*
Thy colde dores, °dorste I for this route;
And farwel shryne, of which the seynt is oute!"   *saint*

Therwith he caste on Pandarus his yë,   *eyes*
555 With chaunged face, and pitous to biholde;   *pitiful*
And whan he myghte his tyme aright aspie,   *see the opportune moment*

---

529 See n. to 1. 35.
530 it seemed to him his sorrowful heart burst in two
552 if I dared before this crowd

Ay as he rood, to Pandarus he tolde *ever*
His newe sorwe, and ek his joies olde,
So pitously and with so ded an hewe, *deadly (pale) a countenance*
560 That every wight myghte on his sorwe rewe. *person, take pity*

Fro thennesforth he rideth up and down,
And every thyng com hym to remembraunce
As he rood forby places of the town *by*
In which he whilom hadde al his plesaunce. *once*
565 "Lo, yonder saugh ich last my lady daunce; *saw I*
And in that temple, with hire eyen cleere,
Me kaughte first my righte lady dere. *lady (subject of sentence)*

"And yonder have I herd ful lustyly
Me dere herte laugh; and yonder pleye
570 Saugh ich hire ones ek ful blisfully. *saw I, once*
And yonder ones to me gan she seye,
'Now goode swete, love me wel, I preye;'
And yond so goodly gan she me biholde, *look on me*
That to the deth myn herte is to hire holde. *bound*

575 "And at that corner, in the yonder hous,
Herde I myn alderlevest lady deere *heard, dearest of all*
So wommanly, with vois melodious,
Syngen so wel, so goodly, and so clere,
That in my soule yet me thynketh ich here
580 The blisful sown; and in that yonder place *sound*
My lady first me took unto hire grace."

Thanne thoughte he thus, "O blisful lord Cupide,
Whan I the proces have in my memorie,
How thow me hast wereyed on every syde, *made war on me*
585 Men myght a book make of it, lik a storie.
What nede is the to seke on me victorie, *for you to seek*
Syn I am thyn, and holly at thi wille? *wholly*
What joie hastow thyn owen folk to spille? *destroy*

263

"Wel hastow, lord, ywroke on me thyn ire,   *avenged*
590 Thow myghty god, and dredefull for to greve!   *terrible to offend*
Now mercy, lord! thow woost wel I desire   *know*
Thi grace moost of alle lustes leeve,   *dear delights*
And lyve and dye I wol in thy byleve;   *creed*
°For which I n'axe in guerdoun but o bone,
595 That thow Criseyde ayein me sende sone.   *again, soon*

"Distreyne hire herte as faste to retorne,   *constrain, firmly*
As thow doost myn to longen hire to see,
Than woot I wel that she nyl naught sojorne.   *know, tarry*
Now blisful lord, so cruel thow ne be   *be not so cruel*
600 Unto the blood of Troie, I preye the,
As °Juno was unto the blood Thebane,
For which the folk of Thebes caughte hire bane."   *death*

And after this he to the yates wente   *gates*
Ther as Criseyde out rood a ful good paas,   *where, rode, distance*
605 And up and down ther made he many a wente,   *turn*
And to hymself ful ofte he seyde, "Allas!
Fro hennes rood my blisse and my solas!   *hence, rode*
As wolde blisful God now, for his joie,   *would God!*
I myghte hire sen ayein come into Troie!   *again*
610 "And to the yonder hille I gan hire gyde,   *guide*
Allas, and ther I took of hire my leve!   *leave*
And yond I saugh hire to hire fader ride,   *saw*
For sorwe of which myn herte shal tocleve.   *split asunder*
And hider hom I com whan it was eve,   *home*
615 And here I dwelle out cast from alle joie,
And shal, til I may sen hire eft in Troie."   *again*

---

594 for which I ask only one favor as a reward (for my fidelity)
601 Juno's hostility towards Thebes is often referred to—cf. Boccaccio's *Teseida* 3.
1; it was owing to her resentment of Jove's infidelities with Theban women, including
Semele (by whom he had Bacchus) and Alcmene (by whom he had Hercules).

And of hymself ymagened he ofte
To ben defet, and pale, and °waxen lesse   *disfigured*
Than he was wont, and that men seyden softe,
620 "What may it be? Who kan the sothe gesse   *truth guess*
Whi Troilus hath al this hevynesse?"
And al this nas but his malencolie,   *was only his*
That he hadde of hymself swich fantasie.

Another tyme ymaginen he wolde   ·
625 That every wight that wente by the weye   *person*
Hadde of hym routhe, and that they seyen sholde,   *pity, say*
"I am right sory Troilus wol deye."   *sorry, die*
And thus he drof a day yet forth or tweye,   *caused to pass, two*
As ye have herd; swich lif right gan he lede,   *straightway, lead*
630 As he that stood bitwixen hope and drede.   *dread*

For which hym likede in his songes shewe   *it pleased him*
Th'enchesoun of his wo, as he best myghte,   *cause*
And made a song of wordes but a fewe,   *only*
Somwhat his woful herte for to lighte.   *cheer*
635 And whan he was from every mannes syghte,   *(away) from*
With softe vois he of his lady deere,
That absent was, gan synge as ye may heere.

Troilus's Song

"O sterre, of which I lost have al the light,
With herte soor wel oughte I to biwaille,   *sore, lament*
640 That evere derk in torment, nyght by nyght,   *dark*
Toward my deth with wynd in steere I saille;   *astern*
For which the tenthe nyght, if that I faille   *am without*
The gydyng of thi bemes bright an houre,   *guiding, beams*
My ship and me °Caribdis wol devoure."

618-19 and that he had grown thinner than he used to be and that men said in whispers

644 Scylla and Charybdis were located between Sicily and Italy. On the latter dwelt

645 This song whan he thus songen hadde, soone *sung*
He fil ayeyn into his sikes olde; *again, sighs*
And every nyght, as was his wone to doone, *custom, do*
He stood the brighte moone to byholde,
And al his sorwe he to the moone tolde,
650 And seyde, "Ywis, whan thow art horned newe, *new (i.e., the new moon)*
I shal be glad, if al the world be trewe!

"I saugh thyn °hornes olde ek by the morwe, *in the morning*
Whan hennes rood my righte lady dere, *hence, very own*
That cause is of my torment and my sorwe;
655 For which, O brighte Latona the clere, *Latona (the moon)*
For love of God, ren faste aboute thy °spere! *run, sphere*
For whan thyne hornes newe gynnen °sprynge,
Than shal she come that may my blisse brynge."

The dayes moore, and lenger every nyght, *more (i.e., longer)*
660 Than they ben wont to be, hym thoughte tho, *used, it seemed to him*
And that the sonne went his cours unright *travelled his course awry*
By lenger weye than it was wont to do; *longer way*
And seyde, "Ywis, me dredeth evere mo, *I fear*
The sonnes sone, °Pheton, be on lyve, *son, alive*
665 And that his fader carte amys he dryve." *father's chariot*

---

a monster, of this name, who swallowed the waters of the channel and spewed them out again. In other accounts Charybdis is simply a whirlpool that sucked in ships, which would suit the present reference.

652 i.e., the moon was in the last quarter

656 The moon's was the first of the seven spheres in which the planets were thought to revolve.

657 spring (i.e., when you are new)

664 Phaethon was Apollo's son; he foolishly demanded to drive his father's chariot, pulled by the immortal horses of the sun; failing to control the chariot, he scorched the earth, whereupon Zeus destroyed him lest he do worse damage.

Upon the walles faste ek wolde he walke,   *resolutely*
And on the Grekis oost he wolde se,   *look*
And to hymself right thus he wolde talke:
"Lo, yonder is myn owene lady free,
670 Or ellis yonder, ther the tentes be.   *where*
And thennes comth this eyr, that is so soote,   *thence, air, sweet*
That in my soule I fele it doth me boote.   *feel, remedy*

"And hardily this wynd, that more and moore   *assuredly*
Thus stoundemele encresseth in my face,   *gradually increases*
675 Is of my ladys depe sikes soore.   *sighs*
I preve it thus, for in noon othere place
Of al this town, save onliche in this space,   *only*
Fele I no wynd that sowneth so lik peyne: *sounds, pain*
It seyth, 'Allas! whi twynned be we tweyne?'"   *separated, two*

680 This longe tyme he dryveth forth right thus,   *makes pass*
Til fully passed was the nynthe nyght;
And ay bisyde hym was this Pandarus,   *ever*
That bisily did al his fulle myght   *solicitously*
Hym to conforte, and make his herte light,   *cheerful*
685 Yevyng hym hope alwey, the tenthe morwe   *giving*
That she shal come, and stynten al his sorwe.   *put an end to*

Upon that other syde ek was Criseyde,
With wommen fewe, among the Grekis stronge;
For which ful ofte a day "Allas!" she seyde,   *many times a day*
690 "That I was born! Wel may myn herte longe
After my deth; for now lyve I to longe.   *for, too*
Allas! and I ne may it nat amende!
For now is wors than evere yet I wende.   *expected*

"My fader nyl for nothyng do me grace
695 °To gon ayeyn, for naught I kan hym queme;

---

695 to go again for anything I can do to please him

And if so be that I my terme pace,   *exceed my term (of ten days)*
My Troilus shal in his herte deme   *assume*
That I am fals, and so it may wel seme;   *seem*
Thus shal ich have unthank on every side.   *blame*
700 That I was born, so weilaway the tide!   *alas the time*

"And if that I me putte in jupartie,   *jeopardy*
To stele awey by nyght, and it bifalle   *steal, happen*
That I be kaught, I shal be holde a spie;   *considered*
Or elles—lo, this drede I moost of alle—   *dread*
705 If in the hondes of som wrecche I falle,   *low-life*
I nam but lost, al be myn herte trewe.   *although*
Now, myghty God, thow on my sorwe rewe!"   *take pity*

Ful pale ywaxen was hire brighte face,   *grown*
Hire lymes lene, as she that al the day   *limbs lean*
710 Stood, whan she dorste, and loked on the place   *dared*
Ther she was born and ther she dwelt hadde ay;   *where*
And al the nyght wepyng, allas, she lay.
And thus despeired out of alle cure   *in despair of all remedy*
She ladde hire lif, this woful creature.   *conducted*

715 Ful ofte a day she sighte ek for destresse,   *sighed, distress*
And in hirself she wente ay purtrayinge   *went picturing to herself*
Of Troilus the grete worthynesse,
And al his goodly wordes recordynge   *recalling*
Syn first that day hire love bigan to springe.   *grow*
720 And thus she sette hire woful herte afire
Thorugh remembraunce of that she gan desire.

In al this world ther nys so cruel herte   *cruel-hearted person*
That hire hadde herd compleynen in hire sorwe,   *if he had heard her*
That nolde han wepen for hire peynes smerte,   *wept*
725 So tendrely she wepte, bothe eve and morwe.
Hire nedede no teris for to borwe!   *she did not need*
And al this was yet the werste of al hire peyne,   *worst*
Ther was no wight to whom she dorste hire pleyne.   *dared, complain*

268

Ful rewfully she loked upon Troie,
730 Biheld the toures heigh and ek the halles.　　　　　*towers*
"Allas!" quod she, "the plesance and the joie,
The which that now al torned into galle is,
Have ich had ofte withinne tho yonder walles!　　　*those*
O Troilus, what dostow now?" she seyde.　　　　*do you do now*
735 "Lord! wheyther thow yet thenke upon Criseyde?　　*do you still think*

"Allas, °I ne hadde trowed on youre loore,
And went with yow, as ye me redde er this!　　　*counselled before*
Than hadde I now nat siked half so soore.　　　　*sighed*
Who myghte have seyd that I hadde don amys　　　*said*
740 To stele awey with swich oon as he ys?　　　　*steal*
But al to late comth the letuarie,　　　　*comes the medicine*
Whan men the cors unto the grave carie.　　　　*corpse*

"To late is now to speke of that matere.
°Prudence, allas, oon of thyne eyen thre　　　　*eyes*
745 Me lakked alwey, er that I come here!　　　　*before*
On tyme ypassed wel remembred me,　　　*past, I remembered*
And present tyme ek koud ich wel ise,　　　　*see*
But future tyme, er I was in the snare,
Koude I nat sen; that causeth now my care.

750 "But natheles, bityde what bityde,　　　　*come what may*
I shal to-morwe at nyght, by est or west,
Out of this oost stele on som manere syde,　　*on one side or another*
And gon with Troilus where as hym lest.　　　*it pleases him*
This purpos wol ich holde, and this is best.

---

736 that I did not follow your advice
744 Prudence, who looks to the past, present, and the future, is one of the four
Cardinal Virtues. Dante refers to the four in *Purg.* 29. 130–2, where the one who
leads the others "has three eyes in her head." She is identified by a fourteenth-century
commentator on Dante as Prudence.

755 °No fors of wikked tonges janglerie,
    For evere on love han wrecches had envye.

"For whoso wol of every word take hede,   *heed*
    Or reulen hym by every wightes wit,   *rule, person's, opinion*
    Ne shal he nevere thryven, out of drede;   *prosper, doubt*
760 For that that som men blamen evere yit,
    Lo, other manere folk comenden it.
    And as for me, for al swich variaunce,   *no matter all such fickleness*
    Felicite clepe I my suffisaunce.   *happiness is enough for me*

"For which, withouten any wordes mo,
765 To Troie I wole, as for conclusioun."   *will go*
    But God it wot, er fully monthes two,   *knows*
    She was ful fer fro that entencioun!   *far from*
    For bothe Troilus and Troie town
    Shal knotteles thorughout hire herte slide;   *knot-less*
770 For she wol take a purpos for t'abyde.

This Diomede, of whom yow telle I gan,
    Goth now withinne hymself ay arguynge   *ever planning*
    With al the sleghte, and °al that evere he kan,   *cunning*
    How he may best, with shortest taryinge,   *least delay*
775 Into his net Criseydes herte brynge.
    To this entent he koude nevere fyne;   *(to achieve) this end, cease*
    To fisshen hire, he leyde out hook and lyne.   *fish (for), laid*

But natheles, wel in his herte he thoughte,
    That she nas nat withoute a love in Troie;
780 For nevere, sythen he hire thennes broughte,   *since, from there*
    Ne koude he sen hire laughe or maken joie.   *see*
    He nyst how best hire herte for t'acoye.   *did not know, tame*

---

755 the prating of wicked tongues does not matter
773 everything that he can do

°"But for t'asay," he seyde, "it naught ne greveth;
For he that naught n'asaieth, naught n'acheveth."

785 Yet seide he to hymself upon a nyght,
°"Now am I nat a fool, that woot wel how
Hire wo for love is of another wight,
And hereupon to gon assaye hire now?
I may wel wite, it nyl nat ben my prow.   *understand, (to my) profit*
790 For wise folk in bookes it expresse,
'Men shal nat wowe a wight in hevynesse.'   *woo a person*

But whoso myghte wynnen swich a flour   *flower*
From hym for whom she morneth nyght and day,   *mourns*
He myghte seyn he were a conquerour."
795 And right anon, as he that bold was ay,
Thoughte in his herte, "Happe how happe may,   *come what may*
Al sholde I dye, I wol hire herte seche!   *although, seek*
I shal namore lesen but my speche."   *lose*

This Diomede, as bokes us declare,
800 Was in his nedes prest and corageous,   *regarding his needs, ready*
With sterne vois and myghty lymes square,   *limbs solid*
Hardy, testif, strong, and chivalrous   *impestuous*
Of dedes, lik his fader Tideus.   *deeds, father*
And som men seyn he was of tonge large;   *free with his tongue*
805 °And heir he was of Calydoigne and Arge.

Criseyde mene was of hire stature,   *average*
Therto of shap, of face, and ek of cheere,   *shape*
Ther myghte ben no fairer creature.
And ofte tyme this was hire manere,   *custom*

783-4 but it does no harm to try ... for he that tries not, achieves not
786 now would I not be a fool, I that know well how her woe is for love of another man, if I went to test her now
805 Tydeus, Diomede's father, was king of Calydon; "Arge" is Argos.

271

810 To gon ytressed with hire heres clere   *with her bright hair braided*
Doun by hire coler at hire bak byhynde,   *collar*
Which with a thred of gold she wolde bynde.

And, save hire browes °joyneden yfere,
Ther nas no lak, in aught I kan espien.   *lack, observe*
815 But for to speken of hire eyen cleere,
Lo, trewely, they writen that hire syen,   *they write who saw her*
That Paradis stood formed in hire yën.   *eyes*
And with hire riche beaute evere more
Strof love in hire ay, which of hem was more.   *strove, greater*

820 She sobre was, ek symple, and wys withal,   *wise*
The best ynorisshed ek that myghte be,   *brought up*
And goodly of hire speche in general,
Charitable, estatlich, lusty, and fre;   *dignified, lively, noble*
Ne nevere mo ne lakked hire pite;
825 Tendre-herted, slydynge of corage;   *unstable of heart*
But trewely, I kan nat telle hire age.

And Troilus wel woxen was in highte,   *grown*
°And complet formed by proporcioun
So wel that kynde it nought amenden myghte;
830 Yong, fressh, strong, and hardy as lyoun;   *lion*
Trewe as steel in ech condicioun;   *every*
Oon of the beste entecched creature   *best endowed*
That is, or shal, whil that the world may dure.   *last*

And certeynly in storye it is yfounde,
835 That Troilus was nevere unto no wight,   *man*
As in his tyme, in no degree secounde   *second*

---

813 Ch considers knit eyebrows a blemish, but it is often a feature of medieval descriptions of women and in ancient Greece a mark of beauty.

828 and fully formed, each part answering to the other proportionately, that nature might not improve on it

272

In durryng don that longeth to a knyght. *daring to do what belongs*
Al myghte a geant passen hym of myght, *although, giant*
His herte ay with the first and with the beste
840 Stood paregal, °to durre don that hym leste. *fully equal*

But for to tellen forth of Diomede:
It fel that after, on the tenthe day *happened*
Syn that Criseyde out of the citee yede, *since, went*
This Diomede, as fressh as braunche in May,
845 Com to the tente, ther as Calkas lay, *where, lodged*
And °feyned hym with Calkas han to doone;
But what he mente, I shal yow tellen soone.

Criseyde, at shorte wordes for to telle, *to put it briefly*
Welcomed hym, and down hym by hire sette; *sat him down beside her*
850 And he was ethe ynough to maken dwelle! *easy*
And after this, withouten longe lette, *delay*
The spices and the wyn men forth hem fette; *fetched*
And forth they speke of this and that yfeere, *together*
As frendes don, of which som shal ye heere. *friends*

855 He gan first fallen of the werre in speche *he began first to speak*
Bitwixe hem and the folk of Troie town;
And of th'assege he gan hire ek biseche *siege, beseech*
To telle hym what was hire opynyoun.
Fro that demaunde he so descendeth down *question, made his way*
860 To axen hire, if that °hire straunge thoughte *ask*
The Grekis gise, and werkes that they wroughte; *ways, deeds, did*

And whi hire fader tarieth so longe *delays*
To wedden hire unto some worthy wight. *marry*
Criseyde, that was in hire peynes stronge *grieving greatly*

---

840 to dare to do what pleased him
846 and pretended he had business to conduct with Calkas
860 to her seemed strange

865 For love of Troilus, hire owen knyght,
    As ferforth as she konnyng hadde or myght, *far, wit*
    Answerde hym tho; but, as of his entente, *as for*
    It semed nat she wiste what he mente. *knew*

    But natheles, this ilke Diomede *nevertheless, same*
870 Gan in hymself assure, and thus he seyde: *increase in self-confidence*
    "If ich aright have taken of yow hede, *have correctly observed you*
    Me thynketh thus, O lady myn, Criseyde, *it seems to me*
    That syn I first hond on youre bridel leyde, *hand*
    Whan ye out come of Troie by the morwe,
875 Ne koude I nevere sen yow but in sorwe. *never could I see you except*

    "Kan I nat seyn what may the cause be,
    But if for love of som Troian it were, *unless*
    The which right sore wolde athynken me, *sorely cause me regret*
    That ye for any wight that dwelleth there *person*
880 Sholden spille a quarter of a tere, *tear*
    Or pitously youreselven so bigile; *delude*
    For dredeles, it is nought worth the while. *doubtless*

    "The folk of Troie, as who seyth, alle and some *so to speak*
    In prisoun ben, as ye youreselven se;
885 Nor thennes shal nat oon on-lyve come *out of there, one, alive*
    For al the gold atwixen sonne and se. *sun*
    Trusteth wel, and understondeth me,
    Ther shal nat oon to mercy gon on-lyve,
    Al were he lord of worldes twiës fyve! *though, twice*

890 "Swiche wreche on hem, for fecchynge of Eleyne, *vengeance, seizing*
    Ther shal ben take, er that we hennes wende, *taken, go from here*
    °That Manes, which that goddes ben of peyne,

892-3 Manes are the shades of the dead, sometimes spoken of as gods; the thrust of the lines seems to be that the Greeks will perform such slaughter as to strike fear even into the gods of pain.

Shal ben agast that Grekes wol hem shende.
And men shul drede, unto the worldes ende,   *shall dread*
895 From hennesforth to ravysshen any queene,   *carry off*
So cruel shal oure wreche on hem be seene.

°"And but if Calkas lede us with ambages,
That is to seyn, with double wordes slye,   *sly*
Swiche as men clepen a word with two visages,   *call, faces*
900 Ye shal wel knowen that I naught ne lye,   *do not lie*
And al this thyng right sen it with youre yë,   *you shall see, eyes*
And that anon, ye nyl nat trowe how sone.   *won't believe how soon*
Now taketh hede, for it is for to doone.   *necessary to do so*

"What! wene ye youre wise fader wolde   *do you think*
905 Han yeven Antenor for yow anon,   *given*
If he ne wiste that the cite sholde   *did not know*
Destroied ben? Whi, nay, °so mote I gon!
He knew ful wel ther shal nat scapen oon   *escape*
That Troian is; and for the grete feere,   *fear*
910 He dorste nat ye dwelte lenger there.   *dared, longer*

"What wol ye more, lufsom lady deere?   *more will you have, lovely*
Lat Troie and Troian fro youre herte pace!   *pass*
Drif out that bittre hope, and make good cheere,   *drive*
And clepe ayeyn the beaute of youre face,   *recall*
915 That ye with salte teris so deface.   *tears*
For Troie is brought in swich a jupartie,   *jeopardy*
That it to save is now no remedie.

"And thenketh wel, ye shal in Grekis fynde   *among the Greeks*
A moore parfit love, er it be nyght,
920 Than any Troian is, and more kynde,

---

897 unless Calkas leads us (astray) with ambiguous words
907 so may I be able to walk (or, more loosely, as I hope to be able to walk)

°And bet to serven yow wol don his myght.
And if ye vouchesauf, my lady bright,   *agree*
I wol ben he to serven yow myselve,
Yee, levere than be lord of Greces twelve!"   *indeed, rather*

925 And with that word he gan to waxen red,   *turn red (in the face)*
And in his speche a litel wight he quok,   *little bit, shook*
And caste asyde a litle wight his hed,   *turned aside*
And stynte a while; and afterward he wok,   *ceased, aroused himself*
And sobreliche on hire he threw his lok,   *glance*
930 And seyde, "I am, al be it yow no joie,   *though*
As gentil man as any wight in Troie.   *person*

For if my fader Tideus," he seyde,
"Ilyved hadde, ich hadde ben, er this,   *lived*
Of Calydoyne and Arge a kyng, Criseyde!
935 And so hope I that I shal yet, iwis.   *shall (be)*
But he was slayn, allas! the more harm is,
Unhappily at Thebes al to rathe,   *too soon*
°Polymytes and many a man to scathe.   *to the harm of*

"But herte myn, syn that I am youre man,—
940 And ben the first of whom I seche grace,—   *(since you) are, seek*
°To serve yow as hertely as I kan,   *earnestly*
And evere shal, whil I to lyve have space,
So, er that I departe out of this place,
Ye wol me graunte that I may to-morwe,   *will you (please) grant me*
945 At bettre leyser, tellen yow my sorwe."   *leisure*

---

921 and one who, to serve you better, will do his utmost
938 Polymytes is Polynices. In the war for control of Thebes (the subject of Statius's *Thebaid*) between the brothers Eteocles and Polynices, sons of Oedipus, Tydeus fought on the side of Polynices. Hence his death was a misfortune ("scathe") to Polynices and his supporters.
941 (and since I am bound) to serve you

What sholde I telle his wordes that he seyde?   *why*
He spak inough, for o day at the meeste.   *spoke enough, one, most*
It preveth wel, he spak so that Criseyde *the event bore it out well*
Graunted, on the morwe, at his requeste,
950 For to speken with hym at the leeste,   *least*
So that he nolde speke of swich matere.   *provided that, matter*
And thus to hym she seyde, as ye may here,   *hear*

As she that hadde hire herte on Troilus
So faste, that ther may it non arace;   *firmly, root out*
955 And strangely she spak, and seyde thus: *distantly, spoke*
"O Diomede, I love that ilke place   *same*
Ther I was born; and Joves, for his grace,   *where*
°Delyvere it soone of al that doth it care!
God, for thy myght, so leve it wel to fare!   *grant*

960 "That Grekis wolde hire wrath on Troie wreke, *wreak*
If that they myght, I knowe it wel, iwis.   *indeed*
But it shal naught byfallen as ye speke,   *happen*
And God toforn! and forther over this, *God willing, furthermore*
I woot my fader wys and redy is;   *know, prudent, ready*
965 And that he me hath bought, as ye me tolde,
So deere, I am the more unto hym holde. *so dearly, beholden*

"That Grekis ben of heigh condicioun,   *high*
I woot ek wel; but certeyn, men shal fynde   *know*
As worthi folk withinne Troie town,
970 As konnyng, and as parfit, and as kynde, *knowledgeable*
°As ben bitwixen Orkades and Inde.
And that ye koude wel yowre lady serve,
I trowe ek wel, hire thank for to deserve.   *also believe*

---

958 deliver it soon from everything that gives it anxiety
971 as are between the Orkney Islands, on the western edge of the world, and India (i.e., in the known world)

"But as to speke of love, ywis," she seyde,   *speaking of love*
975 "I hadde a lord, to whom I wedded was,
The whos myn herte al was, til that he deyde;   *whose, died*
And other love, as help me now °Pallas,
Ther in myn herte nys, ne nevere was.
And that ye ben of noble and heigh kynrede,   *kindred*
980 I have wel herd it tellen, out of drede.   *doubt*

"And that doth me to han so gret a wonder,   *causes*
That ye wol scornen any womman so.   *mock, so (as you are doing me)*
Ek, God woot, love and I ben fer ysonder!   *far asunder*
I am disposed bet, °so mot I go,   *better*
985 Unto my deth, to pleyne and maken wo.   *lament*
What I shal after don, I kan nat seye;   *in the future*
But trewelich, as yet me list nat pleye.   *it does not suit me to play*

"Myn herte is now in tribulacioun,
And ye in armes bisy day by day.   *in fighting*
990 Herafter, whan ye wonnen han the town,   *conquered*
Peraunter, thanne so it happen may,   *perhaps*
That whan I se that nevere yit I say,   *see what I never saw before*
Than wol I werke that I nevere wroughte!   *do what I never did*
This word to yow ynough suffisen oughte.   *ought to be enough*

995 "To-morwe ek wol I speken with yow fayn,   *speak, gladly*
So that ye touchen naught of this matere.   *do not discuss, topic*
And whan yow list, ye may come here ayayn;   *it pleases you*
And er ye gon, thus muche I sey yow here: *say to*
As help me Pallas with hire heres clere,   *bright hair*
1000 If that I sholde of any Grek han routhe,   *have pity*
It sholde be yourselven, by my trouthe!

---

977 Pallas Athena, upon the preservation of whose image (the Palladium) the safety of Troy depended (See, further, above, 1. 153.)
984 See n. to 5. 907.

"I say nat therfore that I wol yow love,
N'y say nat nay; but in conclusioun,   *nor do I say nay*
I mene wel, by God that sit above!"   *mean*
1005 And therwithal she caste hire eyen down,
And gan to sike, and seyde, "O Troie town,   *sigh*
Yet bidde I God, in quiete and in reste   *pray*
I may yow sen, or do myn herte breste."   *see, make, burst*

But in effect, and shortly for to seye,
1010 This Diomede al fresshly newe ayeyn
Gan pressen on, and faste hire mercy preye;   *pray*
And after this, the sothe for to seyn,   *truth*
Hire glove he took, of which he was ful feyn.   *glad*
And finaly, whan it was woxen eve,   *was evening*
1015 And al was wel, he roos and tok his leve.   *rose, took*

°The brighte Venus folwede and ay taughte   *showed*
The wey ther brode Phebus down alighte;   *plainly, set*
And °Cynthea hire °char-hors overraughte
To whirle out of the Leoun, if she myghte;
1020 And Signifer his °candels sheweth brighte,   *Signifer (the Zodiac)*
Whan that Criseyde unto hire bedde wente
Inwith hire fadres faire brighte tente,   *within*

Retornyng in hire soule ay up and down   *considering*
The wordes of this sodeyn Diomede,   *sudden*
1025 His grete estat, and perel of the town,   *peril*
And that she was allone and hadde nede   *need*
Of frendes help; and thus bygan to brede   *grow*

1016 Venus is here the Evening Star, following the setting sun and thus showing the track of its "wey" down.

1018 Cynthea is the moon; in 4. 1591, C had promised that she would return before the moon passed out of the sign of Leo.

1018 reached over her chariot horses (in the act of urging them on)

1020 candles (i.e., stars)

The cause whi, the sothe for to telle,   *truth*
That she took fully purpos for to dwelle.   *decided*

1030 The morwen com, and gostly for to speke,   *truthfully*
This Diomede is come unto Criseyde;
And shortly, °lest that ye my tale breke,   *cut short*
So wel he for hymselven spak and seyde,   *spoke*
That alle hire sikes soore adown he leyde.   *sighs, allayed*
1035 And finaly, the sothe for to seyne,   *truth*
°He refte hire of the grete of al hire peyne.

And after this the storie telleth us
That °she hym yaf the faire baye stede,   *steed*
The which he ones wan of Troilus;   *won*
1040 And ek a broche — °and that was litel nede —   *brooch*
That Troilus was, she yaf this Diomede.   *Troilus's, gave*
And ek, the bet from sorwe hym to releve,   *relieve*
She made hym were a pencel of hire sleve.   *wear, pennon, sleeve*

I fynde ek in the stories elleswhere,
1045 Whan thorugh the body hurt was Diomede
Of Troilus, tho wepte she many a teere,   *by*
Whan that she saugh his wyde wowndes blede;   *wounds*
°And that she took, to kepen hym, good hede;
And for to helen hym of his sorwes smerte,   *heal, painful*
1050 °Men seyn — I not — that she yaf hym hire herte.

1032 lest I weary you with too long a story (and you thus "cut short" my tale)
1036 he took away from her the great part of all her pain
1038 Diomede won the horse in battle and according to other accounts sent it to
C; she here gives it back to him.
1040 and there was little need for that
1048 and that she took good care to look after him
1050 men say — I do not know — that she gave him her heart

But trewely, the storie telleth us,
Ther made nevere woman moore wo
Than she, whan that she falsed Troilus.   *betrayed*
She seyde, "Allas! for now is clene ago   *completely gone*
1055   My name of trouthe in love, for everemo!
For I have °falsed oon the gentileste
That evere was, and oon the worthieste!

"Allas! of me, unto the worldes ende,
Shal neyther ben ywriten nor ysonge
1060   No good word, for thise bokes wol me shende.   *revile*
°O, rolled shal I ben on many a tonge!
Thorughout the world °my belle shal be ronge!
And wommen moost wol haten me of alle.   *hate*
Allas, that swich a cas me sholde falle!   *misfortune, happen to*

1065   "Thei wol seyn, in as muche as in me is,   *say*
I have hem don dishonour, weylaway!   *alas*
Al be I nat the first that dide amys,   *although I am not*
What helpeth that to don my blame awey?   *cause my blame to disappear*
But syn I se ther is no bettre way,
1070   And that to late is now for me to rewe,   *too, repent*
To Diomede algate I wol be trewe.   *in any case*

"But, Troilus, syn I no bettre may,   *since I no better may (do)*
And syn that thus departen ye and I,   *separate*
Yet prey I God, °so yeve yow right good day,   *pray*
1075   °As for the gentileste, trewely,   *(I think of you) as*

1056 Cf. 5. 1845.

1061 The sense is that she (i.e., her name) shall be turned over and over on many a tongue by rumor.

1062 a slang or proverbial expression, meaning something like "rumor shall sound my name and deeds abroad"

1074 so may he give you a very good day (i.e., the best of luck or good chances)

1075 The syntax is very loose and "nervous," in keeping with C's agitated state of mind; the general idea, however, is clear—she thinks of him as a very loving man.

281

That evere I say, to serven feythfully,   *saw, (and one) to serve*
And best kan ay his lady honour kepe";—   *and (one who), lady's*
And with that word she brast anon to wepe.   *burst, into weeping*

"And certes, yow ne haten shal I nevere;   *hate*
1080 And frendes love, that shal ye han of me,   *friend's, have*
And my good word, al sholde I lyven evere.   *even if I should live*
And, trewely, I wolde sory be   *sorry*
For to seen yow in adversitee;
And gilteles, I woot wel, I yow leve.   *believe you (to be)*
1085 But al shal passe; and thus take I my leve."   *leave*

But trewely, how longe it was bytwene
That she forsok hym for this Diomede,
Ther is non auctour telleth it, I wene.   *assume*
°Take every man now to his bokes heede;
1090 He shal no terme fynden, out of drede.   *dates, doubt*
For though that he bigan to wowe hire soone,   *woo*
Er he hire wan, yet was ther more to doone.   *won*

Ne me ne list this °sely womman chyde   *poor, rebuke*
Forther than the storye wol devyse.   *further, suggest (I should)*
1095 Hire name, allas! is punysshed so wide,   *punished with ill repute*
That for hire gilt it oughte ynough suffise.   *guilt*
And if I myghte excuse hire any wise,   *in any way*
For she so sory was for hire untrouthe,   *sorry, infidelity*
Iwis, I wolde excuse hire yet for routhe.   *pity*

1100 This Troilus, as I byfore have told,
Thus driveth forth, as wel as he hath myght.   *marks the time*
But often was his herte hoot and cold,
And namely that ilke nynthe nyght,   *very*

1089 let every man consult his books now
1093 Cf. 5. 529 and n. to 1. 35.
1104 on the morning of which

°Which on the morwe she hadde hym bihight   *promised*
1105 To com ayeyn: God woot, ful litel reste   *knows*
Hadde he that nyght; °nothyng to slepe hym leste.

The laurer-crowned Phebus, with his heete,   *laurel-crowned, heat*
Gan, in his course ay upward as he wente,
To warmen of the °est see the wawes weete,   *wet waves*
1110 And °Nysus doughter song with fressh entente,   *endeavor*
Whan Troilus his Pandare after sente;
And on the walles of the town they °pleyde,
To loke if they kan sen aught of Criseyde.   *look, see*

Tyl it was noon, they stoden for to se   *stood*
1115 Who that ther come; and every maner wight   *sort of person*
That com fro fer, they seyden it was she,   *far*
Til that thei koude knowen hym aright.   *identify him correctly*
Now was his herte dul, now was it light.
And thus byjaped stonden for to stare   *fooled, stood (they)*
1120 Aboute naught this Troilus and Pandare.   *for nothing*

To Pandarus this Troilus tho seyde,
"For aught I woot, °byfor noon, sikirly,   *all I know, certainly*
Into this town ne comth nat here Criseyde.
She hath ynough to doone, hardyly,   *indeed*
1125 To wynnen from hire fader, so trowe I.   *to get away from, believe*
Hire olde fader wol yet make hire dyne   *dine*
Er that she go; God yeve hys herte pyne!"   *pain*

1106 he was not at all interested in sleeping
1109 The "sea in the east" has not been certainly identified.
1110 "Nysus doughter" is Scylla, who, for the love of Minos, caused her father's death. To save her from the vengeance about to overtake her she was changed into a bird.
1112 amused themselves as they passed the time
1122 "Noon" here carries the modern sense; T and P have not yet eaten (line 1129 below), although the usual hour for dinner was ten o'clock.

Pandare answerde, "It may wel be, certeyn.
And forthi lat us dyne, I the byseche,   *therefore, beseech*
1130 And after noon than maystow come ayeyn."
And hom they go, withoute more speche,
And comen ayeyn; but longe may they seche   *seek*
Er that they fynde that they after gape.   *what they are looking for*
Fortune hem bothe thenketh for to jape!   *mock*

1135 Quod Troilus, "I se wel now that she
Is taried with hire olde fader so,   *delayed*
That er she come, it wol neigh even be.   *nearly evening*
Com forth, I wole unto the yate go.   *gate (in the city wall)*
Thise porters ben unkonnyng evere mo,   *unknowing (i.e., incompetent)*
1140 And I wol don hem holden up the yate   *cause, portcullis*
°As naught ne were, although she come late."

The day goth faste, and after that com eve,
And yet com nought to Troilus Criseyde.
He loketh forth by hegge, by tre, by greve,   *hedge, thicket*
1145 And fer his hed over the wal he leyde,   *far, put*
And at the laste he torned hym and seyde,
"By God, I woot hire menyng now, Pandare!   *know, meaning*
Almoost, ywys, al newe was my care.   *renewed*

"Now douteles, this lady kan hire good;   *can look after herself*
1150 I woot, she meneth riden pryvely.   *know, means, secretly*
I comende hire wisdom, by myn hood!
She wol nat maken peple nycely   *stupidly*
Gaure on hire whan she comth; but softely   *stare at, unnoticed*
By nyghte into the town she thenketh ride.   *plans to ride*
1155 And, deere brother, °thynk not longe t'abide.

1141 as though there were no special reason even though she should come late
1155 don't expect to have to wait very long

"We han naught elles for to don, ywis.
And Pandarus, now woltow trowen me?　　　　　*believe*
Have here my trouthe, I se hire! yond she is!　　　*yonder*
Heve up thyn eyen, man! maistow nat se?"　　　*lift, eyes*
1160 Pandare answerede, "Nay, so mote I the!　　　*may I prosper*
Al wrong, by God! °What saistow, man, where arte?
That I se yond nys but a fare-carte."　　　*is only a hauling cart*

"Allas! thow seyst right soth," quod Troilus.　　　*truth*
"But, hardily, it is naught al for nought
1165 That in myn herte I now rejoysse thus.
°It is ayeyns som good I have a thought.
Not I nat how, but syn that I was wrought,　　*I don't know how, made*
Ne felte I swich a comfort, dar I seye;　　　*dare*
She comth to-nyght, my lif that dorste I leye!"　　*I would dare wager*

1170 Pandare answerde, "It may be, wel ynough,"
And held with hym of al that evere he seyde.　　*agreed with him in*
But in his herte he thoughte, and softe lough,　　*quietly laughed*
And to hymself ful sobreliche he seyde,　　　*soberly*
°"From haselwode, there joly Robyn pleyde,
1175 Shal come al that that thow abidest heere.　　*you wait for*
Ye, fare wel al the snow of ferne yere!"　　　*last year*

The warden of the yates gan to calle
The folk which that withoute the yates were,
And bad hem dryven in hire bestes alle,　　　*bade, animals*
1180 Or al the nyght they moste bleven there.　　*remain (out)*

1161 what do you say, man, where are you
1166 I believe it forebodes some good, or I would not feel such a comfort (See 5. 1165; 1168.)
1174 The sense is "will not come at all." But the expression and its exact meaning are unknown. Robin is a common name for a young shepherd in the medieval pastourelle. In Ch *haselwode* always has some connotation besides the literal meaning "a thicket of hazel bushes"–cf. the note to 3. 890.

And fer withinne the nyght, with many a teere, *far, tear*
This Troilus gan homward for to ride;
For wel he seth it helpeth naught t'abide. *sees, linger*

But natheles, he gladed hym in this: *took comfort*
1185 He thought he misacounted hadde his day, *miscounted*
And seyde, "I understonde have al amys. *wrongly*
For thilke nyght I last Criseyde say, *that same, saw*
She seyde, 'I shal ben here, if that I may,
Er that the moone, O deere herte swete,
1190 °The Leoun passe, out of this Ariete.'

"For which she may yet holde al hire byheste." *keep, promise*
And on the morwe unto the yate he wente, *gate*
And up and down, by west and ek by este, *east*
Upon the walles made he many a wente; *turn*
1195 But al for nought; his hope alwey hym blente. *blinded*
For which at nyght, in sorwe and sikes sore *sigh*
He wente hym hom, withouten any more. *without (doing)*

His hope al clene out of his herte fledde;
°He nath wheron now lenger for to honge;
1200 But for the peyne hym thoughte his herte bledde, *it seemed to him*
So were his throwes sharpe and wonder stronge. *torments, amazingly*
For whan he saugh that she abood so longe, *stayed (away)*
He nyste what he juggen of it myghte, *judge*
Syn she hath broken that she hym bihighte. *since, promised*

1205 The thridde, ferthe, fifte, sexte day
After tho dayes ten of which I tolde, *those*
Bitwixen hope and drede his herte lay,
Yet somwhat trustyng on hire hestes olde. *promises*

1190 See 4. 1591–2 and n.
1199 he has nothing to hang onto any longer

°But whan he saugh she nolde hire terme holde,
1210 He kan now sen non other remedie
But for to shape hym soone for to dye.   *arrange, die*

Therwith the wikked spirit, God us blesse,   *protect us (from it)*
Which that men clepeth the woode jalousie,   *call, mad, jealousy*
Gan in hym crepe, in al this hevynesse;   *creep*
1215 For which, by cause he wolde soone dye,
He ne et ne drank, for his malencolye,   *ate*
And ek from every compaignye he fledde:
This was the lif that al the tyme he ledde.

He so defet was, that no manere man   *wasted away*
1220 Unneth hym myghte knowen ther he wente;   *hardly, where*
So was he lene, and therto pale and wan,   *lean*
And feble, that he walketh by potente;   *feeble, with a crutch*
And with his ire he thus hymselve shente.   *rage, injured*
And whoso axed hym wherof hym smerte,   *of what he suffered*
1225 He seyde, his harm was al aboute his herte.   *malady*

Priam ful ofte, and ek his moder deere,   *dear mother*
His bretheren and his sustren gonne hym freyne   *ask*
Whi he so sorwful was in al his cheere,
And what thyng was the cause of al his peyne;
1230 But al for naught. He nolde his cause pleyne,   *explain his case*
But seyde he felte a grevous maladie
Aboute his herte, and fayn he wolde dye.   *gladly*

So on a day he leyde hym doun to slepe,
And so byfel that in his slep hym thoughte   *it seemed to him*
1235 That in a forest faste he welk to wepe   *walked to weep*
For love of here that hym these peynes wroughte;   *her, caused*
And up and doun as he the forest soughte,   *explored*

1209 when he saw that she would not keep to her appointed time (of return)

He mette he saugh a bor with tuskes grete,   *dreamed, saw, boar*
That slepte ayeyn the bryghte sonnes hete.   *slept exposed to, heat*

1240 And by this bor, faste in his armes folde,   *folded*
Lay, kissyng ay his lady bryght, Criseyde.
For sorwe of which, whan he it gan byholde,
°And for despit, out of his slep he breyde,
And loude he cride on Pandarus and seyde:
1245 "O Pandarus, now know I crop and roote   *root and branch*
I n'am but ded; ther nys non other bote.   *remedy*

"My lady bryght, Criseyde, hath me bytrayed,
In whom I trusted most of any wight.   *person*
She elliswhere hath now here herte apayed.   *satisfied*
1250 The blysful goddes, thorugh here grete myght,
Han in my drem yshewed it ful right.   *shown*
Thus in my drem Criseyde have I byholde"—
And al this thing to Pandarus he tolde.

"O my Criseyde, allas! what subtilte,   *subtle (speculation)*
1255 What newe lust, what beaute, what science,   *pleasure, knowledge*
What wratthe of juste cause have ye to me?   *anger*
What gilt of me, what fel experience,   *guilt of mine, dreadful*
Hath fro me raft, allas! thyn advertence?   *taken, attention*
O trust, o feyth, O depe aseuraunce,   *assurance*
1260 Who hath me reft Criseyde, al my plesaunce?   *taken (from)*

"Allas! whi leet I you from hennes go,   *did I let you go from here*
For which wel neigh out of my wit I breyde?   *I'm going out of my mind*
°Who shal now trowe on any othes mo?
God wot, I wende, O lady bright, Criseyde,   *knows, assumed*
1265 That every word was gospel that ye seyde!

1243 and because of indignation, he started out of his sleep
1263 who shall ever believe in oaths again

But who may bet bigile, yf hym lyste,   *beguile, it pleases him*
°Than he on whom men weneth best to triste?

"What shal I don, my Pandarus, allas?
I fele now so sharp a newe peyne,   *feel*
1270 Syn that ther is no remedye in this cas,
That bet were it I with myn honde tweyne   *two hands*
Myselven slow than thus alwey to pleyne.   *slew, complain*
For thorugh my deth my wo shold han an ende,
Ther every day with lyf myself I shende."   *where, life, destroy*

1275 Pandare answerde and seyde, "Allas the while   *hour*
That I was born! Have I nat seyd er this,
That dremes many a maner man bigile?   *manner, beguile*
And whi? For folk expounden hem amys.   *expound them wrongly*
How darstow seyn that fals thy lady ys,   *dare you*
1280 °For any drem, right for thyn owene drede?
Lat be this thought; thow kanst no dremes rede.   *interpret*

"Peraunter, ther thow dremest of this boor,   *where*
It may so be that it may signifie
Hire fader, which that old is and ek hoor,   *white-haired*
1285 Ayeyn the sonne lith, o poynt to dye,   *lies, on the point*
And she for sorwe gynneth wepe and crie,   *weep*
And kisseth hym, ther he lith on the grounde: *where*
Thus sholdestow thi drem aright expounde!"

"How myghte I than don," quod Troilus,   *what*
1290 "To knowe of this, yee, were it nevere so lite?"   *little*
"Now seystow wisly," quod this Pandarus.   *you're talking sense*
"My rede is this, syn thow kanst wel endite,   *advice, compose*
That hastily a lettre thow hire write,

1267 than he in whom men presume it is best and safest to trust
1280 on account of any dream just because your fear forces you to interpret it that way

289

Thorugh which thow shalt wel bryngyn it aboute,
1295 To know a soth of that thow art in doute.   *truth about that of which*

"And se now whi; for this I dar wel seyn,
That if so is that she untrewe be,
I kan nat trowen that she wol write ayeyn.   *imagine*
And if she write, thow shalt ful sone yse   *see*
1300 As wheither she hath any liberte   *as (to)*
To come ayeyn; or ellis in som clause,
If she be let, she wol assigne a cause.   *hindered*

"Thow hast nat writen hire syn that she wente,
Nor she to the; and this I dorste laye,   *dare wager*
1305 Ther may swich cause ben in hire entente,   *understanding*
That hardily thow wolt thiselven saye   *indeed*
That hire abod the best is for yow twaye.   *staying, two*
Now writ hire thanne, and thow shalt feele sone   *write, soon*
A soth of al; ther is namore to done."   *truth*

1310 Acorden ben to this conclusioun,
And that anon, thise ilke lordes two;   *right away, same*
And hastily sit Troilus adown,
And rolleth in his herte to and fro,   *considers*
How he may best discryven hire his wo.   *describe to*
1315 And to Criseyde, his owen lady deere,
He wrot right thus, and seyde as ye may here: *hear*

Troilus's Letter

"Right fresshe flour, whos I ben have and shal,
°Withouten part of elleswhere servyse,
With herte, body, lif, lust, thought, and al,
1320 I, woful wyght, in everich humble wise   *man*
That tonge telle or herte may devyse,   *tongue may tell, invent*

1318 with no part of my service bestowed elsewhere

°As ofte as matere occupieth place,
Me recomaunde unto youre noble grace.

"Liketh yow to witen, swete herte, — *May it please you to recall*
1325 As ye wel knowe, how longe tyme agon
That ye me lefte in aspre peynes smerte, — *bitter, sharp*
Whan that ye wente, of which yit boote non — *yet no remedy*
Have I non had, but evere wors bigon — *worse beset*
Fro day to day am I, and so mot dwelle, — *must*
1330 While it yow list, of wele and wo my welle. — *pleases you, joy*

"For which to yow, with dredul herte trewe,
I write, as he that sorwe drifth to write, — *drives*
°My wo, that everich houre encresseth newe,
Compleynyng, as I dar or kan endite. — *compose*
1335 And that defaced is, that may ye wite — *that it is defaced, blame*
The teris which that fro myn eyen reyne, — *tears, rain*
That wolden speke, if that they koude, and pleyne. — *complain*

"Yow first biseche I °that youre eyen clere
To loke on this, defouled ye nat holde;
1340 And over al this, that ye, my lady deere,
Wol vouchesauf this lettre to byholde. — *grant*
And by the cause ek of my cares colde, — *because also*
That sleth my wit, if aught amys m'asterte, — *slay, escapes from me*
Foryeve it me, myn owen swete herte!

1345 "If any servant dorste or oughte of right — *dared*
Upon his lady pitously compleyne,
Thanne wene I that ich oughte be that wight, — *suppose, person*
Considered this, that ye thise monthes tweyne — *considering this*
Han taried, ther ye seyden, soth to seyne, — *said, truth*

1322 as long as space is filled with matter (i.e., as long as there is a world, life, etc.)
1333 "My wo" is the object of "compleynyng" (1334).
1338 that you do not consider your eyes defiled by looking on this

291

1350 But dayes ten ye nolde in oost sojourne,— *that only, host*
But in two monthes yet ye nat retourne.

"But for as muche as me moot nedes like *must needs*
Al that yow liste, I dar nat pleyne moore, *pleases you, complain*
But humblely, with sorwful sikes sike, *sighs sick*
1355 Yow write ich myn unresty sorwes soore, *(about) my unquiet*
Fro day to day desiryng evere moore
To knowen fully, if youre wille it weere,
How ye han ferd and don whil ye be theere; *have fared*

°"The whos welfare and hele ek God encresse *well-being*
1360 In honour swich, that upward in degree
It growe alwey, so that it nevere cesse. *ceases*
Right as youre herte ay kan, my lady free,
Devyse, I preye to God so moot it be, *imagine and arrange it, may*
And graunte it that ye soone upon me rewe, *take pity*
1365 As wisly as in al I am yow trewe. *certainly, to you true*

"And if yow liketh knowen of the fare *it pleases you, condition*
Of me, whos wo ther may no wit discryve, *describe*
I kan namore but, chiste of every care, *can (say), receptacle*
At wrytyng of this lettre I was on-lyve, *alive*
1370 Al redy out my woful gost to dryve; *though ready, spirit*
Which I delaye, and holde hym yet in honde,
Upon the sighte of matere of youre sonde. *waiting for, message*

"Myn eyen two, in veyn with which I se, *vain*
Of sorwful teris salte arn waxen welles; *have become*
1375 °My song, in pleynte of myn adversitee; *lament*
My good, in harm; myn ese ek woxen helle is;
My joie, in wo; I kan sey yow naught ellis, *say*
But torned is, for which my lif I warie, *because of, curse*
°Everich joie or ese in his contrarie. *into*

1359 i.e., yours
1375 my song (has turned into)
1379 "Joie or ese" is the subject of "torned."

1380 "Which with youre comyng hom ayeyn to Troie
Ye may redresse, and more a thousand sithe   *times*
Than evere ich hadde, encressen in me joie.   *had (before), increase*
For was ther nevere herte yet so blithe
To han his lif as I shal ben as swithe   *soon*
1385 As I yow se; and though no manere routhe   *pity*
Commeve yow, yet thynketh on youre trouthe.   *move*

"And if so be my gilt hath deth deserved,   *guilt, death*
Or if yow list namore upon me se,   *it pleases you, to look*
In guerdoun yet of that I have yow served,   *reward*
1390 Byseche I yow, myn owen lady free,
That hereupon ye wolden write me,
For love of God, my righte lode-sterre,   *lode-star (guiding star)*
That deth may make an ende of al my werre.   *war*

"If other cause aught doth yow for to dwelle,   *reason, causes*
1395 That with youre letter ye me recomforte;
For though to me youre absence is an helle,
With pacience I wol my wo comporte,   *bear my woe*
And with youre lettre of hope I wol desporte.   *console myself*
Now writeth, swete, and lat me thus nat pleyne;   *lament*
1400 With hope, or deth, delivereth me fro peyne.

"Iwis, myne owene deere herte trewe,
I woot that, whan ye next upon me se,   *look*
So lost have I myn hele and ek myn hewe,   *health, color*
Criseyde shal nought konne knowen me.   *be able to recognize*
1405 Iwys, myn hertes day, my lady free,
So thursteth ay myn herte to byholde   *thirsts*
Youre beute, that °my lif unnethe I holde.   *beauty*

"I say namore, al have I for to seye   *though*
To yow wel more than I telle may,

1407 I can hardly sustain my life

293

1410 But wheither that ye do me lyve or deye, *cause*
Yet praye I God, so yeve yow right good day! *give, good fortune*
And fareth wel, goodly, faire, fresshe may, *maid*
As ye that lif or deth may me comande!
And to youre trouthe ay I me recomande, *commend*

1415 °"With hele swich that, but ye yeven me
The same hele, I shal non hele have.
In yow lith, whan yow liste that it so be, *lies, it pleases you*
The day in which me clothen shal my grave; *my grave shall clothe me*
In yow my lif, in yow myght for to save *(lies) my life*
1420 Me fro disese of alle peynes smerte; *distress, bitter*
And far now wel, myn owen swete herte! *fare*
le vostre T." *your T.*

This lettre forth was sent unto Criseyde,
Of which hire answere in effect was this:
Ful pitously she wroot ayeyn, and seyde, *wrote*
1425 That also sone as that she myghte, ywys, *as soon as, certainly*
She wolde come, and mende al that was mys. *mend, amiss*
And fynaly she wroot and seyde hym thenne, *to him then*
She wolde come, ye, but she nyste whenne. *did not know*

But in hire lettre made she swich festes *paid such compliments*
1430 That wonder was, and swerth she loveth hym best; *swears*
Of which he fond but botmeles bihestes. *empty promises*
But Troilus, thow maist now, est or west, *east*
Pipe in an ivy lef, if that the lest! *go whistle, it pleases you*
Thus goth the world. God shilde us fro meschaunce, *mischance*
1435 °And every wight that meneth trouthe avaunce!

1415 and together with that (I also wish) you well-being such that, unless you give
me the same well-being, I shall have none at all
1435 and everyone who intends the truth (may God) further

Encressen gan the wo fro day to nyght   *increase, from*
Of Troilus, for tarying of Criseyde;
And lessen gan his hope and ek his myght,   *decrease*
For which al down he in his bed hym leyde.   *laid*
1440 He ne eet, ne dronk, ne slep, ne no word seyde,   *ate, slept*
Ymagynyng ay that she was unkynde,   *untrue*
For which wel neigh he wex out of his mynde.   *be nearly went out of*

This drem, of which I told have ek byforn,   *already*
May nevere come out of his remembraunce.
1445 He thought ay wel he hadde his lady lorn,   *certainly, lost*
And that Joves, of his purveyaunce,   *foreknowledge*
Hym shewed hadde in slep the signifiaunce   *shown*
Of hire untrouthe and his disaventure,   *misfortune*
And that the boor was shewed hym in figure.   *boar, symbolically*

1450 For which he for °Sibille his suster sente,
That called was Cassandre ek al aboute,   *all about (Troy)*
And al his drem he tolde hire er he stente,   *before he stopped*
°And hire bisoughte assoilen hym the doute
Of the stronge boor with tuskes stoute;
1455 And fynaly, withinne a litel stounde,   *while*
Cassandre hym gan right thus his drem expounde.   *explain*

She gan first smyle, and seyde, "O brother deere,   *smile*
If thow a soth of this desirest knowe,   *truth, to know*
Thow most a fewe of olde stories heere,   *hear*
1460 To purpos, how that Fortune overthrowe   *pertinent to the matter*
Hath lordes olde; thorugh which, withinne a throwe,   *moment*
Thow wel this boor shalt knowe, and of what kynde   *lineage*
He comen is, as men in bokes fynde.   *books*

1450 "Sibille" means "prophetess," strictly speaking, but Ch uses it as another name
for Cassandra; Cassandra is a prophetess cursed by Apollo with the fate of always predict-
ing truly but never being believed.
1453 and asked her to release him from his uncertainty about

"Diane, which that wroth was and in ire   *angry*
1465 For Grekis nolde don hire sacrifise,   *because*
     Ne encens upon hire auter sette afire,   *incense, altar*
     She, for that Grekis gonne hire so despise,   *because*
     Wrak hire in a wonder cruel wise;   *avenged herself, amazingly, way*
     For with a boor as gret as ox in stalle
1470 She made up frete hire corn and vynes alle.   *caused to be consumed*

     "To sle this boor was al the contre raysed,   *slay, enlisted*
     Amonges which ther com, this boor to se,
     A mayde, oon of this world the beste ypreysed;   *maiden, praised*
     And °Meleagre, lord of that contree,
1475 He loved so this fresshe mayden free,
     That with his manhod, er he wolde stente,   *cease*
     This boor he slough, and hire the hed he sente;   *slew, head*

     "Of which, as olde bokes tellen us,
     Ther ros a contek and a gret envye;   *arose, strife*
1480 And of this lord descended °Tideus   *from*
     By ligne, or ellis olde bookes lye.
     But °how this Meleagre gan to dye
     Thorugh his moder, wol I yow naught telle,   *mother*
     For al to longe it were for to dwelle."

1474 Meleager was the son of the Calydonian king and leader of the band that slew the monster (a boar) which was devastating the country. Ovid tells the story at *Metam.* 8. 271–444. The maiden is Atalanta.

1480 Tideus is properly the half-brother, not the descendant of Meleager.

1482 Meleager's mother's brothers protested his giving the head to Atalanta, whereupon he slew them. When he was an infant the Fates had declared that he would die when a certain piece of wood on the hearth was consumed. His mother, Althaea, had extinguished it and concealed it. Now in her rage over her brothers' deaths she threw it into the fire.

1485 °She tolde ek how Tideus, er she stente,   *ceased*
    Unto the stronge citee of Thebes,
    To cleymen kyngdom of the citee, wente,   *claim, rule*
    For his felawe, daun Polymytes,   *in behalf of his friend, lord*
    Of which the brother, daun Ethiocles,
1490 Ful wrongfully of Thebes held the strengthe;
    This tolde she by proces, al by lengthe.   *in due course*

    She tolde ek how °Hemonydes asterte,   *escaped*
    Whan Tideus slough °fifty knyghtes stoute.   *slew*
    She tolde ek °alle the prophecyes by herte,
1495 And how that °seven kynges with hire route   *armies*
    Bysegeden the citee al aboute;   *besieged*
    And of the °holy serpent, and the welle,
    And of the °furies, al she gan hym telle;°

1485 This and the following three stanzas summarize the *Thebaid* of Statius. Eteocles and Polynices (whom Ch calls Polymites), sons of Oedipus, agreed to rule Thebes in alternate years. When at the end of a year Eteocles refused to let Polynices take his turn, the latter enlisted the help of his father-in-law Adrastus, king of Argos. Adrastus's other daughter was married to Tydeus.

1492 Hemonydes is Maeon, son of Haemon.

1493 The "fifty knyghtes" really should read "the other forty-nine." Eteocles had sent the fifty against Tydeus who single-handedly slew them all but Maeon.

1494 Amphiaraus, a great prophet at Argos, had foretold the fatal outcome of the war.

1495 The seven kings are the seven heroes (including Polynices) who besieged Thebes—they are the Seven against Thebes.

1497 A serpent sent by Jove stung to death the child Archemorus when its nurse left it to guide the host of the Seven at one point in their march. The well is the stream to which the nurse was guiding them.

1498 In Statius (Book 5), Hypsipyle recalls how the women of Lemnos, acting like furies, killed all their husbands (for having left them and taken concubines from Thrace).

1498 After this stanza, in all but two of the manuscripts of *T&C*, follows a twelve-line summary in Latin of Statius's *Thebaid*, which in effect Cassandra is here paraphrasing.

Of °Archymoris burying and the pleyes,   *games*
1500 And how °Amphiorax fil thorugh the grounde,   *fell*
How Tideus was sleyn, lord of °Argeyes,   *slain*
And how °Ypomedoun in litel stounde   *time*
Was dreynt, and ded Parthonope of wownde;   *drowned, (how was) dead*
And also how Capaneus the proude
1505 With thonder-dynt was slayn, that cride loude.   *thunder-stroke*

She gan ek telle hym how that eyther brother,   *either*
Ethiocles and Polymyte also,
At a scarmuche ech of hem slough other,   *skirmish, slew*
And of °Argyves wepynge and hire wo;   *weeping*
1510 And how the town was brent, she tolde ek tho.   *burnt, also then*
And so descendeth down from gestes olde   *stories*
To Diomede, and thus she spak and tolde.

"This ilke boor bitokneth Diomede,   *same, signifies*
Tideus sone, that down descended is   *Tideus's son*
1515 Fro Meleagre, that made the boor to blede.   *bleed*
And thy lady, wherso she be, ywis,
This Diomede hire herte hath, and she his.
°Wep if thow wolt, or lef! For, out of doute,
This Diomede is inne, and thow art oute."

1499 For Archymoris, see n. to 5. 1497; "the pleyes" are the Nemean games, instituted by the Seven on their way to Thebes.

1500 On Amphiaraus, see n. to 5. 1494 and 2. 104–5; in addition to being a prophet he was a famous warrior, finally swallowed up by the earth during the Siege of Thebes.

1501 The Argeyes are Argives, citizens of Argos.

1502 Hippomedon was one of the Seven against Thebes, as were also Parthenopeus and Capaneus. Capaneus boasted that even the fire of Zeus would not prevent him from scaling the walls of Thebes, whereupon Zeus struck him with a thunderbolt ("thonder-dynt").

1509 Although the form of the name is peculiar, the mention is usually explained as a reference to Argia, Polynices's wife, whose grief is described in the *Thebaid* (12. 111–16).

1518 weep if you will, or don't ("leave it")

1520	"Thow seyst nat soth," quod he, "thow sorceresse,	*the truth*
	With al thy false goost of prophecye!	*spirit*
	Thow wenest ben a gret devyneresse!	*you think you're, divineress*
	Now °sestow nat this fool of fantasie	
	Peyneth hire on ladys for to lye?	*strains, lies*
1525	Awey!" quod he, "ther Joves yeve the sorwe!	*may Jove give you sorrow*
	Thow shalt be fals, peraunter, yet tomorwe!	*false*

	"As wel thow myghtest lien on °Alceste,	*lie*
	That was of creatures, but men lye,	*unless*
	That evere weren, kyndest and the beste!	*(creatures) that ever were*
1530	For whan hire housbonde was in jupertye	*jeopardy*
	To dye hymself, but if she wolde dye,	*unless*
	She ches for hym to dye and gon to helle,	*chose*
	And starf anon, as us the bokes telle."	*died immediately*

	Cassandre goth, and he with cruel herte	
1535	Foryat his wo, for angre of hire speche;	
	And from his bed al sodeynly he sterte,	*started up*
	As though al hool hym hadde ymad a leche.	*whole, made a physician*
	And day by day he gan enquere and seche	*ask, seek*
	A sooth of this with al his fulle cure;	*truth, care*
1540	And thus he drieth forth his aventure.	*goes through with*

	Fortune, which that permutacioun	*mutation*
	Of thynges hath, as it is hire comitted	*to her*
	Thorugh purveyaunce and disposicioun	*foresight*
	Of heighe Jove, as °regnes shal be flitted	*high*
1545	Fro folk in folk, or when they shal be smytted,	*to, sullied*

1523 now do you not see that this victim of foolish imaginings (The question is generalized, not directed at Cassandra.)

1527 Alcestis's husband, Admetus, had been promised by the Fates deliverance from death if his father, mother, or wife would die for him. She is the principal character in the "Prologue" to Ch's *Legend of Good Women*.

1544 kingdoms shall be transmitted

Gan pulle awey the °fetheres brighte of Troie   *feathers*
Fro day to day, til they ben bare of joie.

Among al this, the fyn of the parodie   *end, (life-)period*
Of Ector gan aprochen wonder blyve.   *approach amazingly fast*
1550 The fate wolde his soule sholde unbodye,   *leave his body*
And shapen hadde a mene it out to dryve,   *arranged, means*
Ayeyns which fate hym helpeth nat to stryve;   *against, it helps*
But on a day to fighten gan he wende,   *go*
At which, allas! he caught his lyves ende.   *life's*

1555 For which me thynketh every manere wight
That haunteth armes oughte to biwaille   *haunts (practices), lament*
The deth of hym that was so noble a knyght;
For as he drough a kyng by °th'aventaille,   *drew*
Unwar of this, Achilles thorugh the maille   *without his knowing it*
1560 And thorugh the body gan hym for to ryve;   *pierce*
And thus this worthi knyght was brought of lyve.   *taken from life*

For whom, as olde bokes tellen us,
Was mad swich wo, that tonge it may nat telle;   *made*
And namely, the sorwe of Troilus,   *especially*
1565 That next hym was of worthynesse welle.   *next to (Hector)*
And in this wo gan Troilus to dwelle,
That, what for sorwe, and love, and for unreste,   *a disturbed mind*
Ful ofte a day he bad his herte breste.   *bade, burst*

But natheles, though he gan hym dispaire,   *despair*
1570 And dradde ay that his lady was untrewe,   *dreaded*
Yet ay on hire his herte gan repaire.   *ever, return (as to home)*
And as thise loveres don, he soughte ay newe   *anew*
To gete ayeyn Criseyde, brighte of hewe;   *get*

1546 Cf. 1. 353.
1558 a wide band of chain-mail protecting the lower part of the face, the neck, and the upper chest

And in his herte he wente hire excusynge,   *went on excusing her*
1575 That Calkas caused al hire tariynge.   *delay*

And ofte tyme he was in purpos grete   *serious purpose*
Hymselven lik a pilgrym to desgise,   *disguise*
To seen hire; but he may nat contrefete   *so as to see, counterfeit*
To ben unknowen of folk that were wise,   *so as*
1580 Ne fynde excuse aright that may suffise,
If he among the Grekis knowen were;   *should be discovered*
For which he wep ful ofte and many a tere.   *wept*

To hire he wroot yet ofte tyme al newe   *wrote*
Ful pitously,—he lefte it nought for slouthe,—   *remissness*
1585 Bisechyng hire, syn that he was trewe,   *faithful*
That she wol come ayeyn and holde hire trouthe.
For which Criseyde upon a day, for routhe,—   *pity*
I take it so,—touchyng al this matere,
Wrot hym ayeyn, and seyde as ye may here:

Criseyde's Letter

1590 "Cupides sone, ensample of goodlyheede,   *example*
O swerd of knyghthod, sours of gentilesse,   *sword, source*
How myght a wight in torment and in drede   *person, dread*
And heleles, yow sende as yet gladnesse?   *devoid of well-being*
I herteles, I sik, I in destresse!   *dispirited, sick*
1595 Syn ye with me, nor I with yow, may dele,   *deal*
°Yow neyther sende ich herte may nor hele.

"Youre lettres ful, the papir al ypleynted,   *filled with complaint*
°Conceyved hath myn hertes pietee.
I have ek seyn with teris al depeynted   *painted*
1600 Youre lettre, and how that ye requeren me

1596 I can send you neither courage nor well-being
1598 has aroused (engendered) my heart's pity

301

To come ayeyn, which yet ne may nat be.
But whi, lest that this lettre founden were,
No mencioun ne make I now, for feere.   *fear*

"Grevous to me, God woot, is youre unreste,
1605 Youre haste, and that the goddes ordinaunce   *impatience*
It semeth nat ye take it for the beste.
Nor other thyng nys in youre remembraunce,
As thynketh me, but only youre plesaunce.   *so it seems to, pleasure*
But beth nat wroth, and that I yow biseche;   *angry*
1610 For that I tarie is al for wikked speche.   *the reason that, rumor*

"For I have herd wel moore than I wende,   *expected*
Touchyng us two, how thynges han ystonde;   *stood*
Which I shal with dissymulyng amende.   *dissembling*
And beth nat wroth, I have ek understonde   *angry*
1615 °How ye ne do but holden me in honde.
But now no force, I kan nat in yow gesse   *no matter, suppose*
But alle trouthe and alle gentilesse.   *(anything) but*

"Come I wole; but yet in swich disjoynte   *will, difficult straits*
I stonde as now, that what yer or what day   *year*
1620 That this shal be, that kan I naught apoynte.   *appoint*
But in effect I pray yow, as I may,   *ask you*
Of youre good word and of youre frendship ay.   *for*
For trewely, while that my lif may dure,   *last*
As for a frend ye may in me assure.   *friend, feel secure*

1625 "Yet preye ich yow, on yvel ye ne take   *take it not amiss*
That it is short which that I to yow write;
I dar nat, ther I am, wel lettres make,   *dare, where*
Ne nevere yet ne koude I wel endite.   *compose*
°Ek gret effect men write in place lite;

1615 only lead me on with false expectation
1629 also people write matters of great consequence in little space

302

1630 Th'entente is al, and nat the lettres space.   *letter's length*
   And fareth now wel, God have yow in his grace!
                 La vostre C."   *your C.*

   This Troilus this lettre thoughte al straunge,
   Whan he it saugh, and sorwfullich he sighte.   *sighed*
   Hym thoughte it lik a °kalendes of chaunge.   *seemed to him*
1635 °But fynaly, he ful ne trowen myghte   *might not fully believe*
   That she ne wolde hym holden that she hyghte;   *keep, promised*
   °For with ful yvel wille list hym to leve,
   That loveth wel, in swich cas, though hym greve.

   But natheles, men seyen that at the laste,   *say*
1640 For any thyng, men shal the soothe se.   *despite everything, truth*
   And swich a cas bitidde, and that as faste,   *happened, very soon*
   That Troilus wel understood that she   *(such) that*
   Nas nought so kynde as that hire oughte be.
   And fynaly, he woot now, out of doute,   *knows*
1645 That al is lost that he hath ben aboute.

   Stood on a day in his malencolie
   This Troilus, and in suspecioun   *(and stood also) in suspicion*
   Of hire for whom he wende for to dye.   *expected*
   And so bifel that thorughout Troye town,   *happened*
1650 As was the gise, iborn was up and down   *custom, carried*
   °A manere cote-armure, as seith the storie,   *says*
   Byforn °Deiphebe, in signe of his victorie;

1634 beginning, first day of the month (See 2. 7.)

1635-6 The sense is: he could not bring himself to believe that she would really break her promise.

1637-8 for reluctantly is someone who loves well satisfied to believe (the evidence), in such a case, although he is troubled (by the evidence)

1651 a type of coat-armor ("Coat-armor" is a tunic with heraldic devices worn over armor—here, an anachronism.)

1652 T's brother (Cf. 2. 1398.)

303

The whiche cote, as telleth Lollius,
Deiphebe it hadde rent fro Diomede   *torn from*
1655 The same day. And whan this Troilus
It saugh, he gan to taken of it hede,   *pay attention to it*
Avysyng of the lengthe and of the brede,   *observing, breadth*
And al the werk; but as he gan byholde,   *workmanship*
Ful sodeynly his herte gan to colde,   *did grow cold*

1660 As he that on the coler fond withinne   *collar*
A broche, that he Criseyde yaf that morwe   *morning*
That she from Troie moste nedes twynne,   *must, depart*
In remembraunce of hym and of his sorwe.
And she hym leyde ayeyn hire feith to borwe   *laid, in pledge*
1665 To kepe it ay! But now ful wel he wiste,   *ever, knew*
His lady nas no lenger on to triste.   *a person to trust*

He goth hym hom, and gan ful soone sende   *home*
For Pandarus; and al this newe chaunce,   *unexpected occurrence*
And of this broche, he tolde hym °word and ende,
1670 Compleynyng of hire hertes variaunce,   *mutability*
His longe love, his trouthe, and his penaunce.   *suffering*
And after deth, withouten wordes moore,   *upon death*
Ful faste he cride, his reste hym to restore.   *cried (i. e., called)*

Than spak he thus, "O lady myn, Criseyde,
1675 Where is youre feith, and where is youre biheste?   *faith, promise*
Where is youre love? where is youre trouthe?" he seyde.   *loyalty*
"Of Diomede have ye now al this feeste!   *enjoyment*
Allas! I wolde han trowed atte leeste   *believed at least*
That, syn ye nolde in trouthe to me stonde,
1680 °That ye thus nolde han holden me in honde!

1669 properly *ord and ende*, "beginning and end"
1680 that you wouldn't have thus led me on with false expectation (Cf. 5. 1615.)

304

°"Who shal now trowe on any othes mo?
Allas! I nevere wolde han wend, er this,   *believed*
That ye, Criseyde, koude han chaunged so;
Ne, but I hadde agilt and don amys,   *unless, been guilty*
1685 So cruel wende I nought youre herte, ywis,   *I would not have believed*
To sle me thus! Allas, youre name of trouthe   *slay*
Is now fordon, and that is al my routhe.   *lost, (source of) pity*

"Was ther non other broche yow liste lete   *it pleased you to let go*
°To feffe with youre newe love," quod he,
1690 "But thilke broch that I, with teris wete,   *wet tears*
Yow yaf, as for a remembraunce of me?   *gave*
Non other cause, allas, ne hadde ye
But for despit, and ek for that ye mente   *except spite*
Al outrely to shewen youre entente.   *outwardly to display*

1695 "Thorugh which I se that clene out of youre mynde   *clean*
Ye han me cast; and I ne kan nor may,
For al this world, withinne myn herte fynde   *find (a way)*
To unloven yow a quarter of a day!
In corsed tyme I born was, weilaway,   *cursed, alas*
1700 That yow, that doon me al this wo endure,   *cause, (to) endure*
Yet love I best of any creature!

"Now God," quod he, "me sende yet the grace
That I may meten with this Diomede!   *encounter*
And trewely, if I have myght and space,
1705 Yet shal I make, I hope, his sydes blede.   *sides, bleed*
O God," quod he, "that oughtest taken heede
To fortheren trouthe, and wronges to punyce,   *further, punish*
Whi nyltow don a vengeaunce of this vice?   *perform, evil*

1681 Cf. 5. 1263.
1689 with which to enfeoff (i.e., with which to endow)

305

"O Pandarus, that in dremes for to triste   *trust*
1710 Me blamed hast, and wont art oft upbreyde,   *accustomed, to chide*
Now maistow se thiself, if that the liste,   *it pleases you*
How trewe is now thi nece, bright Criseyde!
In sondry formes, God it woot," he seyde,   *sundry, knows*
"The goddes shewen both joie and tene   *show, sorrow*
1715 In slep, and by my drem it is now sene.   *seen*

"And certeynly, withouten moore speche,
From hennesforth, as ferforth as I may,   *as far as I am able*
Myn owen deth in armes wol I seche.   *seek*
I recche nat how soone be the day!   *do not care*
1720 But trewely, Criseyde, swete may,   *maid*
Whom I have ay with al my myght yserved,
That ye thus doon, I have it nat deserved."

This Pandarus, that al thise thynges herde,
And wiste wel he seyde a soth of this,   *knew, truth*
1725 He nought a word ayeyn to hym answerde;   *again*
For sory of his frendes sorwe he is,
And shamed for his nece hath don amys,
And stant, astoned of thise causes tweye,   *stands, amazed, two*
As stille as ston; a word ne kowde he seye.   *he could not say*

1730 But at the laste thus he spak, and seyde:
"My brother deer, I may do the namore.   *for you*
What sholde I seyen? I hate, ywys, Cryseyde;
And, God woot, I wol hate hire evermore!   *knows*
°And that thow me bisoughtest don of yoore,
1735 Havyng unto myn honour ne my reste
Right no reward, I dide al that the leste.

1734-7 and what you once besought me to do for you, I did for you, all just as it pleased you, with no regard to my own honor or comfort

"If I dide aught that myghte liken the,   *please*
It is me lief; and of this tresoun now,   *I am glad, treason*
God woot that it a sorwe is unto me!   *knows*
1740 And dredeles, for hertes ese of yow,   *doubtless, ease*
Right fayn I wolde amende it, wiste I how.   *gladly, if I knew*
And fro this world, almyghty God I preye
Delivere hire soon! I kan namore seye."

Gret was the sorwe and pleynte of Troilus;   *lament*
1745 But forth hire cours Fortune ay gan to holde.   *course*
Criseyde loveth the sone of Tideus,   *son*
And Troilus moot wepe in cares colde.   *must weep*
Swich is this world, whoso it kan byholde: *whoever*
In ech estat is litel hertes reste.   *each estate*
1750 God leve us for to take it for the beste!   *grant*

In many cruel bataille, out of drede,   *battles*
Of Troilus, this ilke noble knyght,   *same*
As men may in thise olde bokes rede,   *read*
Was seen his knyghthod and his grete myght.
1755 And dredeles, his ire, day and nyght,   *doubtless*
Ful cruwely the Grekis ay aboughte;   *cruelly, bought*
And alwey moost this Diomede he soughte.

And ofte tyme, I fynde that they mette
With blody strokes and with wordes grete,   *great*
1760 Assayinge how hire speres weren whette;   *testing, sharpened*
And, God it woot, with many a cruel hete   *burning blow*
Gan Troilus upon his helm to bete!   *beat*
But natheles, Fortune it naught ne wolde,   *would not have it*
°Of oothers hond that eyther deyen sholde.

1765 And if I hadde ytaken for to write   *undertaken to*
The armes of this ilke worthi man,   *deeds of arms, same*

1764 that either of the other's hand should die

307

Than wolde ich of his batailles endite;   *battles, compose*
But for that I to writen first bigan
Of his love, I have seyd as I kan,—
1770 His worthi dedes, whoso list hem heere,   *deeds (of arms), wants*
Rede °Dares, he kan telle hem alle ifeere—   *all together*

Bysechyng every lady bright of hewe,   *complexion*
And every gentil womman, what she be,   *whoever she be*
That al be that Criseyde was untrewe,   *although*
1775 That for that gilt she be nat wroth with me.   *guilt, angry*
Ye may hire giltes in other bokes se;
And gladlier I wol write, if yow leste,   *it pleases you*
°Penelopeës trouthe and good Alceste.

N'y sey nat this aloonly for thise men,   *I say not, solely*
1780 But moost for wommen that bitraised be   *betrayed*
Thorugh false folk; God yeve hem sorwe, amen!   *give*
That with hire grete wit and subtilte   *subtlety*
Bytraise yow! And this commeveth me   *betray, moves*
To speke, and in effect yow alle I preye,
1785 Beth war of men, and herkneth what I seye!—   *wary, hearken*

Go, litel book, go, litel myn tragedye,   *my little*
Ther God thi makere yet, er that he dye,   *author*
So sende myght to make in som comedye!   *compose*
But litel book, °no makyng thow n'envie,   *verbal making, envy*
1790 But subgit be to alle poesye;   *subject, poetry*
And kis the steppes, where as thow seest pace   *kiss, steps, pass*
Virgile, Ovide, Omer, Lucan, and Stace.   *Homer, Statius*

1771 See 1. 146 and n.
1778 Penelope is famous for her fidelity to Ulysses during his twenty years of war
and wandering; on Alceste, see 5. 1527.
1789 do not vie with other poetry

And for ther is so gret °diversite
In Englissh and in writyng of oure tonge,
1795 So prey I God that non myswrite the,
Ne the mysmetre °for defaute of tonge.   *mis-meter*
And red wherso thow be, or elles songe,   *wherever you may, else*
That thow be understonde, God I biseche!
But yet to purpos of my rather speche.—   *earlier*

1800 The wrath, as I bigan yow for to seye,
Of Troilus the Grekis boughten deere.   *bought dearly*
For thousandes his hondes maden deye,   *made to die*
As he that was withouten any peere,   *peer*
Save Ector, in his tyme, as I kan heere.   *except*
1805 But weilawey, save only Goddes wille!   *alas, except it was*
Despitously hym slough the fierse Achille.   *(that) pitilessly slew him*

And whan that he was slayn in this manere,
His lighte goost ful blisfully is went   *soul*
Up to the holughnesse of the °eighte spere,   *hollowness*
1810 °In convers letyng everich element;   *leaving behind*
And ther he saugh, with ful avysement,   *saw, contemplation*
°The erratik sterres, herkenyng armonye
With sownes ful of hevenyssh melodie.   *sounds, heavenly*

1793 Cf. 2. 22–5.

1796 on account of deficiency in the English tongue

1809 The reading *eighte* is found in only three MSS, including Caxton (the others reading *seventhe*), but is the number in Ch's source for this passage, or Boccaccio's *Teseida*. It is uncertain whether Ch counted the spheres outward from the earth or inward from that of the fixed stars. The former is suggested by the phrase *up to the holughnesse of*, in which case the sphere referred to would be that of the fixed stars, next to the outermost or *primum mobile*.

1810 "In convers" appears to be a mistranslation or intentional alteration of Boccaccio's *convessi* ("convexities"). Ch's phrase means "on the other side, behind." As the spirit of T rose through the spheres it left behind "everich element."

1812 "The erratik sterres" are the seven planets; "herkenyng armonye" indicates that

309

And down from thennes faste he gan avyse   *fixedly, contemplate*
1815 This litel spot of erthe, that with the se   *sea*
Embraced is, and fully gan despise
This wrecched world, and held al vanite
To respect of the pleyn felicite   *in comparison with, perfect*
That is in hevene above; and at the laste,
1820 Ther he was slayn, his lokyng down he caste.   *where, gaze*

And in hymself he lough right at the wo   *laughed*
Of hem that wepten for his deth so faste;   *wept, hard*
And dampned al oure werk that foloweth so   *condemned all our doings*
The blynde lust, the which that may nat laste,
1825 And sholden al oure herte on heven caste.   *(when we) should*
And forth he wente, shortly for to telle,
°Ther as Mercurye sorted hym to dwelle.

Swich fyn hath, lo, this Troilus for love!   *such an end*
Swich fyn hath al his grete worthynesse!
1830 Swich fyn hath his estat real above,   *royal estate*
Swich fyn his lust, swich fyn hath his noblesse!
Swich fyn hath false worldes brotelnesse!   *insecurity*
And thus bigan his lovyng of Criseyde,
As I have told, and in this wise he deyde.   *way*

1835 O yonge, fresshe folkes, he or she,
In which that love up groweth with youre age,
Repeyreth hom fro worldly vanyte,   *repair (return) home from*
And of youre herte up casteth the visage   *cast the countenance*
To thilke God that after his ymage   *according to his image*
1840 Yow made, and thynketh al nys but a faire   *fair*
This world, that passeth soone as floures faire.   *flowers*

---

he is listening to the music of the spheres, in which the planets revolve, as he observes the planets.

1827 to the place which Mercury, the Psychopomp or guide of souls, allotted him to dwell (See also 5. 321.)

And loveth hym, the which that right for love   *who*
Upon a crois, oure soules for to beye,   *cross, buy*
First starf, and roos, and sit in hevene above;   *died, rose, sits*
1845 °For he nyl falsen no wight, dar I seye,
That wol his herte al holly on hym leye.
And syn he best to love is, and most meke,   *meek*
What nedeth feynede loves for to seke?   *feigned and illusory, seek*

Lo here, of payens corsed olde rites!   *pagans'*
1850 Lo here, what alle hire goddes may availle!
Lo here, thise wrecched worldes appetites!
Lo here, the fyn and guerdoun for °travaille   *end, reward*
Of Jove, Appollo, of Mars, of swich rascaille!   *a worthless bunch*
Lo here, the °forme of olde clerkis speche
1855 In poetrie, if ye hire bokes seche!   *search*

O moral °Gower, this book I directe
To the and to the, philosophical °Strode,
To vouchen sauf, ther nede is, to correcte,   *consent, where need*
Of youre benignites and zeles goode.   *out of, zeals*
1860 And to that sothefast Crist, °that starf on rode,   *true*
With al myn herte of mercy evere I preye,   *for*
And to the Lord right thus I speke and seye:

1845-6 for he will not play false with anyone, I dare to affirm, who will fully invest his heart's devotion in him (lit., "lay his heart all wholly on him")

1852 lit., "labor," perhaps best construed as "service of" or even "worship of"

1854 informing principle of old clerks' speech

1856 John Gower was a poet contemporary with Ch and at one time apparently his close friend.

1857 The reference is perhaps to Ralph Strode (the identification is vexed) who was a contemporary philosopher and theologian, a fellow of Merton College, Oxford. He may be the same as the Ralph Strode who is found later practicing law in London and who died in 1387.

1860 that died on the cross

°Thow oon, and two, and thre, eterne on lyve,   *eternally alive*
    That regnest ay in thre, and two, and oon,
1865 Uncircumscript, and al maist circumscrive,
    Us from visible and invisible foon   *foes*
    Defende, and to thy mercy, everichon,   *protect, everyone*
    So make us, Jesus, for thy mercy digne,   *worthy*
    For love of mayde and moder thyn benigne.   *for the sake of, mother*
                        Amen.

1863 Ch refers to the Trinity—Father, Son, and Holy Spirit—translating Dante, *Para*.
14. 28–30.